Loomis J. Campbell, Charles A. Goodrich

A Concise School History of the United States

based on Seavey's Goodrich's History - Vol. 2

Loomis J. Campbell, Charles A. Goodrich

A Concise School History of the United States
based on Seavey's Goodrich's History - Vol. 2

ISBN/EAN: 9783337885854

Printed in Europe, USA, Canada, Australia, Japan

Cover: Foto ©Paul-Georg Meister /pixelio.de

More available books at **www.hansebooks.com**

A CONCISE

SCHOOL HISTORY

OF THE

NITED STATES

BASED ON

SEAVEY'S GOODRICH'S HISTORY.

L. J. CAMPBELL

With Maps and other Illustrations

NEW YORK:
TAINTOR BROTHERS, MERRILL & CO.
BOSTON:
WILLIAM WARE & CO.
(SUCCESSORS TO BREWER & TILESTON.)

Entered, according to Act of Congress, in the year 1870,
BY BREWER AND TILESTON,
In the Office of the Librarian of Congress, at Washington.

PREFACE.

In preparing this little book, the writer has endeavored to relate briefly, but clearly and accurately, the leading events in the history of our country. Much care and labor have been expended, with the view not only to make a judicious selection of facts, but to present them in such a form as to render the work acceptable as a lesson-book.

The effort has been made not only to avoid statements erroneous in themselves, but also those which might lead to wrong inferences, or in any way give false impressions; and although events are concisely narrated, yet their relative importance has not been overlooked.

The writer believes that the history of our country deserves a prominent place in the school-room; but he is aware of the fact that the time which can be devoted to this department of study in common and grammar schools, and even in academies, is, in most cases, very much limited. Therefore, without intending to dwarf his book to a size which would admit but little more than a full chronology, he has kept the narrative within such bounds that the recitation of only two pages a day would take the learner to the end of it in less than half a year.

The work differs from many other school histories especially in a more sparing use of dates, and in the omission of less important details, such as the losses in indecisive or minor battles. The History is divided into five Periods, and at the close of each, except the last, is found a chapter describing the condition of the country. In these chapters much important information is given, which should not be passed over by even the smallest histories.

The questions at the foot of the pages have been carefully prepared.

Those teachers — and there are many such — who prefer to frame their own questions, will, it is believed, find an advantage in the plan which has been adopted, of printing the leading or key words of the paragraphs in a more conspicuous type. This feature, by bringing out prominently the leading topics, seems also well fitted to assist the learner in preparing his lessons.

The teacher, it is suggested, should not require the scholar to commit to memory and recite the language of the text, word for word, but rather to gain clear and accurate ideas of the subject, and to express them in his own language.

The maps, with which the work is fully supplied, should be put to constant use in the preparation of the lessons. It will be a most profitable exercise for the scholars to draw maps upon the blackboard, showing the positions of the places named in each lesson.

Chronological Reviews have been scattered throughout the book, one at the end of each Period. These are designed to be studied and faithfully committed to memory. Some useful tables have been inserted after the narrative of the events; also the Declaration of Independence and the Constitution of the United States. To the latter, questions have been added, and such explanation of terms and other information as might be needed.

Attention is particularly called to the Review Questions at the close of the book. These are of the utmost importance for enabling scholars to group events and gain a more comprehensive view of them. They may be put to use after an entire Period has been studied, or sooner, at the teacher's discretion.

This History is based, in part, on the excellent larger history prepared, a short time before his death, by that experienced teacher, Mr. William H. Seavey, late principal of the Girls' High and Normal School of this city. Mrs. WM. H. Seavey has aided in the preparation of this volume, especially by valuable suggestions and criticisms.

L. J. C.

BOSTON, September 1, 1870.

LIST OF CHRONOLOGICAL TABLES.

	Page
CHRONOLOGICAL REVIEW FROM 1492 TO 1606	22
CHRONOLOGICAL REVIEW FROM 1607 TO 1763	72
CHRONOLOGICAL REVIEW FROM 1764 TO 1788	112
CHRONOLOGICAL REVIEW FROM 1789 TO 1861	165
CHRONOLOGICAL REVIEW FROM 1861 TO 1879	221

LIST OF MAPS.

Known World in the 15th century.	7
Known World in the 19th century.	7
Discoveries.	11
European Claims in America.	19
Indian Families and principal Tribes. . . . . *facing*	20
Jamestown and Vicinity.	23
Eastern Colonies.	28
Middle Colonies.	43
Carolinas.	52
Intercolonial Wars.	56
Intercolonial Wars.	57
Lake Champlain and Vicinity.	64
War of the Revolution in the South.	80
War of the Revolution in the North.	81
Boston and Vicinity.	84
New York and Vicinity.	88
Philadelphia and Vicinity.	92
Burgoyne's Expedition. Saratoga and Vicinity.	94
Yorktown.	107
Country east of the Mississippi at the beginning of Washington's administration. . . . *facing*	110
War of 1812.	124
War of 1812.	125
Baltimore and Vicinity.	125
Niagara Frontier.	125
Vicinity of Detroit.	125
New Orleans and Vicinity.	136
Florida War.	142
Mexican War.	149
General Taylor's March.	149
General Scott's March.	149
Seat of War in Virginia.	172
War of the Rebellion.	184
Vicksburg and Vicinity.	184
Georgia and South Carolina Coast.	184
War of the Rebellion.	185
Charleston and Vicinity.	185
United States in 1870. . . . . *following*	212
Territorial Growth. . . . . *following*	220

REVIEW QUESTIONS, *Appendix*, p. 31.

(5)

THE NORTHMEN IN AMERICA.

MORE than six hundred years before Columbus sailed to America, the Northmen, bold sea-rovers, discovered **Iceland**, an island remote from their home in the north of Europe, and peopled it. These colonists went from Norway. Only a few years after they began to colonize this island, one of their vessels was driven, by storms, farther to the west, and came in sight of Greenland.

A little more than a hundred years later, in 986, Eric ($ĕr'ik$) the Red sailed from Iceland, and established a colony in **Greenland**. A very few years afterwards an Icelander, named Biörn (*be-urn'*), seeking Greenland, was driven far out of his course by northern gales, and saw a much more southern land, covered with forests. This was some part of the *north-eastern coast of the American continent.*

Afterwards exploring and trading voyages were made from Greenland and Iceland to the unknown country in the south-west. The first explorers, who went out in the year 1000, named the most southern tract which they visited, **Vinland**, from finding there vines and grapes. Their Vinland was, it seems, the *southern coast of New England.*

The Northmen found savage tribes in the new countries, probably the same race called by other discoverers, at a much later date, Indians. They trafficked with the savages for furs and skins, and from the "endless forests" collected wood; but no permanent settlements were made. Those formed in Greenland disappeared, after some centuries, swept away, it is believed, by epidemics and conflicts with the savages. For a long time the country was lost sight of, and remained to be discovered anew.

We should remember that the Northmen did not know that they had discovered a New World. They supposed the strange lands they had found, to be part of Europe.

MAPS OF THE KNOWN WORLD.

THE KNOWN WORLD IN THE 19TH CENTURY.

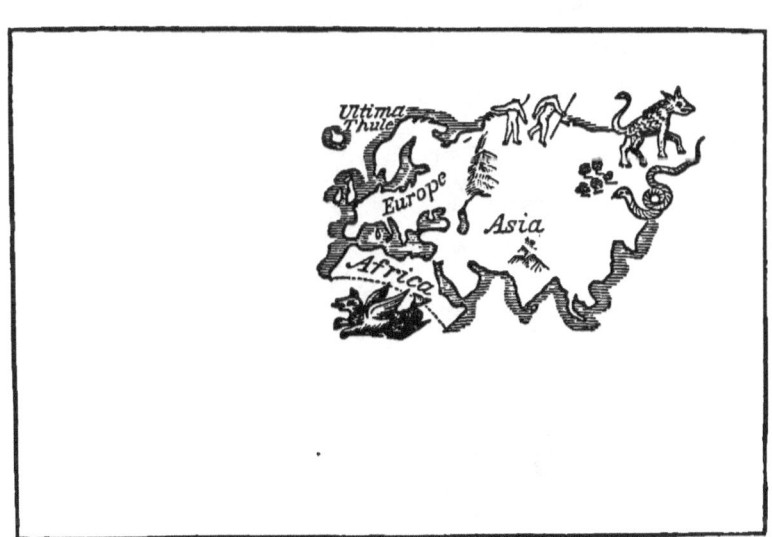

THE KNOWN WORLD IN THE 15TH CENTURY.

The old geographers used to place upon their maps figures of strange animals and headless men, as above, to denote that the regions thus marked were unknown, and supposed to abound in horrible monsters.

LANDING OF COLUMBUS.

PERIOD I. — DISCOVERIES.

FROM THE DISCOVERY OF SAN SALVADOR, IN 1492, TO THE SETTLEMENT OF JAMESTOWN, IN 1607.

I. SPANISH EXPEDITIONS.

1. *Christopher Columbus. Amerigo Vespucci.*

1. THE discovery of America was made in the year 1492, by **Christopher Columbus**, a native of Gen'o-a, in Italy. Believing the earth to be a globe, Columbus conceived the project of sailing west, and thus reaching, by a new route, the wealthy regions of the east, called India.

2. After seeking aid elsewhere without success, he applied to Ferdinand and Isabella, sovereigns of **Spain**, to furnish him with ships to test his theory. For years he fruitlessly urged his project upon the attention of the Spanish sovereigns. He was an elderly man when, at last, the queen, **Isabella**, was persuaded to aid him.

Christopher Columbus.

3. On the morning of Friday, August 12,* Columbus sailed from the harbor of Palos (*pah'-l̇s*) with three small vessels and ninety seamen, and on the morning of Friday, October 21,† just ten weeks after leaving Spain, **he discovered** one of the Baha'ma Islands. Landing with his men, he set up the royal banner, and took

---
* August 3, O. S. † October 12, O. S.

QUESTIONS. — 1. When and by whom was America discovered? What project did Columbus conceive?
2. What is said about his seeking aid? Who, at length, aided him?
3. What can you tell of the sailing of Columbus? What did he discover? What more can you tell of this expedition?

(9)

solemn possession of the island for the king and queen of Spain, naming it San Salvador. He came to other islands soon afterwards, among the rest to Cuba and Hayti (*ha'tĭ*).

4. Columbus supposed the islands which he had discovered to be a part of India; and as they lay west from Europe, they were called the **West Indies**, and their inhabitants **Indians**—a name which was afterwards also given to the natives of the adjacent continent.

5. The news which Columbus carried back to Spain created great excitement; and soon ships, commanded by other courageous mariners, sailed for the strange lands in the west. The great navigator himself made three **other voyages**. On his third voyage, he reached, in 1498, the main land of South America. **He died** in 1506, a few months after his return from a fourth voyage. Long afterwards his remains were carried to Cuba, where they now repose.

6. The New World was named America, from **Amerigo Vespucci** (*ah-mā-re'go ves-poot'che*), a Florentine merchant, who accompanied a Spanish expedition which touched the coast of South America some months after Columbus had discovered it. A narrative written by Amerigo was the cause of his name's being given to the western continent — an honor which did not belong to him.

2. *The Spaniards in the South.*

7. It was not long before the Spaniards had taken possession of the principal islands of the West Indies, and from their colonies there they despatched expeditions to the main land. **Balboa** (*bahl-bo'ah*), in 1513, crossing the isthmus which connects North and South America, discovered the Pacific Ocean, at first called the South Sea.

8. Not very long afterwards **Ma-gel'lan**, a Portuguese in the service of Spain, sailing far south, passed through the straits which bear his name, and entered this ocean. He

---
4. What names were given to the islands and the inhabitants, and why?
5. Effect of the news of Columbus's discovery? What is said of his other voyages and of his discovery of the main land? Of his death?
6. What can you tell about Amerigo Vespucci and the name *America*?
7. What is said of the Spaniards in the West Indies? Of Balboa?
8. What can you tell of Magellan, and of the first voyage round the world?

called it *the Pacific*, because he found it so calm and free from storms. Magellan was killed by the Indians; but his vessel doubled the Cape of Good Hope, and reached Spain in 1522, thus making *the first voyage round the world*.

9. **Hernando Cortes** (*kor'tĕz*), with a few hundred soldiers, conquered the rich and populous empire of Mexico in 1521, and it became a province of Spain. With a smaller force **Francisco Pizarro** (*pe-zăr'ro*) subjugated Peru—a land abounding in the precious metals.

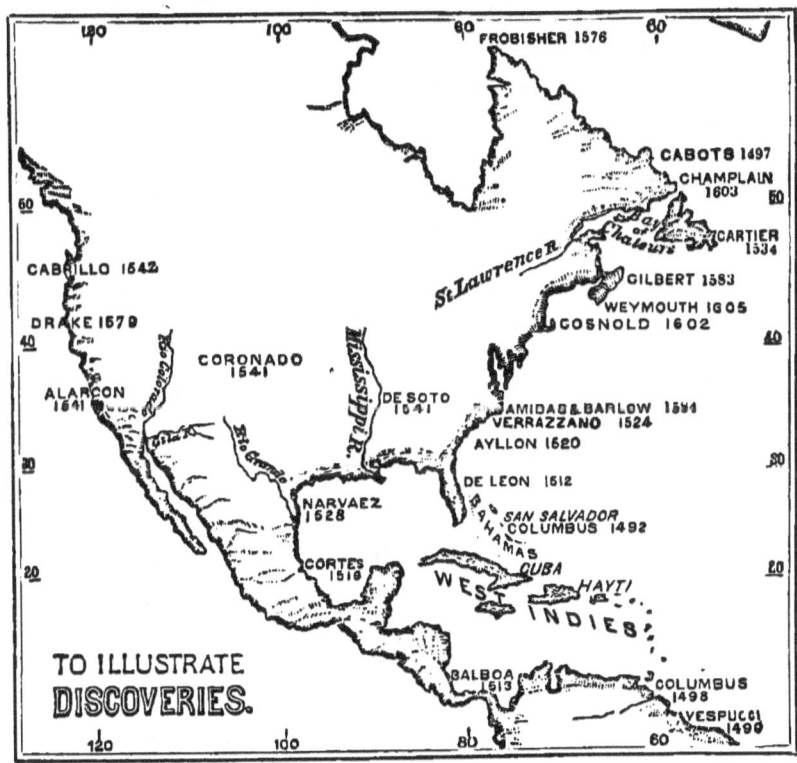

3. *The Spaniards in the United States.*

10. **Ponce de Leon** (*pōne'thā dā-lā-ōne'*), an aged soldier, was the first Spaniard who explored any part of what is now the United States. He fitted out an expedition to

---

9. What can you tell of Hernando Cortes and Francisco Pizarro?
10. Give an account of Ponce de Leon's expedition.

seek for gold, and also for a fountain whose waters were fabled to restore youth. In 1512, on Easter Sunday, called by the Spaniards Pascua Florida (*pahs-koo'ah flo-re'dah*), he came in sight of land, which, from its flowery appearance and from the day, he named *Florida*.

11. Some years later **Ponce** came again to colonize the land he had discovered; but the Indians furiously attacked the Spaniards, and forced them to take to their ships. Ponce was mortally wounded. A Spanish leader, named **Narvaez** (*nar-vah'eth*), afterwards sailing from Cuba with three hundred men, attempted the conquest of Florida. Nearly all perished. Only four of his company, after long wanderings, reached a Spanish settlement in Mexico.

12. A rich man named **Ayllon** (*ile-yōne'*), with the help of a few associates in Hayti, fitted out an expedition in 1520, which reached the coast of Carolina. Their object was to capture the natives as slaves. A few years afterwards Ayllon endeavored to conquer the country, but was unsuccessful. Most of his men sickened and died, or were slain by the Indians.

13. The conquest of Florida was next attempted by **Fernando de Soto** (*dā so'to*), a famous commander, and a companion of Pizarro, the conqueror of Peru. At the head of more than six hundred brave soldiers, De Soto landed on the western shore of Florida, and pushed inland. He believed that he should find opulent cities to plunder, and a land abounding in gold. He found neither cities nor gold.

14. In the spring of 1541, after wandering two years, and marking his course with the blood of the natives, De Soto came to the **Mississippi River**, near the southern limit of the present State of Tennessee. Broken in spirit by disappointments and hardships, he died the next year by the side of the great river he had discovered, and was buried in its waters. A miserable remnant of the brilliant expedi-

---

11. What is said of Ponce's second expedition? What of Narvaez?
12. Give an account of Ayllon's expeditions to the coast of Carolina.
13. What is said of De Soto and the conquest of Florida? What did he expect to find?
14. What is said of his discovery of the Mississippi? His fate? His followers?

tion that had set out with De Soto at last reached a settlement which the Spaniards had already established on the western coast of the Gulf of Mexico.

15. Nearly a quarter of a century later **Menendez** (*ma-nen'deth*), a fierce warrior, received a commission from the king of Spain to conquer and colonize Florida. He was also ordered to destroy a colony of French Protestants who had lately come into that country.* Immediately after landing, in 1565, he founded **St. Augustine** (*-teen'*), the oldest European town in the United States. He next surprised the French fort, and put to the sword nearly all the colonists: even those who surrendered were massacred.

16. From Mexico Spanish discovery was extended northward. **Coronado** (*ko-ro-nah'do*), departing from this province in 1540, with a body of soldiers, explored the country about the upper Rio Grande (*ri'o grand*).† At the same time another Spaniard sailed along the coast of California. The region which Coronado traversed was afterwards called *New Mexico*, and possession of it was taken for Spain. Santa Fé, its chief town, is, next to St. Augustine, the oldest European settlement in the United States.

II. FRENCH EXPEDITIONS.

1. Early Expeditions in the North.

1. The fishing-grounds off the north-eastern coast of America were early visited by French ships; but the first explorer sent out by France to the New World was **John Verrazzano** (*ver-rat-sah'no*), a Florentine, who made a voyage of discovery, in the service of the French king, in 1524. Reaching land, near Wilmington, North Carolina, Verrazzano first sailed south some distance, and then north, along the coast, to Newfoundland (*nu'fund-land*). He named the country *New France*.

* See p. 14, ¶¶ 3, 4.   † *Spanish pron.* re'o-grahn'dā.

15. What commission did Menendez receive, and what was he ordered to do? What was done by him in Florida? Where is St. Augustine? (See Map, p. 19.)
16. What is said of Coronado? The coast of California? Of New Mexico and Santa Fé? Where is Santa Fé? (See Map, p. 19.)
1. What is said of the first expedition sent to the New World by France?

2. Ten years later, that is, in 1534, **James Cartier** (*kar-te-a'*) was sent to explore the northern coast of the New World. He entered the Gulf of St. Lawrence, and claimed the adjacent country for his king. The next year he came again, and ascended the River St. Lawrence till he reached the spot where now is Montreal. Several years afterwards, Cartier and a French nobleman were unsuccessful in an attempt to plant a colony in this region. The discoveries of Verrazzano and Cartier gave France its claim to the northern part of the American continent.

2. *The Huguenots.*

3. Coligny (*ko-leen'ye*), admiral of France, and a distinguished leader of the Huguenots, — as the French Protestants were called, — desiring to plant a Protestant colony in America, sent out an expedition to our shores in 1562. A small fort was built near Port Royal entrance, in South Carolina, and thirty men were left as colonists. They fell into extreme want, and the next year sailed for France.

4. **A second colony** of Huguenots, in 1564, reached the mouth of the St. John's, in Florida, and a few miles up the river built a fort, which, in honor of their king, Charles (in Latin *Carolus*), they named Fort Caroline. Several hundred other colonists soon came over with Ribault (*re-bo'*), who had led the first expedition. But Spain claimed the country, and the Spaniard, **Menendez**, as we have told, captured the fort in 1565, and slaughtered the greater part of the colonists in the most cruel manner.

A French nobleman, named **Gourgues** (*goorg*), who was a deadly enemy to the Spaniards, fitted out an expedition to avenge this horrible deed. He sailed to Florida, assailed the Spanish forts on the St. John's, and put to death the garrisons. Gourgues then sailed home again, and Florida remained a Spanish province.

---

2. What is said of two voyages by James Cartier? What was attempted several years afterwards? Upon what did the French base their claim to the northern part of America?
3. Who sent out a colony of French Protestants, and when? What can you tell of this colony?
4. Where and when was a second colony of Huguenots established? Fate of this colony? What revenge was taken for the cruel deed of Menendez?

3. Acadia.

5. A considerable period elapsed before the French attempted to plant another colony in America. Early in the seventeenth century, the king of France granted to **De Monts** (*duh mawn[g]*)* a territory, called *Acadia*, extending from the southern part of Pennsylvania to the northern part of Nova Scotia. Under this grant the first permanent French settlement in America was made in 1605, on the western coast of Nova Scotia, and named *Port Royal*. With the expedition of De Monts came Samuel de Champlain (*sham-plane'*), afterwards the able leader of the French colonists of Canada.

III. ENGLISH EXPEDITIONS.

1. *The Cabots. Francis Drake.*

1. England was the first to compete with Spain for the honors and advantages of western discovery. **John Cab'ot** and his son Sebastian, sailing in behalf of the English king, in the summer of 1497 fell in with land, which is believed to have been the coast of Labradōr'. Thus the continent of America was discovered by Cabot more than a year before Columbus saw it. The next year **Sebastian Cabot** made another voyage, and explored the coast from Labrador to Albemarle Sound, North Carolina.

2. The great sea-captain **Francis Drake** was the first Englishman who visited the western coast of America. Passing through the stormy Straits of Magellan, Drake sailed along the coast of California. Claiming the country for England, he named it *New Albion*. He then steered boldly out into the Pacific, and reached home in 1579, by the way of the Cape of Good Hope; and thus has the honor of being the first Englishman who sailed round the world. After his return home Queen Elizabeth knighted him.

* This nasal sound stops before the sound *ng* is formed.

5. What is said of Acadia? Of Port Royal? Of Samuel de Champlain?
1. What is said of England in connection with western discovery? Give an account of Cabot's discovery of the continent of America. What is said of another voyage?
2. What can you tell of Francis (afterwards Sir Francis) Drake's voyage?

2. *Attempts to form Settlements.*

3. About this time **Sir Humphrey Gilbert**, by permission of Queen Elizabeth, endeavored to plant a colony in America. The enterprise was unsuccessful. On his homeward voyage, while a violent storm was raging, Sir Humphrey sat on deck calmly reading. To those in the other and stronger vessel he cried out, "Be of good heart, my friends; we are as near to heaven by sea as by land." In that storm his frail bark went down, and all on board perished.

4. His half brother, **Sir Walter Raleigh** (*raw'lĭ*), another adventurous sailor and accomplished gentleman, now obtained a commission from Elizabeth, and despatched Am'idas and Barlow, with two small vessels, to make explorations. They reached the coast of North Carolina, and spent a short time trafficking with the natives. On their return home they gave a brilliant description of the country, and the name of *Virginia* was bestowed upon it, in honor of Elizabeth, the Virgin Queen.

5. The next year, namely, in 1585, Raleigh sent out **a colony**, with Ralph Lane as governor. They landed on Roanoke Island, in Albemarle Sound, where they remained nearly a year, when they were glad to be taken to England by Sir Francis Drake, who stopped there on his way home from the West Indies. **Another colony** sent out by Raleigh, with John White as governor, arrived at Roanoke in 1587. White soon went to England for supplies, leaving more than a hundred colonists, among them his infant granddaughter, Virginia Dare, the first child born of English parents within the limits of the present United States. When he returned, after three years, the colonists had disappeared. They were never heard of more.

6. In 1602 **Bartholomew Gosnold** (*goz'nuld*) visited the coast of New England. He discovered Cape Cod, and

---

3. What can you tell of Sir Humphrey Gilbert?
4. What is said of Sir Walter Raleigh, and the exploring expedition sent out by him? Why was Virginia so named?
5. When did Raleigh send out his first colony, and what was the result? When did his second colony reach Roanoke? What further is said of these colonists?
6 What can you tell of Gosnold's voyage? What of other explorers?

named it from his catching a great number of codfish there. On one of the Elizabeth Islands he built a fort and a storehouse, with the design of leaving a small colony; but before he sailed, those who were to remain became faint-hearted and discontented; so all embarked for England. Gosnold carried home a very flattering account of the country, and other explorers, after a year or two, followed in his track.

0. *North and South Virginia.*

7. **England** was now ready to take possession of her **claims in America.** Accordingly James I. granted, under the name of *Virginia*, a territory between the 34th and 45th degrees of north latitude — that is, from Cape Fear to the northern limit of the coast of Maine — to two companies. The southern portion, called *South Virginia*, was granted to the **London Company,** whose prominent members lived in London. The northern portion, called *North Virginia*, was granted to the **Plymouth Company,** whose prominent members lived in Plymouth.

8. Each company sent out **colonists** in 1607. Those who came to the present Virginia effected a permanent settlement, those who landed in Maine abandoned the country the next year. These events will be related in the next Period.

CONDITION, AT THE CLOSE OF THIS PERIOD, OF WHAT IS NOW THE UNITED STATES.

1. Progress of Discovery.

1. At the beginning of this Period the existence of the **American Continent** was unknown in Europe. When first discovered, it was supposed to be a part of Asia; but those who sailed upon the Pacific Ocean proved it to be widely separated from that country. A hundred years had elapsed

---

7. What is said of an English grant to territory in America? Name the companies receiving the grant and give residence of prominent members.
8. What can you tell of colonists sent out by these companies?
1. When first discovered, what was America supposed to be? What was afterwards proved? What was the object of many of the early navigators?

since the last voyage of Columbus, and the general outline of the continent, except at the extreme north, had now been determined. Various voyages, which we have not mentioned in this little History, had been made to the Western World. The object of many of the early navigators was to find a passage through to the Pacific Ocean. This was called the **North-west Passage**, and was long sought for.

2. *Claims of Spain, France, and England.*

2. **Spain, England, and France claimed**, at the close of this Period, in right of the discoveries and explorations of their famous navigators, the immense region known as North America. The **Spanish claim** above the southern boundary of the present United States extended indefinitely northward, under the name of Florida on the east, and New Mexico in the interior and on the west. In these provinces Spanish settlements had been made at St. Augustine and Santa Fé.

3. The **French claim** extended southward, under the name of Acadia, to the latitude of Philadelphia, and under the name of New France, indefinitely. The French had established a colony at Port Royal. The **English claim**, as made by the charter of Virginia, was based on the discoveries of the Cabots, and included regions claimed by both France and Spain, but not those actually occupied by them.

3. *The Aborigines or Indians.*

4. When the Europeans first landed upon the shores of the **New World** they found it an almost unbroken wilderness. There were herds of deer living in the depths of the forests, together with bears, wolves, panthers, beavers, foxes, and many other wild animals. A countless number of buffaloes fed in the grassy plains.

5. This country was also the native home of numerous tribes of men, called by the Europeans, **Indians**, each tribe

---

2. What nations claimed North America? What is said of the Spanish claim?
3. What is said of the French claim? Of the English claim?
4. What was the condition of the New World at the time of its discovery?
5. Who inhabited America? What is said of the number of the Indians?

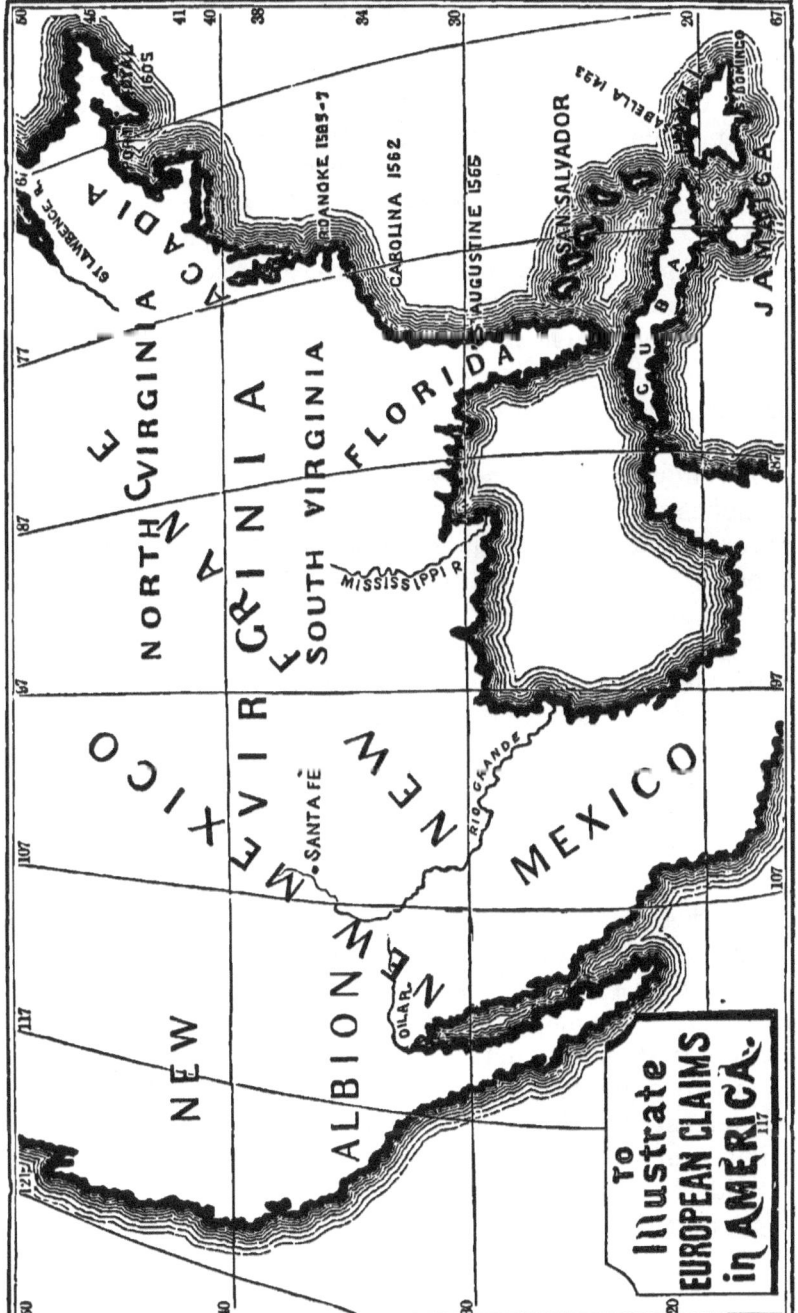

under its own sachem or chief. The number of the Indians, when the English came to settle this country, is not known; but it probably did not exceed two hundred thousand in that part of the United States east of the Mississippi.

6. The natives were generally tall, straight, and well-formed. Their skin was of a cinnamon or **copper-brown color**; and from this reddish hue they are sometimes called Red Men. They had long, black, coarse hair, a scant beard, and high cheek-bones. Their eyes were small, deep-set, and snaky. By way of ornament they sometimes painted their faces and bodies with streaks and with hideous devices.

7. They lived in **wigwams** or huts, made of poles or branches of trees, erected so as to converge at the top, and covered with mats or pieces of bark. For **their food** they depended, for the most part, upon the wild beasts they killed and the fish they caught. Sometimes the women, or **squaws**, would raise a little patch of corn or beans, cultivated with a hoe, made, perhaps, from a clam-shell, or a moose's shoulder-blade, fastened into a handle. The squaws had to do all the work; they were the slaves and drudges of their lazy lords. In summer **the Indians wore** only a little piece of deer-skin around the loins; but in winter they clothed themselves with the undressed skins of deer and other wild animals.

8. These men of the woods were very **revengeful** if any injury was done them; and, on the other hand, it is said, they seldom forgot a benefit. **War**, they thought, was the most honorable employment. Armed with war-clubs, tomahawks or stone hatchets, and bows and arrows, they would go stealthily through the forest, to rush upon their enemy when least expected. The one who could show the greatest number of **scalps**, torn from the heads of his foes, was considered the bravest warrior.

9. Sometimes, when they took a **prisoner**, they would

---

6. What is said of the bodily appearance of the Indians?
7. Give some account of their dwellings. Their food. Squaws. Dress.
8. What is said of their disposition? Their employment? Their custom in war?
9. How would they sometimes torture a prisoner? His behavior?

burn him at the stake by a slow fire, and torture him horribly in every way. It was great glory for the dying warrior to bear all without any signs of anguish. He would shout out his death-song, and with his last breath taunt his tormentors with their want of skill in torturing, and deride them as squaws and cowards.

10. They had **no books**, but they sometimes communicated with each other by rude figures traced on bark or rocks. Their language being destitute of abstract terms, caused the frequent use of metaphors in speech, such as may be derived from familiar appearances of nature and the habits of animals.

11. As to the **religion** of the Indians, we are told that they believed there were good and bad spirits in the invisible world; that there was a superior Being, whom they called the Great Spirit; and that the human spirit, released from the body, speeded away to the happy hunting-grounds. The **origin** of the Indians is involved in obscurity. It is most generally supposed, however, that they originated in Asia, and migrated from that country to America across Behring's (*beer'ingz*) Straits.

---

10. How did they sometimes communicate with each other? What is said of their language?
11. What is said of the religion of the Indians? Of the origin of the Indians?

See Map facing p. 20.

The Indians who lived in the United States, east of the Mississippi River, have been divided into eight groups or families. Three, the **Natchez**, the **U'chees**, and the **Catawbas**, possessed but a small space of territory.

The range of the **Cher'okees** was wider; that of the **Iroquois** (*Ĭr'o-kwoi*), or Five Nations, wider still. This last group occupied the northern part of New York, from the Hudson River to Lake Erie. The names of the Five Nations were the Mohawks, the Oneidas (*o-ni'dahs*), the Onondagas (*on-on-daw'gahs*), the Cayu'gas, and the Sen'ecas. At a later period the Tuscaro'ras, a kindred nation, from North Carolina and Virginia, joined them.

The **Mobilians** (*mo-bil'yanz*), composed of Choctaws, Chickasaws, Creeks, and Seminoles (*sem'i-nōlz*), lived in the extreme southern region, and occupied a space of territory more extensive than that of the Iroquois.

But the largest domain of all was that of the **Algonquins**. It extended entirely around that of the Iroquois, and on the Atlantic from the Gulf of St. Lawrence to Pamlico Sound. To this group belonged all the Indians living in New England, the Powhatans', the Illinois, the Chippewas, the Sacs and Foxes, the Ottawas, and many other well-known tribes.

The **Da-ko'tas**, or Sioux (*soo*), dwelt, for the most part, west of the Mississippi but one tribe, the Winneba'goes, established itself east of the river and west o Lake Michigan. — *Chiefly from Dr. Palfrey's History of New England.*

CHRONOLOGICAL REVIEW.

NOTE. — The figures at the end of the paragraphs refer to the pages upon which the events are mentione !.

1492. Columbus discovered America, 9.
1497. John and Sebastian Cabot discovered the continent of America, probably Labrador, 15.
1498. Columbus discovered the continent of America, 10.
1499. Amerigo Vespucci, from whom America was named, visited the Western Continent, 10.
1512. Ponce de Leon discovered Florida, 11.
1513. Balboa discovered the Pacific, at first called the South Sea, 10.
1520. Magellan discovered the Straits of Magellan, and entered and named the Pacific Ocean. One of his ships completed the first circumnavigation of the globe in 1522, 10.
1521. Cortes completed the subjugation of Mexico, 11.
1524. Verrazzano explored the coast of America from North Carolina to Nova Scotia, 13.
1534. Cartier explored the shores of the Gulf of St. Lawrence, 14.
1541. Coronado explored the country about the upper Rio Grande, 13. De Soto discovered the Mississippi, 12.
1562. The Huguenots attempted to form a settlement in South Carolina, 14.
1564. The Huguenots attempted to form a settlement in Florida, 14.
1565. St. Augustine, the oldest European town in the United States, was founded by Menendez, 13.
1579. Drake visited the western coast of North America, named it New Albion, and claimed it for England, 15.
1584. Raleigh sent out, under Amidas and Barlow, an expedition, which reached the coast of North Carolina. The country was named Virginia, 16.
1585. Raleigh attempted to plant a colony at Roanoke, 16.
1587. Raleigh again attempted to plant a colony at Roanoke, 16.
1602. Gosnold discovered and named Cape Cod, 16.
1605. Port Royal (now Annapolis), Nova Scotia, was settled by the French, 15.
1606. James I. granted the Charter of Virginia, 17.

PERIOD II.
SETTLEMENTS AND INTERCOLONIAL WARS.
FROM THE SETTLEMENT OF JAMESTOWN, IN 1607, TO THE BEGINNING OF THE REVOLUTIONARY PERIOD, IN 1764.

I. VIRGINIA.

1. IN May, 1607, a colony of one hundred and five persons, under the auspices of the London Company, began the settlement of **Jamestown**, on the James River, in Virginia. This was the *first permanent English settlement in America.*

2. It was not long before the **colonists** began to experience severe troubles. They were, for the most part, poor gentlemen and broken-down tradesmen, unused to labor, many of them despising it. Their provisions were unwholesome, and the spot where they landed was unhealthy. Soon the air was filled with the complaints and groans of the sick. Before autumn near half of their number had perished, among them Bartholomew Gosnold, a leading spirit of the enterprise.

3. Under the **first charter** the colony was governed by two councils, the superior one resident in England, the other, which managed local affairs, resident in the colony. The local council had power to choose a president, who was to be the chief officer in the colony.

QUESTIONS.—1. Name the first permanent English settlement in America. When, where, and by whom was it made?
2. What can you tell about the character of the colonists and the hardships they had to undergo? How many perished before autumn?
3. Under the first charter, how was the colony governed?

4. **Wingfield**, the first president, was soon accused of misconduct in office, and, although he vigorously defended himself against the charges, was deposed. At length the management of affairs was intrusted to **Captain John Smith**, the ablest man of all. He was of a bold and roving disposition, and his life had been full of the most exciting and romantic adventures. He became the master-spirit and the preserver of the colony.

5. Smith explored the neighboring country, and forced the Indians to supply him with corn. A **well-known story** is related of his escape from death at their hands. We are told that on one of his expeditions he was taken prisoner by the Indians, and brought before their great chief, Pow-hat-an'; and that a council of grim warriors, arrayed in their best attire, was held to determine the fate of the captive. They decided that he should be put to death. His head was placed upon a stone, and two strong Indians had raised their clubs to strike the fatal blows, when **Po-ca-hon'tas**, Powhatan's daughter, a young and beautiful girl, sprung to the side of Smith, clung to his neck, and begged her father to spare his life. Her prayer was granted, and Smith was allowed to return to Jamestown.

6. We do not know that **this story** of Captain Smith and the young Indian princess is true; but we do know that there was an Indian maiden by the name of **Pocahontas**, who was a daughter of Powhatan, and that, several years after this event is said to have occurred, she was married to an Englishman named John Rolfe, with whom she visited England, where she was treated with great favor.

7. **More settlers** came over from England, but they were of the same sort as the former. They would neither build nor plant, but wasted their time searching for gold. At last Smith made a rule that all should work six hours a

---

4. What is said of the first president? What of Captain John Smith?
5. Relate the well-known story of Smith's capture by the Indians, and his rescue by Pocahontas.
6. What is said of this story? What do we know about Pocahontas?
7. What is said of new settlers? What rule did Smith make?

day. "He that will not work," Smith said, "shall not eat." A better state of things soon began to prevail.

8. Two years after the founding of the colony the London Company obtained a **second charter** from the king. The territory granted by this charter extended along the coast two hundred miles north of Old Point Comfort, and the same distance south, and throughout the land from sea to sea. The council in England was now authorized to appoint a governor for the colony.

9. About this time Smith returned to England, and his departure was the signal for disorder and idleness. The Indians became hostile. All the provisions were quickly consumed, and the horrors of famine ensued. This period, in 1610, was long remembered as the **starving time.** Some of the English were killed by the savages; others sailed away to turn pirates. Smith left in the colony near five hundred persons; within a few months the number was reduced to sixty.

10. In this time of extreme distress **Lord Delaware,** the new governor, arrived with men and provisions, just in season to prevent the wretched colonists from abandoning the country. By his judicious management matters presently wore a better aspect. From time to time the company sent over **emigrants,** by whom the soil was successfully cultivated and new settlements were formed.

11. A **third charter** was granted in 1612. The control of affairs, heretofore committed by the king to a council, was now given to the Company. Till 1619 the colonists had no voice in making their laws; but that year, under the administration of Sir George Yeardley (*yard'lĭ*), they were allowed to elect **representatives** (called burgesses), who convened at Jamestown, and formed *the first legislative assembly in America.*

---

8. What territory was granted by the second charter? What was the council in England now authorized to do? Where is Old Point Comfort? (See Map.)
9. What happened to the colonists after Smith's return to England?
10. Who arrived in the time of extreme distress? What was prevented? What is said of Delaware's management? What of new emigrants?
11. When was a third charter granted, and what change was then made in the control of affairs? When and under what governor, did the first legislative assembly in America convene?

12. In the year 1619 a Dutch ship, from Africa, landed twenty negroes at Jamestown, who were sold as slaves for life. The arrival of this first ship-load of negroes marks the beginning of **negro slavery** in the English colonies of America. In the same year nearly a hundred young English women, of good character, were sent over, and sold to the planters for **wives**. The price of a wife was a hundred and twenty pounds of tobacco,—this being the cost of her passage across the ocean. Afterwards, when more came over, the price was somewhat higher. **Tobacco** had already become a staple product for export to England.

13. The colony was in a flourishing condition, when, in 1622, it experienced a stroke which nearly proved fatal. **Opechancanough** (*op-e-kan'ka-no*), a bold and wily Indian chief, **laid a plot** to destroy all the whites at a single blow. The Indians professed the warmest friendship. "Sooner," said they, "shall the sky fall than peace be violated on our part;" but at midday they fell upon the unsuspecting **settlers**, and **massacred** nearly three hundred and fifty persons. Jamestown and a few of the neighboring settlements were saved by the warning of a Christian Indian.

14. The English immediately rose against the savages, destroyed many of them, and drove the rest far into the wilderness. Somewhat more than twenty years after this massacre the Indians made **another attack**, by which several hundred colonists lost their lives. Again the savages were pursued and killed without mercy.

15. Dissatisfied with the proceedings of the London Company, the king wrongfully took away its charter, and made **Virginia a royal province** in 1624. The governor and council were to be appointed by the crown, but the colony was permitted to retain its legislative assembly. So long

---

12. When and how was negro slavery introduced? How were the colonists supplied with wives? Price of a wife? What of tobacco?
13. What can you tell of a plot to destroy the English? How many whites were massacred, and how were some of the settlements saved?
14. How did the English avenge this massacre? When was another attack made, and with what result?
15. When, and for what cause, was Virginia made a royal province? What is said of the government of the colony? What of the right of the colonists to elect representatives? Conduct of some of the royal governors?

as the colonists had the right to elect their representatives to help make laws, the principle of popular liberty was preserved. This right was the more precious as the conduct of some of the **royal governors** was odious and oppressive.

16. During the time of the Commonwealth in England, after the execution of King Charles I., **Virginia** enjoyed the highest measure of freedom and prosperity; but after monarchy was restored, in 1660, a different state of things began to prevail. Certain laws of England, called the Navigation Acts,* secured to the mother country a rigorous monopoly of colonial commerce. Besides this grievance the Virginia planters had others. While **Sir William Berkeley**† was governor, exorbitant taxes were levied, and the people were much restricted in their liberties. To make this state of affairs worse, a war began with the Indians.

17. The tyrannical course of Berkeley, and his neglect to provide for defence against the savages, caused many of the planters, in 1676,‡ to rise against his government, under the lead of Nathaniel Bacon. During this outbreak, known as **Bacon's Rebellion**, the governor was driven from Jamestown, which was burned by the insurgents, to prevent its again being a harbor for the enemy. In the midst of his successes Bacon suddenly died, and as there was no one to fill his place, the popular forces dispersed. Berkeley regained his power, and cruelly wreaked his vengeance on those who had opposed him.

18. Notwithstanding these troubles, and the greedy and arbitrary dispositions of many of the governors after Berkeley's time, **the colony** continued to grow and prosper; but its history henceforth, till the beginning of the French and Indian War, is marked by no events of sufficient importance to be noticed in these pages.

---

* See Navigation Acts, p. 71, ¶ 8.   † *berk'li.*
‡ One hundred years before the Declaration of Independence.

---

16. What was the state of things in Virginia during the time of the Commonwealth? What after monarchy was restored in England? What is said of the Navigation Acts and other grievances while Berkeley was governor?
17. What caused an outbreak, and when did it occur? What more can you tell of Bacon's Rebellion?
18. **What is said of the colony of Virginia after Bacon's Rebellion?**

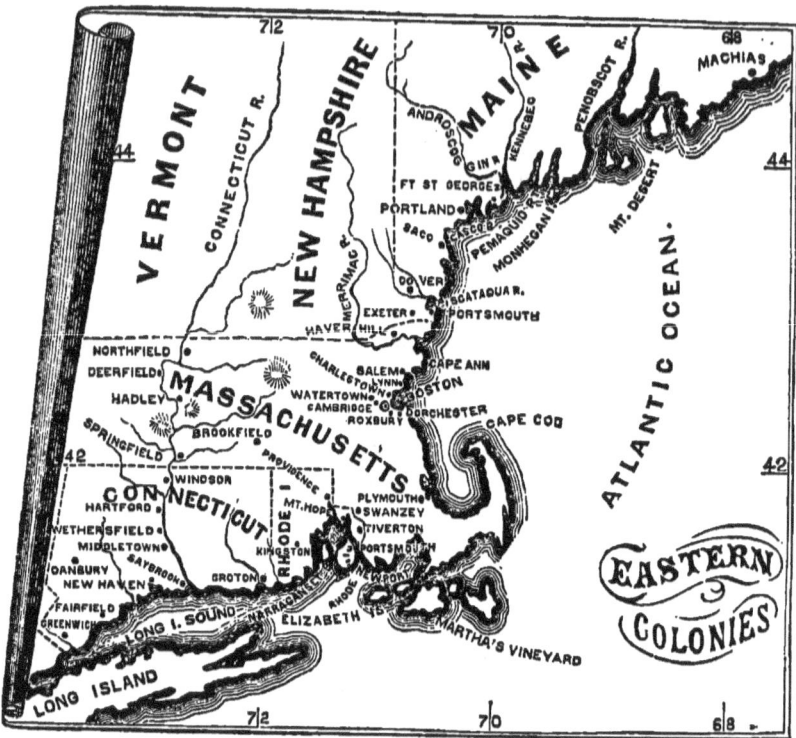

II. MASSACHUSETTS.

1. *North Virginia. The Council for New England.*

1. The same year in which Jamestown was settled, the Plymouth Company attempted to plant a colony in America. A party of emigrants, under **George Popham** (*pop'am*), landed near the mouth of the Kennebec River, in Maine, and erected a fort; but discouraged by the severe cold of the winter and the death of their leader, they returned the next year to England.

2. Seven years later, in 1614, **Captain John Smith**, so famous in the early history of Virginia, came again to America, sailing from England with two ships, for the pur-

---

1. Give an account of an unsuccessful attempt to plant a colony in Maine. What fort did the emigrants erect? *Ans.* Fort St. George.
2. What expedition was undertaken to America in 1614? What coast did Smith explore, and what name did he give the country?

pose of trade and discovery. He examined the coast from the Penobscot River to Cape Cod, made a map of it, and named the country *New England*.

3. The old Plymouth Company was dissolved in 1620, and a new company formed, called the **Council for New England**.* To this company the king, James I., granted, under the name of New England, the territory between the 40th and 48th degrees of north latitude, — that is, from the southern part of Pennsylvania to near the middle of Newfoundland, — and extending westward from the Atlantic to the Pacific. But this country was destined to be first settled by Englishmen, without permission from either the Council or the king.

2. Colony of Plymouth.

4. A company of **Puritans**, as certain dissenters from the Church of England were called, to escape persecution at home, fled to Holland. After some years they determined to remove to the wilderness of America, that they might follow their own ideas of worship and government.

5. Accordingly they embarked for Southampton, England, where they were joined by others from London. **They set out** at first in two vessels, the Speedwell and the Mayflower. But the Speedwell springing aleak, they twice put into port, the last time at Plymouth, where that ship was dismissed as unseaworthy. The Mayflower finally set sail alone for the New World, having on board one hundred and two of the Pilgrims—men, women, and children. After a long and stormy voyage, they entered harbor at Cape Cod.

6. Before landing, the male immigrants signed **a compact**, by which they formed themselves into a body politic, and declared that they would enact just and equal laws for the

---

* Also called the " Council of Plymouth."

---

3. When was the old Plymouth Company dissolved, and what company took its place? What territory was granted to the Council for New England?
4. Who were the Puritans, and where did some of them take refuge? What did they determine to do, and why?
5. What occurred at Southampton? After the Puritans set out for the New World, what occurred? How many Pilgrims sailed in the Mayflower? What of the voyage? Meaning of the word Pilgrim?
6. What took place before landing? Who were the most prominent Pilgrims?

general good, and obey them. The most prominent among the colonists were John Carver, who was chosen to be the first governor; William Bradford, the second governor; the cultivated Edward Winslow; William Brewster, their ruling elder, and Miles Standish, their military leader.

7. Many days were spent in selecting a spot for a settlement. The last of the exploring parties, sent out from the Mayflower, landed December 21,* 1620, at **Plymouth**, and here all the Pilgrims came, a few days afterwards, and began the *first permanent settlement in what is now called New England.*

8. **They suffered** severely during the first winter. Many fell sick with colds and lung fevers. When in March, as it is recorded, "'a south wind brought fine weather, and the birds sang in the woods most pleasantly,' the sun shone and the birds sang over many graves." Within four months from the time of their landing, nearly half of the little band had perished, among these Governor Carver.

9. Fortunately **the Indians** did not molest them during the time of their severest trials. Massasoit', "the chief of the Wampano'ags" (*wom-*), formed a treaty of friendship with them, which was not violated for more than fifty years — till King Philip's War. Canon'icus, the powerful chief of the Narragansetts, was at first hostile, but the determined course of Governor Bradford caused him to conclude that it was best to be on friendly terms with the white men.

10. The spring after their arrival **the Pilgrims** began to till the ground; but, during the first three years, they often suffered from the want of food. Afterwards they raised corn enough for themselves, and had some to trade with the Indians for furs. The colony of Plymouth grew very slowly. In 1692, by command of the English king, it was united with that of Massachusetts Bay.

* New Style, or December 11, Old Style. Owing to an error made in changing the date from Old to New Style, the anniversary has commonly been celebrated on the 22d.

---

7. When and where was the first permanent settlement in New England made?
8. What is said of sickness and death among the Pilgrims?
9. What of the Indians? Of Massasoit? Of Canonicus?
10. What did the Pilgrims do in the spring? Their condition afterwards? To what colony was the colony of Plymouth united, and when?

3. *Colony of Massachusetts Bay.*

11. In the year 1628, **John Endicott** and a small party of Puritans settled at **Salem**, and thus laid the foundation of the Colony of Massachusetts Bay. These emigrants were sent out from England by a company which had obtained a grant of land from the Council for New England.*

12. The next year King Charles I. granted the company a **charter**.† More colonists were now sent over, some of whom settled at **Charlestown**. In a short time the proprietors decided to transfer the charter and powers of government from England to the colony in America. The wisdom of this policy was seen in the increased number of emigrants who now sought homes in the new land. About a thousand, with the excellent **John Winthrop** as governor, came over in 1630, and founded **Boston**, and other neighboring settlements. Winthrop ably managed affairs. Not only while he was governor, but at all times the welfare of the colony was first in his thoughts.

13. **The colonists** suffered severely in many ways, as had those at Plymouth; but their privations and distress were overcome by their energy and fortitude. From time to time the colony was increased by the arrival of **Puritans**, who sought safety from persecution in England, and many new towns were settled.

14. The **chief officers** of the colony were a governor, a deputy governor, and assistants, sometimes called magistrates. After the settlements became numerous, the towns

---

* This grant comprised the lands extending from a line three miles north of every part of the Merrimack River, to a line three miles south of the Charles River, and from ocean to ocean.

† The patent from the council gave the company the territory, the charter from the king secured to the company the right to choose officers and make laws.

---

11. What is said of the settlement at Salem, and of the emigrants sent there? Whence is the name of Massachusetts derived? *Ans.* From the name of a tribe of Indians,— the tribal name probably signifying *great hill people.*
12. What was obtained from the king the next year? What of new colonists? What was decided in regard to the charter and powers of government? Result of this policy? What of John Winthrop and other emigrants?
13. What is said of the sufferings and privations of the colonists? How was the colony increased?
14. What officers of the colony are mentioned? Who alone were voters? What wish had the Fathers of Massachusetts?

were allowed to send deputies to assist in making laws. The legislative body formed by these various officers was called the General Court. Among the rules adopted was this — that only church members should be allowed to vote for the civil officers. This rule existed for many years. The Fathers of Massachusetts wished to found a religious commonwealth.

Log-house of an early Settler.

15. The Puritans living on Massachusetts Bay were soon disturbed by dissensions. The first serious contest was with Roger Williams, a young minister of Salem. His opinions in regard to civil and religious affairs being considered dangerous, the magistrates banished him from the colony. But they were soon much more alarmed and troubled by the conduct of Mrs. Ann Hutchinson. She held meetings, and taught doctrines which most of the Puritans

---

5. What is said of dissensions? Of Roger Williams? Of Mrs. Ann Hutchinson?

believed to be false and pernicious. At last, determined to have peace in the community, they banished her and the most obnoxious of her followers.

16. Severer punishments were inflicted upon the **Quakers**, who were filled with fanatical zeal, and very unlike the Quakers of our day. They began to come to Massachusetts in 1656. The first who came were sent away; but soon others appeared. Some of the Quakers were whipped, some put into prison, some had the right ear cut off, and four, who came again and again into the colony, were hanged. But these cruel measures of the Puritans did not keep away their disagreeable visitors, and after a few years such penalties were not inflicted.

17. Very early in the history of Massachusetts care was taken to provide for **education**. When Boston was only six years old, the General Court appropriated four hundred pounds to found a college. This, the oldest college in America, was established at Cambridge, and named after the Rev. John Harvard, who, dying in 1638, gave it several hundred pounds and his library. Not many years after this, it was ordered that each town of fifty families should maintain a school to teach reading and writing, and each town of a hundred families should set up a grammar school. It would be difficult to estimate too highly the good which has resulted from these wise orders.

18. Impelled by a sense of common danger from the Indians, and by the encroachments of the Dutch and the French,* the colonies of Massachusetts Bay, Plymouth, Connecticut, and New Haven, in 1643, formed themselves into a confederacy, styled the **United Colonies of New England**. This league for mutual protection is famous in our colonial history. It continued more than forty years.

---

* The Dutch in what is now New York, and the French upon the eastern frontier of the English colonists.

---

16. Describe the first Quakers in Massachusetts. When did they begin to come? What cruelties were inflicted upon them? Effect?
17. What is said of education in the early history of Massachusetts? What of Harvard College? What of schools in towns?
18. What confederacy was formed in 1643, and for what causes? How long did this league continue?

19. In 1675, a hundred years before the beginning of the Revolution, a terrible contest, called **King Philip's War**, began with the Indians. King Philip, as the English named him, was the son and successor of the friendly Massasoit, chief of the Wampanoags. His home was at Mount Hope, in Bristol, Rhode Island. For several years the colonists had suspected him of being unfriendly, and of plotting for their destruction. The **immediate cause** of the war was the execution of three Indians, by the English, for the murder of an Indian who had come to them and accused Philip of hostile intentions. Furious with rage, Philip's men began hostilities, in which they were joined by most of the New England tribes.

20. For more than a year this **savage warfare** spread devastation and ruin among the scattered settlements of the English. Connecticut alone, of all the New England colonies, escaped its ravages; yet she liberally contributed to the common defence. The principal battle, known as the **swamp fight**, took place in a swamp, in South Kingston, Rhode Island, where the powerful Narragansetts were defeated with great slaughter. The **death of Philip**, who was shot by an Indian fighting on the side of the whites, brought the war to a close, except in Maine, where it lasted some time longer. This contest broke the spirit of the New England Indians.

21. Many complaints having been made to the king, Charles II., that Massachusetts had violated the Navigation Acts, and in other respects had disregarded the royal authority and the laws of England, he determined to take away her form of government. To carry out this design the highest English court, in 1684, declared the **charter of Massachusetts null and void**. The colony now lay at the king's mercy.

---

19. When did King Philip's War begin? Who was Philip, and where did he live? Give an account of the origin and beginning of the war?
20. What was the nature of this warfare, and how long did it last? What of Connecticut? Where, and with what tribe, was the principal battle fought? What of the death of Philip? Result of the contest to the Indians?
21. What complaints were made against Massachusetts to the king? With what result? What can you tell of the Navigation Acts? (See p. 71, ¶ 8) How and when was the charter of Massachusetts declared null and void?

22. The king dying before he had time to adjust colonial affairs, his successor, James II., sent over **Sir Edmund Andros** as governor of all New England. For more than two years the people endured Sir Edmund's tyrannical sway; but in 1689, when news reached the colonies that the king had been driven from the throne, the inhabitants of Boston seized Andros and put him into prison. The colonies of New England then resumed their former modes of government.

23. William and Mary, successors to James II., granted a **new charter** to Massachusetts, in 1691, by which the limits of the province were so extended as to embrace the Plymouth colony. Maine and Nova Scotia were also placed under her jurisdiction. But this charter was far less liberal than the old; the governor and other high officers were hereafter to be appointed by the king. In May, 1692, **Sir William Phipps** arrived from England, as the first governor under the new charter, which he brought with him.

24. At this time there prevailed in Massachusetts that strange delusion, known as the **Salem Witchcraft**. Some girls in Danvers, then a part of Salem, were, or pretended to be, strangely affected, and they accused certain persons of bewitching them. Those whom they "cried out" against were arrested, and soon, new accusers arising, the mania spread throughout the community.

25. Within a few months twenty persons were tried and executed; more than fifty were frightened into confessing themselves guilty, and the jails were full of prisoners. **Accusations** fell upon some high in social position before the people began to come to their senses. At length the frenzy spent itself; those in prison were liberated, and the awful tragedy closed. In that age the belief in witchcraft was common in all civilized countries.

---

22. Who was sent over as governor of New England? How long did the people endure Sir Edmund's rule? How and when was it terminated?
23. What happened to Massachusetts in 1691? How did the new charter differ from the old? Who was the first governor under the new charter?
24. What prevailed in Massachusetts in 1692? Give an account of the origin and progress of the delusion.
25. How many persons were executed, and how many confessed themselves guilty? What is said of accusations and of the close of the tragedy? What is said of the belief in witchcraft in that age?

4. Maine.

26. The first settlers in what is now the State of Maine were fishermen, who built a few huts here and there along the coast, but a little while after the landing of the Pilgrims at Plymouth.

27. In 1639 **Sir Ferdinando Gor'ges** obtained a royal charter, constituting him lord proprietor of a tract of land reaching from the Piscataqua to the Kennebec. This territory he called the *Province of Maine.** The charter made good a grant which Gorges had already obtained from the Council for New England.

28. But Massachusetts also claimed to the Kennebec, and after some years asserted her jurisdiction over the district. At length the claims of the heir of Gorges were bought by Massachusetts, and in the course of time the region farther east was joined to that province. Maine continued a part of Massachusetts till 1820.

III. NEW HAMPSHIRE.

1. Two years after the landing of the Pilgrims at Plymouth, **Sir Ferdinando Gorges** and **Captain John Mason** obtained from the Council for New England a grant of lands lying between the Merrimack and the Kennebec. In the following year, 1623, the proprietors sent out a few colonists, and two settlements were made — one near **Portsmouth**, and the other at **Dover**.

2. The partnership between Gorges and Mason being dissolved, the latter, in 1629, obtained a new grant for a territory between the Merrimack and the Piscataqua, and

---

* This eastern country had been called the *Mayne* [main] land in distinction from the islands along the coast, and thus the province probably obtained its name.

26. Who were the first settlers of Maine?
27. What royal charter did Sir Ferdinando Gorges obtain in 1639? Where is the Piscataqua? the Kennebec? the Merrimack? (See Map, p. 28.) What did Gorges call his province? What grant had Gorges previously obtained? Whence does Maine derive its name? See note above.
28. What is said of Massachusetts and this district? What of the region farther east? Till what year was Maine connected with Massachusetts?
1. What grant of lands was obtained by Gorges and Mason? When and where were the first settlements made in New Hampshire?
2. What new grant did Mason obtain in 1629? Whence does New Hampshire derive its name? See note, p. 37. Under whose jurisdiction did the settlements in New Hampshire place themselves?

named it *New Hampshire.** The feeble settlements of **New Hampshire** voluntarily placed themselves under the jurisdiction of Massachusetts in 1641, and under her charge they continued for nearly forty years.

3. In 1679 New Hampshire was made a **royal province** — the first so constituted in New England. Afterwards it was united with Massachusetts for a long time, so far as to have the same governor, but with its own legislative body and laws. A final separation took place in 1711, just a hundred years from the first union.

4. The settlers of New Hampshire were harassed for many years by lawsuits, brought against them by those into whose hands Mason's claim to the soil had come. At length the long **controversy** was ended, the claimants under Mason's grant consenting to take only the unoccupied portion of the province.

IV. CONNECTICUT.

1. The soil of **Connecticut**† was assigned to Lord Say and Seal, Lord Brooke, and others, in 1632, by the Earl of Warwick, who was president of the Council for New England. The earl had already received, or was expecting to receive, a grant of this territory from the Council. Before the proprietors could take possession of the lands which they had thus obtained, others had begun to occupy them.

2. Some years after the **Dutch** had formed settlements in what is now New York, they built a fort where Hartford stands, and began to buy furs of the Indians. In the autumn of the same year, namely, 1633, **Captain Holmes** (*hōmz*), with a party of men from the Plymouth colony, sailed up the Connecticut. When he reached the Dutch fort, the

---
* After the county of Hampshire, England, in which Mason lived.
† So named from the Indian name of its principal river — a word signifying *long river.*

---
3. What is said of New Hampshire as a royal province? What of a later connection with Massachusetts? When did a final separation take place?
4. How were the settlers of New Hampshire long harassed? How was the controversy settled?
1. When and by whom was the soil of Connecticut assigned? What is said of the Earl of Warwick's right to this territory? Whence does Connecticut derive its name? See note above.
2. Give an account of the Dutch in Connecticut and of Capt. Holmes's expedition.

officer in command there ordered him to stop; but Holmes kept on, and erected a trading-house at Windsor.

3. The colonists on Massachusetts Bay had also heard of the rich meadow-lands in this region, and emigrants from the neighborhood of Boston, making their way across the wilderness, began the settlement of Connecticut in earnest in 1635, at **Wethersfield, Windsor, and Hartford.**

4. But the largest emigration took place the next summer, when about a hundred persons, of both sexes and all ages, led by their pastor, Thomas Hooker, "the light of the western churches," came through the pathless forests, driving their herds of cattle before them. Most of this company settled at Hartford. The settlements in these parts formed the **Connecticut Colony.**

5. Meanwhile John Winthrop, son of the Massachusetts governor, had come over from England, as the agent of Lord Say and Seal, Lord Brooke, and the other proprietors. He built a fort at the mouth of the Connecticut in 1635, and here a settlement, called Saybrook, was made. After a few years the **Saybrook Colony** was united with the Connecticut colony, farther up the river.

6. The year 1637 is marked in the history of Connecticut by the **Pequot War**, the first contest in New England between the whites and the Indians. The Pequots were the most formidable Indian nation in New England. They had murdered, with horrible cruelty, many of the colonists, when Captain John Mason, with a small force of Englishmen and friendly Indians, marched against their principal stronghold in the south-eastern part of Connecticut. The savages were attacked by surprise, but they fought desperately till their fort and wigwams were set on fire. Few indeed escaped, while hundreds perished in the flames and by the weapons of the colonists. The war was soon ended, but not till the Pequots had ceased to exist as a people.

---
3. Give an account of the settlement of Wethersfield, Windsor, and Hartford.
4. Give an account of the emigration under the Rev. Thomas Hooker. What did the settlements on this part of the Connecticut form?
5. What can you tell of John Winthrop and the Saybrook colony?
6. When did the Pequot war break out? Who were the Pequots, and what had they done to the colonists? Tell what you can about Mason's expedition, and the result of the war to the Pequots.

7. The founders of the Connecticut colony, finding themselves beyond the bounds of Massachusetts, organized a **government** for themselves, modelled on that of Massachusetts, but more liberal, since the right of voting was not restricted to church members.

8. **New Haven** was founded in 1638, by emigrants under the lead of John Davenport, a distinguished minister from London, and Theoph'ilus Eaton, an eminent London merchant. This and the neighboring towns, which were settled soon after, were known as the **New Haven Colony**. The Scriptures were adopted here as the rule in public affairs, and only members of the church were voters.

9. Both the colonists at New Haven and those on the Connecticut came near having a strife in arms with the **Dutch**, in New Netherland, who claimed the soil as far as, and even beyond, the river; but the disputes were finally settled without bloodshed. Fear of these neighbors, as we have already said, was one of the causes for forming the Confederacy of the New England colonies.

10. In the year 1665, under a **charter** granted three years before by the English king, Charles II., Connecticut and New Haven were united, and styled the *Colony of Connecticut*. The charter was so liberal, that the privileges conveyed by it almost amounted to colonial independence. A little more than twenty years later, **Andros**, "glittering in scarlet and lace," landed at Boston, as governor of New England. Within a year he appeared at Hartford, and, dissolving the colonial government, asserted his own authority.

11. **A story** relates that Andros, at this time, demanding possession of the charter, a discussion arose, which was prolonged into the evening, when the precious writing was brought in and laid upon the table. Suddenly the lights

---

7. What is said about the government of the Connecticut colony?
8. Give an account of the founding of New Haven. What of the government of the New Haven colony?
9. What is said of difficulties with the Dutch?
10. When, and under what charter, were the colonies of Connecticut and New Haven united? What further is said of this charter? What is said of Andros at Boston and at Hartford?
11. Relate the story of the hiding of the charter. When was the charter government resumed?

were extinguished; when they were rekindled the charter had disappeared. Captain Wadsworth had taken it away, and secreted it in the hollow trunk of an oak, afterwards known as the *Charter Oak*. The charter government was resumed after news came that Andros had been deposed in Boston.

V. RHODE ISLAND.

1. The founder of Rhode Island was **Roger Williams**, who was banished from Massachusetts. He left his home, and for more than three months was a wanderer in the wilderness, "sorely tossed in a bitter winter season," as he says, "not knowing what bread or bed did mean."

2. At last, with five associates who had joined him, he went to a point of land above Narragansett Bay, and made a settlement, which he called **Providence**, to express his confidence in "God's merciful providence to him in his distress." This was in 1636, the same year in which Hooker and his company migrated to Connecticut. Williams bought of the Narragansett sachems, Canonicus and Mianton'omoh, lands to be occupied by his colony.

3. He was soon followed by other exiles from Massachusetts. By his advice some friends of the celebrated Mrs. Hutchinson purchased of the Indians the island now called Rhode Island,* and settled there, founding **Portsmouth** in 1638, and the next year **Newport**, now so famed as a sea-side resort. Both the Providence colony and that of Rhode Island granted **religious freedom** to all. This was the great idea that Roger Williams advocated. His liberal views and kind heart have gained him an honored name.

4. Williams went to England, and obtained from Parlia-

---

* The Dutch had called this island, from its reddish appearance, *Roodt Eylandt* — Red Island. This became the English *Rhode Island*.

---

1. Who was the founder of Rhode Island? What is said of Williams after his banishment?
2. What can you tell of the settlement of Providence?
3. Give an account of the settlement of Portsmouth and Newport. What is said of religious freedom in the colonies of Providence and Rhode Island? What of Roger Williams? Whence does Rhode Island derive its name? See note.
4. What is said of a charter from the English Parliament? What was the distinguishing feature of the government?

ment, then controlling public affairs, a **charter**, by which the two colonies were united. Religious toleration was the distinguishing feature of the government which the colonists afterwards organized.

5. The settlements prospered, and Charles II., in 1663, granted to them, under the name of the Rhode Island and Providence Plantations, a **royal charter**, as liberal as that of Connecticut. This was set aside by Andros, but after his overthrow it was resumed, and henceforth, till a very recent date, was the only constitution of Rhode Island, as the colony came to be called.

VI. NEW YORK.

1. New York under the Dutch.

1. **Henry Hudson**, an Englishman, sailing in the service of a company of Dutch merchants in 1609, to find a northern passage to India, explored part of the eastern coast of America, entered New York harbor, and ascended to a considerable distance the noble river which now bears his name. The Dutch claim to territory in America was based upon the discoveries of Hudson.

2. Dutch ships were soon sent out to the newly discovered river, and a traffic for furs was begun with the Indians. A few huts to shelter traders were built on Manhattan Island,* and a fortified trading-house was erected in 1614, within the limits of the present city of Albany.

3. Actual **colonization** began in 1623, under the patronage of a great trading association, called the Dutch West India Company. Permanent settlements were then made at *New Amsterdam*, now **New York**; and *Fort Orange*, where now stands **Albany**. The region claimed by the Dutch reached, under the name of *New Netherland*,† from the southern shore of Delaware Bay to the peninsula of Cape Cod.

---

* The site of New York city. † The *th* of *Netherland* pron. as *th* in *this*.

5. When was a royal charter obtained, and what is said of it?
1. Who was Henry Hudson, and what exploring voyage did he make in 1609? Upon what was the Dutch claim to territory in America based?
2. What is said of Dutch ships? Of traders and a fortified trading-house?
3. When and how was actual colonization begun? What permanent settlements were then made? What region was claimed as New Netherland?

4. **Peter Minuit** (*min'u-it*) arrived in 1626 as governor of New Netherland. During his administration the company adopted a scheme to promote colonization. Any one who would plant a colony of fifty persons was allowed to select lands many miles in extent, which should descend to his posterity forever. Such as availed themselves of this privilege were called **patroons**, or lords of the manor.

5. The next governor was **Wouter Van Twiller**. During his time the English made their first settlements in Connecticut, and thus entered upon territory claimed by the Dutch. The controversy which now began with the English settlers in Connecticut was continued by **Sir William Kieft** (*keeft*), who succeeded Van Twiller.

6. But an **Indian war** was Kieft's most serious trouble. His treatment of the natives was marked by extreme cruelty, and they, with the fury of revenge, wasted the settlements, nearly all of which were destroyed before the long and bloody contest ended.

7. The last and ablest Dutch governor was **Peter Stuyvesant** (*sti'ves-ant*). He arranged a boundary with the English in Connecticut, and conquered a colony of Swedes, on the Delaware, who were, the Dutch claimed, within the bounds of New Netherland.

8. The **English** had never ceased to regard New Netherland as belonging to them, on the ground of the discoveries of the Cabots, and therefore King Charles II. made a grant of it to his brother, the Duke of York and Albany (afterwards King James II.), and Colonel Nic'olls and despatched, with a fleet, to take possession of the province.

9. When the English ships entered the harbor of **New**

---

4. When did Peter Minuit arrive, and what scheme to promote colonization was adopted?
5. Who was the next governor? What was done by the English during his time? Who succeeded Van Twiller?
6. What is said of an Indian war in New Netherland?
7. Who was the last and ablest governor of New Netherland? What proceedings of his are mentioned?
8. How did the English regard New Netherland? What grant was made, and what measures taken, to gain New Netherland for the English?
9. What can you tell of the capture of New Amsterdam?

Amsterdam, Stuyvesant, who was a stout old soldier, resolved to defend the city to the last. But the people thought that resistance would be useless, and refused to fight the invaders. Hence Stuyvesant was obliged to yield.

2. *New York under the English.*

10. The whole province was reduced without a battle, and thus, in 1664, **New Netherland** came under the dominion of England. The country and its chief city were named New York. The settlement at Fort Orange was called Albany. It is reckoned that New Netherland, at the time of its surrender, contained ten thousand inhabitants.

---

10. In what year did the English conquer New Netherland? What names did the English give to the province and the two principal settlements? Whence does New York derive its name? *Ans.* It was so named in honor of the Duke of York and Albany. Number of inhabitants in all New Netherland?

11. **Colonel Nic'olls** was the first English governor of New York. The colonists were sadly disappointed in the hope which they had had of obtaining greater freedom under the new rule. Hence they did not regret it when, after a few years, a **Dutch squadron** appeared in the harbor of New York, and compelled the surrender of the city. But after little more than a year, in 1674, the province was restored to the English, and **Edmund Andros** was appointed governor. Several years later Andros was recalled; but he was again sent to America, as has been told, to play the tyrant in New England.

12. In the year 1683 the colonists of New York were granted a right which they had long ardently desired. The governor, by permission from the Duke of York, called an **assembly of representatives** of the people. The duke not long afterwards becoming king of England, under the title of James II., refused to allow the people to hold their assembly; but this state of things lasted only a few years, and then the colonists again helped make their own laws.

13. About the close of this century pirates were infesting almost all seas. **William Kidd**, a New York shipmaster, was sent with an English ship to cruise against them. But soon Kidd himself turned pirate, and became the most notorious of them all. After a long cruise he returned to the colonies, and was seen in the streets of Boston. The Earl of Bellamont, who was then governor of both New York and Massachusetts, caused Kidd to be seized and sent to England, where he was hanged.

14. In the year 1741 the city of **New York** was thrown into dreadful alarm. Many fires having taken place, a report was circulated that the **negroes** had devised a plot to burn the town, murder the citizens, and take the government into their own hands. Without sufficient proof that any plot of this kind existed, more than thirty negroes

---

11. What of Colonel Nicolls and the colonists? After a few years what took place? When was New York restored to the English? What is said of Edmund (afterwards Sir Edmund) Andros?
12. What can you tell of an assembly of representatives?
13. Relate the story of William Kidd.
14. Give an account of the supposed negro plot in New York city.

were condemned and burned at the stake or hanged. The existence of any real plot is doubtful; but it is certain that many innocent persons were put to a cruel death. When they were tried no one was willing to say a word in their defence.

VII. NEW JERSEY.

1. The territory included in New Jersey was a part of the grant made by King Charles II. to the Duke of York, and came into the possession of the English with the rest of New Netherland. But even before the surrender of the Dutch the duke had conveyed New Jersey* to **Lord John Berkeley** (*berk'lĭ*) and **Sir George Car'teret**.

2. While the **Dutch** held sway over this territory, they formed a few feeble settlements within its limits. As early as 1623 they erected a fort on the east side of the Delaware River; and still earlier, it is asserted, they had a trading-post at Bergen.† But the settlement made at **Elizabeth** in 1664, by persons from Long Island, is generally regarded as the beginning of colonization in New Jersey.

3. The following year the proprietors sent over **Philip Carteret**, as the first governor. The liberal constitution which they granted the colonists, together with the mildness of the climate and the fertility of the soil, soon induced many people from New England and New York to settle in the province.

4. Lord Berkeley sold his share of New Jersey to certain English Quakers; after the purchase, a party of this sect made a settlement at Salem. The province was now divided into **East and West Jersey** — the eastern portion becoming Sir George Carteret's property, the western that of the Quaker proprietors.

5. In 1682, after Carteret's death, East Jersey was sold

---

* It was so named in honor of Sir George Carteret, who had been governor of the Island of Jersey. † *g* in *Bergen* sounded as *g* in *get*.

1. In what grant was the territory of New Jersey included? Whence does New Jersey take its name? See note above.
2. Give an account of the Dutch in this territory. What is considered the beginning of the colonization of New Jersey?
3. Who was the first governor? What induced colonists to settle in New Jersey?
4. What is said of Quakers? How was the province divided?
5. To whom was East Jersey sold? Who settled in New Jersey?

to **William Penn** and other Quakers. English Quakers, Puritans from New England, and Dutch colonists formed settlements in New Jersey. Many Scotch Presbyterians, fleeing from their native land to escape persecution, also became planters in this province.

6. The various proprietors surrendered the government of East and West Jersey to the crown in 1702. The two Jerseys were then reunited as a **royal province**, and placed under the same governor with New York. In 1738 the king appointed Lewis Morris governor of New Jersey only, and from this time the government of the province was kept entirely distinct from that of New York.

VIII. DELAWARE.

1. The permanent colonization of the present State of Delaware* was begun in 1638, by a company of **Swedes and Finns**, conducted by Peter Minuit, who had been governor of New Netherland. The plan of founding a colony in America for the benefit of all persecuted Christians had been formed by the famous Protestant king, Gusta'vus Adolphus, of Sweden. He was killed in battle, but the colonists were sent to carry out his wish.

2. They purchased of the Indians a tract of land on the Delaware, and near the present site of Wilmington made their first settlement, which they called **Christina** (*kris-te'nah*), after the young Queen of Sweden. Afterwards more colonists arrived, and other settlements were made farther up the river. The territory lying along the western shore of Delaware Bay and River, as far as the falls at Trenton, was named *New Sweden*.

3. **The Dutch** claimed this region as a part of their New Netherland, and built a fort a few miles from Christina.

---
* The state takes its name from Lord Delaware, one of the governors of Virginia.

6. When did New Jersey become a royal province? In what way, and till what year, was its government connected with that of New York?
1. When and by whom was Delaware colonized? Whence does Delaware derive its name? See note above. What plan had Gustavus Adolphus formed?
2. Where was the first settlement made, and what called? Other settlements? Extent and name of the Swedish province?
3. What can you tell of the conquest of New Sweden by the Dutch?

This fort the Swedish governor seized; but his success cost him dear, for Peter Stuyvesant, the governor of New Netherland, soon came with a force and conquered the whole province. Such of the inhabitants as swore allegiance to Holland were allowed to stay; the rest were sent out of the country. Thus, in 1655, New Sweden came to an end.

4. When the Duke of York took possession of New Netherland, the territory west of the Delaware became part of the province of **New York**. In the year 1682, the duke having sold it to William Penn, it became part of **Pennsylvania**, and was known as "the territories, or three lower counties, on the Delaware." Twenty years later this district was so far separated from Pennsylvania as to have a distinct legislative assembly, but the same governor presided over both colonies till the Revolution.

IX. MARYLAND.

1. Sir George Calvert, the first **Lord Baltimore**, obtained from King Charles I. of England a grant of a tract of land east of the Potomac, and along the shores of Chesapeake Bay. It was the wish of Lord Baltimore to provide a place of refuge for Roman Catholics, then persecuted in England. His territory was called *Maryland*.*

2. This nobleman dying before the charter had been issued, it was made out in favor of his son, **Cecil Calvert**, who inherited his father's title. He sent out his brother, Leonard Calvert, as governor, with about two hundred colonists, who arrived in 1634, and began the settlement of **St. Mary's**, near the mouth of the Potomac.

3. The charter created Lord Baltimore and his heirs

---

* Named in the charter Terra Mariæ (*Mary's Land*), in honor of the queen, Henrietta Maria. *Terra* is a Latin word, meaning "a land."

---

4. What is said of the territory west of the Delaware when the English seized New Netherland? To whom was it sold, and when, and what was it called? What further is said of this district?
1. What grant did the first Lord Baltimore obtain? His wish? Whence does Maryland derive its name? See note above.
2. To whom was the charter issued? What settlement was made, and when?
3. What is said of the charter?

"lords and proprietors" of the province; but it also granted to the colonists the right of choosing representatives for a legislative assembly. The proprietor of Maryland was a Roman Catholic; but the colonists were allowed to worship God as they pleased, and after some years, in 1649, the assembly sanctioned this wise policy by a law, called the **Toleration Act**, which declared that no one professing to believe in Jesus Christ should be molested on account of his religion.

4. A man by the name of **William Clayborne**, who had lived in Virginia, caused a great deal of trouble in the colony. He made the first settlement in Maryland on **Kent Island**, in Chesapeake Bay, as early as 1631. The English king had given him a license to trade with the Indians. After the colonists came, he attempted, by force of arms, to withstand the authority of Lord Baltimore; but he was overcome, and forced to flee. Some years afterwards he reappeared in Maryland, and, inciting a rebellion, obliged the governor to take refuge in Virginia, where he obtained troops who helped him suppress the revolt.

5. But the contests of **the Protestants and the Roman Catholics** caused much more serious trouble in the colony. After the Puritans in England had overthrown monarchy there, those in Maryland disregarded the rights of Lord Baltimore, and, having obtained the power, they ungratefully ordained that no Catholic should be entitled to the protection of the laws. **Civil war** followed, and the Protestants were victorious. But after a very few years the government was restored to Lord Baltimore.

6. For a long period the mild and liberal principles of the proprietor held sway in Maryland, and the **colony** became very **prosperous**. But when William and Mary came to the throne of England this tranquillity was interrupted. The delay on the part of the governor to pro-

---

3. What of religious freedom and the Toleration Act?
4. Who caused much trouble in Maryland? What is said of the first settlement? What more can you tell of Clayborne?
5. What can you tell of trouble between the Protestants and Roman Catholics?
6. What is said of a prosperous period? What of an absurd rumor? How and when was Maryland made a royal province?

claim the new sovereigns, and **an absurd rumor** that the Catholics were plotting the destruction of the Protestants, roused the latter to seize the government, which remained in their hands until the king, in 1691, deprived Charles Lord Baltimore (son of Cecil the founder of Maryland) of his political rights as proprietor, and Maryland became a **royal province**.

7. In the year 1715 Maryland was restored to the infant heir of Lord Baltimore. It remained a **proprietary province** until the Revolution, when the people assumed the government, and confiscated the rights of the proprietor.

X. PENNSYLVANIA.

1. An extensive tract of land west of the Delaware River was granted to **William Penn**, in 1681, by Charles II. of England, and named by the king *Pennsylvania.** After receiving his patent from the king, Penn obtained from the Duke of York a grant of the "territories or three lower counties" now forming the State of Delaware.

2. The father of William Penn was a distinguished English admiral. When he died the government owed him a large sum of money, and in payment of the debt the province in America was granted to his only son. This son belonged to the society of **Friends**, or Quakers, who at that time were despised and persecuted in England. He desired to found a colony where freedom and peace could be enjoyed by all.

3. **Colonists** were sent out to the new province by the proprietor, and in 1682 he himself came over, and was soon followed by a large number of emigrants, chiefly Quakers. The Swedes and Dutch, who had already settled on the banks of the Delaware, and elsewhere within the

---

* Penn's Woodland. *Sylva* is a Latin word, meaning "a wood."

7. What occurred in 1715? What more can you tell of Maryland?
1. What grant of land did William Penn obtain, and when? Tell who named Pennsylvania, and give the meaning of the name. What grant did Penn obtain from the Duke of York?
2. What can you tell of William Penn's father? To what society did William Penn belong? His object in founding a colony?
3. What is said of colonists? Who had already settled within Penn's domain?

4

bounds of Penn's domain, were not disturbed, but were allowed the same privileges as the English.

4. The **government** which Penn established for his province was marked by a spirit of great liberality. The people chose their own representatives for an assembly to aid in making laws. It was agreed that no one who believed in "one Almighty God" should be molested for his religious opinions.

5. Soon after his arrival, Penn made his **famous treaty** with the Indians. He met them under a great elm by the side of the Delaware, in what is now a part of Philadelphia. After hearing the words of peace and kindness with which he addressed them, the Indians declared that they would live in love with William Penn and his children as long as the sun, moon, and stars should endure. The treaty thus established remained uninterrupted for more than seventy years — till Pennsylvania had passed from the control of the Quakers.

6. Near the close of the year 1682 Penn laid out a capital for his province, and named it **Philadelphia** — a name which signifies *brotherly love*. Before the end of the next year it contained nearly a hundred houses. None of the other colonies planted in America had so rapid and prosperous a growth as Pennsylvania.

7. The affairs of his province caused **Penn** a great deal of trouble. The laws which the assembly made were often not to his mind, and the settlers were unwilling to pay the small rent by which the proprietor hoped to remunerate himself for the large sums of money he had spent in founding his colony.

8. He was also harassed by a controversy with Lord Baltimore, in respect to the boundary between **Pennsylvania and Maryland**. This question was not settled till two eminent surveyors, named Mason and Dixon, came over

---

4. What can you tell of the government established by Penn?
5. Give an account of Penn's famous treaty with the Indians.
6. What is said of the founding of Philadelphia, and its growth?
7. How did the affairs of his province give Penn trouble?
8. What controversy harassed Penn? Tell all you can of Mason and Dixon's line.

from England, long after Penn's death, and determined the line separating Pennsylvania from Maryland and Virginia. This is famous in American history as "Mason and Dixon's line," and was, till a recent day, a bound for the free and the slave states.

9. Penn died in 1718, leaving a name conspicuous among those which designate the benefactors of the human race. His sons became proprietors of the flourishing colony he had founded, and appointed deputies to administer the government. At the beginning of the American Revolution the people of Pennsylvania purchased the proprietary claims for more than half a million of dollars.

XI. NORTH AND SOUTH CAROLINA.

1. In 1663 Lord Clarendon, and seven other persons of high rank, obtained from their king, Charles II. of England, a patent for a vast territory south of Virginia. The king afterwards enlarged the boundaries of this province, which was named *Carolina*.*

2. The proprietors of Carolina found that **planters from Virginia** had already settled on the northern shore of Albemarle Sound. The very year in which the grant was made, a liberal government was instituted for this little plantation, which received the name of the **Albemarle Colony**. In 1665 a company from Barbadoes (*bar-ba'doze*), formed a settlement near the mouth of Cape Fear River. This was called the **Clarendon Colony**. Both of these settlements were within the present limits of North Carolina.

3. In 1670 a third colony, called the **Carteret Colony**, was founded by emigrants from England. The colonists sailed into Ashley River, and began their first town ; but ten

---
* In honor of the English king, Charles (Latin *Carolus*) II.

9. How was the colony governed after Penn's death ? What did the people of Pennsylvania do at the beginning of the Revolution?
1. What can you tell of the grant of Carolina ? Whence do the Carolinas derive their names ? See note above.
2. What settlement had already been made ? What name was given to this plantation ? What can you tell of the Clarendon colony ? What is Barbadoes ? *Ans.* It is a small island in the south-eastern part of the archipelago formed by the West Indies. Where is Cape Fear River ? (See Map, p. 52.)
3. Give an account of the Carteret colony and the founding of Charleston.

years later they removed to a point of land between the Ashley and Cooper Rivers, and there laid the foundation of the present city of **Charleston.**

4. Most of the inhabitants of the middle, or Clarendon colony, removing after a few years to Charleston, the affairs of the province were administered by two governments — one for the northern, or Albemarle, and another for the southern, or Carteret colony. Thus were created the two colonies of **North and South Carolina.** They were increased by people from New England, and Dutch families from New York. The persecuted Huguenots of France and Puritans of England also came to find homes in the Carolinas.

5. Both colonies suffered much from wars with the Indians. In the year 1711, the **Tuscaro'ras** in North

---
4. How were the three colonies reduced to two, and what was thus created? What colonists came to Carolina?
5. Give an account of the war with the Tuscaroras in North Carolina.

Carolina, suddenly fell upon the whites and massacred many persons. By the aid of a force from South Carolina the savages were conquered, and soon afterwards they migrated north, and joined the Iroquois of New York, forming the sixth nation of that powerful confederacy. A few years later the **Yam'as-sees** and other Indians attacked the settlers in South Carolina, but they were subdued after some severe fighting.

6. In 1729 the two Carolinas, which had hitherto been considered as one province, were separated, and the proprietors having ceded to the crown their rights of government and seven eighths of the soil, North and South Carolina became distinct **royal provinces.** So they remained till the Revolution.

XII. GEORGIA.

1. To **James O'glethorpe**, an officer in the English army, belongs the honor of founding in America a refuge for the poor of his own country, and the persecuted of all nations. In 1732 George II. granted to him and twenty associates, "in trust for the poor," the territory between the Savannah and the Altamaha (*al-ta-ma-haw'*).* This territory was named *Georgia*, in honor of the king.

2. Oglethorpe himself led the first colony, numbering about one hundred and twenty-five persons. They landed early in 1733, and began to build the town of **Savannah**, on the southern bank of the river of the same name.

3. The **project** of founding a colony for poor debtors, and other indigent persons, excited great interest, and many benevolent Englishmen gave money in aid of the enterprise. More emigrants soon followed the first company. A band of German Lutherans and a party of

* After the treaty of Aix-la-Chapelle, ending King George's war, the St. Mary's was made the southern boundary of Georgia.

---

5. Where did the Tuscaroras go after this war ? What is said about the Yamassees in South Carolina?
6. When and how did the two Carolinas become distinct royal provinces.
1. What is said of James Oglethorpe? What grant of land was made to him and associates?
2. What can you tell of the first colonists and the founding of Savannah?
3. How was Oglethorpe's project aided? What is said of German, Scotch, and English colonists? When and how did Georgia become a royal province?

Scotch Highlanders formed thriving settlements in Georgia; but the **colonists** sent over from England were, for the most part, idle, thriftless, and discontented. The trustees surrendered their charter to the crown in 1752, and Georgia became a **royal province.**

XIII. THE FRENCH AND THE SPANIARDS.

1. While the English were taking possession of a narrow strip along the coast from Maine to Georgia, the **French** were exploring the St. Lawrence, the Great Lakes, the Mississippi, and their tributaries.

2. **Champlain,** "the father of New France," founded Quebec in 1608, and thus began the settlement of **Canada,** which became the principal French province in America. The next year he discovered the lake that still bears his name. In the northern and central parts of New York dwelt the Iroquois, or **Five Nations,** of all Indians the most powerful and warlike. Champlain made alliances with tribes hostile to them, and invaded their country. Hence the Five Nations became bitter enemies to the French, and fought them with the greatest fury; but they held the English as friends.

3. In the summer of 1673, James Marquette (*mar-ket'*), a French Jesuit, and Louis Joliet,* with five of their countrymen, entered **the Mississippi** from the Wisconsin, and in two birch-bark canoes, floated down its current below the mouth of the Arkan'sas. Nine years afterwards, in 1682, the adventurous and daring La Salle (*lah-sal'*) completed the discovery of the great river of the west by descending to its mouth. Naming the whole region drained by it and its branches *Louisiana,* in honor of his king, Louis XIV., he claimed it for France.

---

* English pronunciation *jo'li-et*, French *zho-le-a'*.

---

1. While the English were taking possession of a strip along the Atlantic how were the French employed?
2. What is said of the founding of Quebec, and what of Canada? What can you tell of the Five Nations, and of their relations to the French and the English?
3. What Frenchmen first explored the Mississippi, and when? Who completed the discovery of this river, and when? What region was claimed by La Salle?

1718.] THE FRENCH AND THE SPANIARDS. 55

4. **The vast domain of France** in America now lay north and west of the English colonies, and stretched southward to the Gulf of Mexico. The French followed up their discoveries by establishing forts, missions, and trading-posts, and by making settlements both in the south and the west. In the southern part of their dominion they formed settlements at Biloxi, at Mobile, at Natchez, and at New Orleans. This last town was founded by colonists under Bienville (*be-an[g]ʹ-veel'*) in 1718.

5. Before the "French and Indian War,"—the last struggle between the American colonies of France and England,—the French had constructed a chain of **military posts** from Montreal to New Orleans. This they did with the design of confining the English to the territory between the Alleghany Mountains and the sea. The most famous of these forts were Detroit, Niag'ara, and Crown Point.

6. **Spain** made but few settlements in her Florida and New Mexico. She regarded both the French and the English in the south as intruders upon her soil. Alarmed at the efforts of the former to colonize the country at the mouth of the Mississippi, the Spaniards built a fort at Pensaco'la, and formed a settlement there as early as 1699. They also built forts in Texas. In this region, and farther north on the Rio Grande, Spanish priests founded missions to convert the Indians.

To complete the early history of the English colonies in America we shall now give an account of several wars, sometimes called the **Intercolonial Wars**, in which the colonies of England fought those of France or of Spain.

* This nasal sound stops before the sound *ng* is formed.

4. Describe the French domain in America. What did the French do after making discoveries in the south and the west? What settlements of theirs in the south are mentioned? Where is Biloxi (*be-lok'sĭ*)? (See Map facing p. 110.) Mobile (*mo-beel'*)? Where is Natchez? New Orleans (*or'le-anz*)?
5. What military posts were constructed by the French, and with what design? Name the most famous of these posts, and tell where they were situated.
6. What is said of Spanish settlements? How did Spain regard the French and English in the south? What forts did the Spaniards build? What of Spanish priests?
What were the Intercolonial Wars?

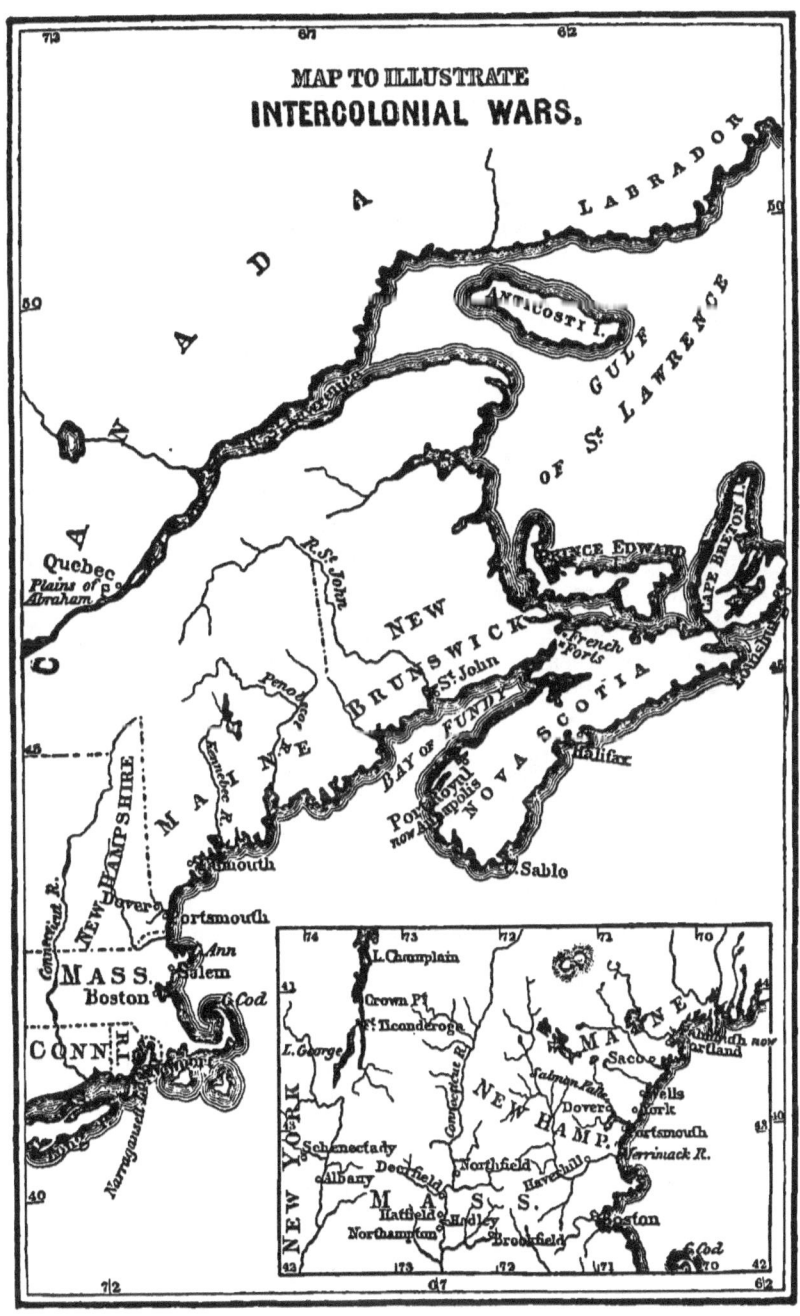

THE INTERCOLONIAL WARS.

I. KING WILLIAM'S WAR.

1. After James II. fled from England, he sought protection of Louis XIV., king of France, who tried to reseat him on his throne. This kindled between the two countries, in 1689, the flames of a war, which extended to their colonies. The contest in America is known as *King William's War*. The Indians of Canada and Maine aided the French; the Five Nations aided the English.

2. Most of the **frontier settlements** in Maine and New Hampshire were broken up or destroyed by the French and the savages. In the winter of 1690 a war party of French and Indians came through the wilderness from Canada, and in the dead of night fell upon the little village of **Schenectady**, in New York, and burned it. Sixty of the inhabitants were killed. Of the rest, those not taken captive fled half naked through the deep snow to Albany.

3. A few months later Sir William Phipps, in command of a small fleet from Massachusetts, captured the old French settlement of **Port Royal**, in Nova Scotia, and obtained considerable booty. After this success a plan was formed for the conquest of **Canada**. Troops from Connecticut and New York were sent against Montreal, by the way of the valley of the Hudson and Lake Champlain, while Phipps, with a naval force from Massachusetts, sailed against Quebec. Both expeditions met with disaster, and effected nothing.

4. The war lasted almost eight years. In 1697 a **treaty**, which put an end to it, was signed at Ryswick (*riz'wik*), a town in Holland. Each party was to have the same territory as before the war.

---

1. Give the cause of King William's war, and the year in which it began. What Indians aided the French, and what the English?
2. What fate befell the frontier settlements in Maine and New Hampshire? Give an account of the attack upon Schenectady (*ske-nek'ta-di*). Where is Schenectady? (See Map, p. 56.)
3. What can you tell of the capture of Port Royal? Of expeditions sent for the conquest of Canada? Where is Port Royal? (See Map, p. 57.)
4. How long did King William's war last, and what treaty put an end to it? How did this treaty affect territorial claims?

II. QUEEN ANNE'S WAR.

1. The peace of Ryswick did not last long. In 1702 England declared war against France and Spain, and the American colonies took part in the contest, which is commonly called in America *Queen Anne's War*.

2. As the Spaniards in Florida were now enemies of the English colonists, South Carolina hastened to send a force against the old settlement of **St. Augustine.** The town was easily captured, but the fort held out till two Spanish ships entered the harbor, when the invaders retreated in great haste. A few years later a French and Spanish naval force made an attack upon **Charleston,** but the assailants were soon driven away with loss.

3. The **contest in the north** took the same form as the preceding war. The French, from Canada, and their Indian allies laid waste the frontier settlements of New England, and committed terrible acts of cruelty. The Five Nations, always friendly to the English, had lately made a treaty with the governor of Canada, and agreed to be neutral; but by their situation they shielded New York from hostile incursions.

4. In 1710 **Port Royal** was again wrested from the French by a combined force from New England and the mother country. In honor of Queen Anne, the name of the place was changed to *Annapolis*. The next year an **English fleet,** with regular and colonial soldiers, proceeded against Quebec. But many of the transports were dashed upon the rocks in the St. Lawrence, and nearly a thousand men perished. After this disaster the commander sent home the colonial troops, and sailed with his fleet for England.

5. After continuing eleven years, Queen Anne's war was closed by a **treaty** made in 1713, at Utrecht (*yoo'trekt*),

---

1. When did Queen Anne's (*anz*) war begin, and what nations were engaged in it?
2. What expedition was sent from South Carolina, and with what result? What happened a few years later?
3. What is said of the contest in the north? What befell New England settlements? What is said of the Five Nations?
4. When and how was Port Royal captured, and what was it named? State what you can of the unsuccessful expedition against Quebec?
5. How long did Queen Anne's war continue, and what treaty put an end to it? What did England gain in America by this treaty?

a town in Holland. By this treaty England gained in America possession of a vast region about Hudson's Bay, of Newfoundland, and of Acadia, afterwards called Nova Scotia.

III. THE SPANISH WAR.

1. After the lapse of little more than a quarter of a century there was another intercolonial war. In 1739 England and Spain again made war upon each other.

2. The next year **General Oglethorpe**, the founder of Georgia, marched against St. Augustine, with an army collected from the southern colonies, and a large body of Indians. He was unsuccessful, as were the Spaniards, who in turn invaded Georgia. General Oglethorpe had too small a force openly to withstand the invaders, but by an artifice he frightened them away.

3. During the contest the American colonies were called upon to furnish troops to aid an English fleet and army in capturing Spanish settlements in the **West Indies**. The enterprise ended disastrously, and of the four thousand men from the colonies but a few hundred ever returned to their homes. The Spanish war was marked by no very important events in America, and after about five years it became merged in King George's war.

IV. KING GEORGE'S WAR.

1. News of another war between England and France reached America in 1744. By the English colonists it was called *King George's War*, from George II.

2. The most important event of the war in America was the **capture of Louisburg** from the French. This fortress

---

1. When did another intercolonial war begin, and what nations were engaged in it?
2. Give an account of Oglethorpe's expedition against St. Augustine. What did the Spaniards afterwards do, and with what result?
3. For what enterprise did the American colonies furnish troops? Result? In what war was the Spanish war merged?
1. When did news of another war reach America? What was this war called in America?
2. What was the most important event in America of this war? When and how was Louisburg taken? What is the fortress of Gibraltar (*jib-rawl'tar*)? *Ans.* It is a fortress in the southern part of Spain, so situated upon a rock as to be almost impregnable.

was of such strength as to be called the Gibraltar of America; but it was taken early, in the summer of 1745, by an army from New England, under command of William Pep'perrell, of Maine, aided by an English fleet.

3. King George's War was brought to a close in 1748, by the treaty of Aix-la-Chapelle (*āks-lah-sha-pel'*), as it was called, from a place in Prussia. It was agreed that both countries should restore their respective conquests.

V. THE FRENCH AND INDIAN WAR.

1. It was not long before **another war** — the last and severest of the intercolonial struggles — broke out between the English and the French. The Indians fought for each party, but much the greater number joined the side of the latter. This contest is known in America as the *French and Indian War*. It was caused by **conflicting claims** of England and France to territory in America. When war was actually declared, both countries had formed alliances which were followed by the mighty struggle in Europe called the *Seven Years' War*.

2. **The French** had determined to confine the English to a belt of land along the coast, and to keep in their own hands the lucrative fur trade with the Indians west of the Al'-leghany Mountains. But the **English** also claimed this interior region, and refused to be thus hemmed in.

3. An association, called the **Ohio Company**, having obtained from the English king the grant of a large tract of land on the Ohio River, prepared to form settlements and open trade with the Indians; but the designs of the company were frustrated by the **governor of Canada**, who sent troops across the lakes to build forts in the disputed territory.

4. Governor Dinwiddie, of Virginia, determined to send

---
3. When and how was King George's war brought to a close? What was agreed by the treaty?
1. What part did the Indians take in the last war between the French and English colonies? Name and cause of the war? What of the war in Europe?
2. What had the French determined to do?
3. What can you tell of the Ohio Company? How were its designs frustrated?
4. What did Governor Dinwiddie determine to do?

a letter to the commander of the French, to demand his reasons for invading the country, and to require him to depart. **George Washington**, not yet twenty-two years old, was selected by the governor to execute this commission. Late in the autumn of 1753, he set out from Williamsburg, the capital of Virginia, for the north-west corner of Pennsylvania, where the French commander had established his post.

5. **His journey**, for several hundred miles, was through the heart of a wilderness, containing rugged mountains and swollen streams, and infested by savages. The peril of the way was increased by cold and stormy weather; but at the end of eleven weeks, Washington delivered to Governor Dinwiddie, in Williamsburg, **the reply** of the French commander, St. Pierre (*pe-are'*). By this reply it was seen that the French intended to hold the country.

6. It was resolved by the governor of Virginia to build **a fort** where Pittsburg now stands, and to send an armed force to drive away the intruders. The men were building the fort, when the French came upon them, and compelled them to retire. The French then completed the works, which they called *Fort Duquesne* (*du-kāne'*).

7. **Washington** became **the leader** of the force which was collected to go against the enemy in the Ohio Valley. While on the march through the wilderness in the spring of 1754, he was warned by an Indian chief to be on his guard, for a party of French soldiers was near, with hostile designs. Washington surprised this party, lurking near his camp. The French commander and ten of his men were killed. This was the *first conflict of arms in the war.*

8. Not much more than a month after this event, a large force of French and Indians marched against Washington, who had hastily thrown up a fortification, which he named *Fort Necessity.* After a brave defence he was obliged to

---

4. Who was sent to the French commander, and when? Where had the French commander established his post?
5. Give an account of Washington's journey. What of the reply of the French?
6. What is said of Fort Duquesne? Where was this fort built? (See Map, p. 56.)
7. What can you tell of the first conflict of the war?
8. What is said of the erection of Fort Necessity, and of its capture?

surrender this fort, July 4, 1754. The English were allowed to retire with the honors of war — drums beating and colors flying.

9. **Events of 1755.** — Early in the spring of 1755, **General Braddock** landed in Virginia, with two British regiments. He had been appointed commander-in-chief of all the forces in the provinces. **Four expeditions were planned.** These were to be sent against Fort Duquesne, Nova Scotia, Crown Point, and Niagara.

10. The force which went against the French on the Ohio was led by **Braddock** himself, **Colonel Washington** acting as an aide-de-camp. The British general was ignorant of Indian warfare, yet too self-confident to heed the prudent counsels which Washington gave him. When within a few miles of Fort Duquesne, his army was surprised, July 9, by a small party of French, with their Indian allies, and routed with terrible slaughter. Braddock was mortally wounded. The ability and bravery which Washington showed at the battle of **Monongahe′la,** as it was called, won for him great regard throughout the colonies.

11. The expedition against **Acadia**, or Nova Scotia, captured the French forts in that province, and the whole region east of the Penobscot fell under British authority. But this success was disgraced by a terrible act of violence and cruelty. Several thousands of **the Acadians,** or French colonists, were assembled, unsuspicious of the designs formed against them, and driven on board ships by British soldiers. These unfortunate people were carried off, and scattered among the English colonies. Thus torn from their homes, wives were separated from their husbands, and children from their parents, never to see each other again.

12. General William Johnson, of New York, commanded the troops collected to go against **Crown Point.** At the

---

9. Who landed in Virginia as commander-in-chief? What expeditions were planned for 1755? Where is Crown Point? Niagara?
10. What is said of Braddock and Washington, and of the expedition against the French on the Ohio? Conduct of Washington at the battle?
11. Give an account of the expedition against Acadia. What can you tell of the cruel treatment of the Acadians?
12. Give an account of the battle of Lake George.

southern end of Lake George, he encountered a French force led by the Baron Dieskau (*dees'kow*), who had come from Montreal by the way of Lake Champlain. The battle finally resulted in a victory for the English. The Baron Dieskau was badly wounded and taken prisoner. After the **battle of Lake George**, Johnson gave up the attempt upon Crown Point. Building Fort William Henry, near the battle-ground, and leaving a garrison in it, he finally disbanded the rest of his troops.

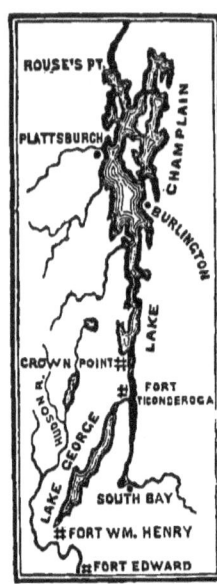

Lake Champlain and Vicinity.

13. The expedition against **Niagara** also proved a failure. The troops commanded by General Shirley, of Massachusetts, advanced as far as Os-we′go, where they built a new fort. At last, owing to the lateness of the season and to other causes, the enterprise was abandoned. Leaving men to garrison the defences at Oswego, Shirley went back to Albany.

14. **Events of 1756-7.** — **War** was not formally **declared** till 1756. During this and the next year the English had little success, but met with serious disasters.

15. In the summer of 1756, the French, under their distinguished leader, the **Marquis de Montcalm** (*mont-kahm'*), captured the forts at **Oswego**. Many prisoners, and a great quantity of stores, fell to the victors. Almost exactly a year later, this bold and vigilant commander struck the English another heavy blow.

16. Ascending Lake George with a large force of French and Indians, he laid siege to **Fort William Henry**, and, after some days, compelled its garrison to surrender. A few miles below this fort was another English post, held by

---

12. After this battle what did General Johnson do?
13. Give an account of the expedition against Niagara.
14. When was war formally declared? Result of the war for the next two years?
15. What is said of Montcalm and his successes?
16. Give an account of the capture of Fort William Henry.

General Webb, with four thousand soldiers; but this officer, to his lasting disgrace, made no attempt to aid the brave Colonel Mon-ro' and his troops in Fort William Henry. The English were promised a safe escort to the fort held by Webb. But the infuriated savages fell upon them as they began their march, and, in spite of the efforts of the French officers, the defenceless prisoners were plundered, and some of them massacred.

17. Nor was the loss of those important forts the only disaster which the English suffered. The savages, fighting for the French, devastated the whole north-western frontier, and **war parties** carried the brand and the tomahawk into the heart of the English settlements. Thus far in the struggle the French had had much the best of it. The English forces in America, during two disastrous years, had been under the command of **an inefficient general**, Lord Loudoun (*lou'dun*), who was always ready to quarrel with the colonies, but never ready to meet the enemy.

18. **Events of 1758.** — In the year 1758, the war assumed a different aspect. The celebrated William Pitt, afterwards Earl of Chatham (*chat'am*), was now the leading spirit of the British ministry, and the supreme direction of the war was in his hands. **Three expeditions** were proposed — one against Louisburg, another against Ticondero'ga and Crown Point, and a third against Fort Duquesne.

19. A large fleet aided the powerful army of General Amherst (*am'erst*), who was sent to capture **Louisburg.** Both the English and the French fought bravely, and for many days the siege went on; but at last, in July, the fortress was won by the English. The French fleet in the harbor was destroyed or captured, and the whole island of Cape Breton (*brit'un*) reduced. The English also became

---

16. What is said of Webb? What did the savages do to the prisoners?
17. What other disasters did the English suffer? What is said of the British general, Loudoun (*lou-dun, ou* as in *house*)?
18. When did affairs take a different aspect? What famous British statesman was then directing the war? What expeditions were proposed for 1758?
19. Give an account of the capture of Louisburg. What besides Louisburg fell into the hands of the English?

masters of Prince Edward Island, and of the coast as far north as the St. Lawrence.

20. While the siege of Louisburg was going on, the largest army as yet seen in America moved against **Fort Ticonderoga**. It was more than fifteen thousand strong, British and provincial troops, under the command of the incompetent Abercrombie (*ab'er-krum-bĭ*), now the general-in-chief of all the English forces in America.

21. On the 5th of July, more than a thousand boats, full of soldiers, with waving flags and strains of martial music, swept down Lake George. All anticipated an easy victory. On the fourth day afterwards the boats bore back the shattered columns of this grand army in disorderly retreat. They had assaulted the defences of the French at Ticonderoga, and Montcalm had beaten them back with heavy loss. Lord Howe, a gallant young English officer, whom all loved, fell dead in the first skirmish.

22. The disgrace of this repulse was in some degree retrieved by Colonel Bradstreet, who, with three thousand men from Abercrombie's army, crossed Lake Ontario and captured **Fort Fron'tenac,** where Kingston now is. This was a severe blow to the French, as they lost a great quantity of stores and several ships on the lake. The fort was blown up by the English.

23. The expedition for the capture of **Fort Duquesne** was commanded by General Forbes. His army pushed forward, Colonel Washington with the Virginians leading the advance. After a long and laborious march through the wilderness, late in November, General Forbes took possession of what was left of Fort Duquesne. The French had abandoned it the day before, and set fire to it. In honor of the illustrious British minister, the name of the stronghold was changed to *Fort Pitt.*

---

20. What is said of the army which moved against Fort Ticonderoga, and of the British general? Where was Fort Ticonderoga? (See Map, p. 56.)
21. Describe the movement of the army against this fort, and tell the result? What is said of Lord Howe?
22. Give an account of the capture of Fort Frontenac. Where was this fort? (See Map, p. 56.)
23. Give an account of the expedition against Fort Duquesne. How was the name of the fort changed?

24. Events of 1759. — The campaign of 1759 had for its object the conquest of Canada. The following plan was formed. One expedition was to reduce Niagara, while another was to capture Ticonderoga and Crown Point. Both armies were then to go down the St. Lawrence, to coöperate with a third expedition, which should go up the river to attack Quebec.

25. Niagara was invested by troops under the English General Prideaux (*prĭd'o*). This officer having been killed, Sir William Johnson took the command, and in July put to rout a strong force of French and Indians, who attempted to relieve the besieged garrison. The next day the fort was surrendered to the English. In the same month, General Amherst, now the commander-in-chief, approached **Ticonderoga and Crown Point** with the main army. As the French could not hope to make a successful resistance, they deserted these strongholds. But after these successes, Amherst and Johnson did not advance to coöperate with the English fleet and army before Quebec.

26. The command of the most important expedition was given to **General James Wolfe.** His forces in June ascended the St. Lawrence to **Quebec.** This town was so strongly situated, and had been so well fortified on all sides, that it seemed impregnable. Below Quebec, Wolfe failed in an assault upon the defences which the skilful Montcalm had constructed; but, above the town, one dark night he silently landed his troops — near five thousand veterans — and they clambered up the precipice to the **Plains of Abraham.** When the day dawned, the French saw with astonishment a British army ranged in order of battle before their intrenchments.

27. **The battle** which took place that day, September 13, decided the fate of France in America, and won for

---

24. What was the object of the campaign of 1759, and what plan was formed?
25. Give an account of the capture of Fort Niagara. Who was now the British commander-in-chief in the colonies, and what resulted from his movement against Ticonderoga and Crown Point?
26. Who commanded the expedition against Quebec? What is said of this town? Give an account of Wolfe's operations before the battle.
27. When was the battle fought, and what did it decide?

Great Britain a noble territory. **Wolfe**, pressing forward in the thickest of the fight, received a mortal wound. He was carried to the rear, where he lay faint and bleeding. While his life was fast ebbing away, he heard the cry, "They run! they run!" "Who run?" he asked. "The French," was the answer. "God be praised," said he; "I die happy." **Montcalm** was also mortally wounded. When the surgeon informed him that he could survive but a few hours, "So much the better," said he; "I shall not live to see the surrender of Quebec." Five days after the battle the city was given up to the English.

28. **Events of 1760, and the Peace of Paris.** — Early in the spring the French made an attempt to recapture Quebec, but they were unsuccessful. In September, General Amherst collected a large army around Montreal. The French governor, seeing that resistance would be useless, now **surrendered all Canada** to the English.

29. England made peace with France and her ally, Spain, by a **treaty** signed at Paris in 1763. All the territory which France had claimed east of the Mississippi, she ceded to England, except two small islands south of Newfoundland, retained as fishing stations, and the island* and town of New Orleans. This island and town, with all the French possessions west of the great river, France ceded to Spain. By the same treaty Spain ceded Florida to England.

30. **The Cherokee War.** — During the war with the French and Indians in the north, the Cherokees ravaged the frontier settlements of **the Carolinas**, in revenge for some gross wrongs which they had suffered. After a long and bloody strife, the Indian villages were destroyed, and the Cherokees compelled to sue for peace.

31. **Pontiac's War.** — In the year 1763, many tribes of

---

* The Island of New Orleans is a strip of land south of the River I'berville, and between the Mississippi and the lakes north and east of New Orleans.

---

27. What is said of Wolfe? Of Montcalm? When was the city surrendered?
28. State further operations of the French and English in Canada.
29. When was the treaty of Paris signed? What was ceded by France to England? What by France to Spain? What by Spain to England?
30. Give an account of the Cherokee war.
31. What war with the Indians began in the year 1763?

the **north-western Indians**, under the lead of a great Ottawa chief, named Pon'ti-ac, united to drive out the English, who now occupied the posts which the French had established in the west. In a short time most of the forts west of Niagara were surprised, and taken by the savages. The border settlements of Pennsylvania and Virginia were laid waste, and hundreds of families driven from their homes or massacred. For several months the fort at Detroit was besieged by Pontiac and his warriors, but the garrison withstood every attack. Expeditions were sent into the Indian country, and the year after the first outbreak most of the tribes that had taken up arms were glad to make peace with the English.

CONDITION, AT THE CLOSE OF THIS PERIOD, OF WHAT IS NOW THE UNITED STATES.

1. **France** had now lost her domain in America. **Spain**, at the close of this period, claimed the whole country west of the Mississippi. The island and the town of New Orleans were hers; but all else east of the great river had come under the power of England. The north-west corner of the continent, now called Alas'ka, was claimed by **Russia**, Vi'tus Behring (*beer'ing*), a Dane in the Russian service, having discovered the main land in 1741, while on a second voyage in these waters.

2. **England** now possessed thirteen colonies along the Atlantic coast. In these colonies there prevailed three **forms of government** — charter, proprietary, and royal.*

---

* The *charter governments* were those of Massachusetts, Rhode Island, and Connecticut. In these colonies important rights and powers were vested in the colonists by charters from the king.

The *proprietary governments* were those of Maryland, Pennsylvania (with Delaware), and at first New York, New Jersey, and the Carolinas. Here the proprietors were authorized, under certain restrictions, to establish governments.

The *royal governments* were those of New Hampshire, Virginia, New York, New Jersey, the Carolinas, and Georgia. Over these colonies the king placed governors, who ruled according to his instructions.

---

31. What forts were captured by the savages? What of settlements and families? What of Detroit? How and when was the war brought to a close?
1. What is said of France at the close of this Period? What was claimed by Spain in America? What by Russia, and from what discoveries?
2. What possessions had England along the Atlantic coast? What is said of the government of the thirteen English colonies?

Under all these forms the people had helped to make laws and had become accustomed to share in the administration of affairs.

3. The **population** of the thirteen English colonies, at the close of this Period, was not far from two millions. Eleven years later, at the breaking out of the Revolutionary War, it is estimated to have been something less than three millions.

4. During the early years of the colonies there prevailed almost everywhere an intolerant spirit in matters of **religion**, showing itself in unjust and cruel laws and deeds. But at the close of this Period the severities of early times, practised in the name of religion, were not sanctioned by any of the colonies. The French and Spanish settlements were exclusively Roman Catholic. The English colonies were Protestant — even in Maryland the adherents to this faith being by far the more numerous.

5. Steps were taken in most of the colonies at an early date to provide for the **education** of youth. But to New England must be accorded the high honor of first instituting and liberally maintaining common schools. The first **printing-press** in the English colonies was set up at Cambridge, Massachusetts, in 1639. Most of the **books** published in the earliest times were on religious subjects. The first permanent **newspaper** printed in America was the "Boston News-Letter," issued in 1704.* Before the close of this Period, Benjamin Franklin had made great **discoveries** in science. By means of a kite he drew lightning from the clouds, in 1752, and proved it to be really the same as electricity.

6. The colonists not only supplied themselves with food from the **cultivation of the soil**, but had a large sur-

---

* A single number of a newspaper was published in Boston in 1690.

3. State the population of these colonies at this time, and at the breaking out of the Revolutionary War in 1775.
4. What statement is made in regard to religion in the early years of the colonies, and at the close of this Period? What was the religion of the French and Spanish colonists? Of the English colonists?
5. What is said of education? When and where was the first printing-press set up? What of books? Give the name and date of the first newspaper issued in America. What is said of Benjamin Franklin?
6. What is said of agriculture? Of tobacco and cotton?

plus to export. Tobacco was an important product of the southern colonies. Cotton, which afterwards became so valuable a staple, was first raised in Virginia, in 1621.

7. **Manufactures** were of slower growth, but before the close of this Period various articles of which the inhabitants stood most in need were made in the colonies. The weaving of cloth was first introduced into America by some Yorkshire clothiers, who settled in Massachusetts, in 1638.

8. **Trade and commerce** from the beginning had steadily increased, although fettered by the **Navigation Acts**, which were laws made by England to benefit her merchants and ship-owners. By these acts the colonies could send their products to England in no ships but those owned by English subjects; their principal exports they were obliged to sell in England or her colonies, and from these countries to buy their principal imports. For a hundred years the colonies had been subjected to these restrictions in their commerce.

9. In the same selfish spirit **other laws** were made by the mother country, which prohibited the colonists from manufacturing certain articles, and from exporting other articles even from one colony to another. The English merchants often complained that the acts of trade were violated by the colonists, as indeed they were. Royal custom-houses were established to collect duties. Most of the **colonial ships** were built and owned in New England. There fishery was an important means of support and gain.

10. **Slavery**, at an early period, found its way into all the colonies, first silently permitted, then regulated by law. In the northern colonies slave labor was not generally lucrative; but in the south, negro slaves were much more numerous, and their labor became a source of wealth in the culture of tobacco, rice, and, after this Period, especially of cotton.

7. What can you tell of manufactures? Of the weaving of cloth?
8. What is said of trade and commerce? Give an account of the Navigation Acts.
9. Give some account of other laws of trade. What is said of royal custom-houses? What of colonial ships, and of fishery?
10. State what you can about slavery in the colonies.

CHRONOLOGICAL REVIEW.

NOTE. — The figures at the end of the paragraphs refer to the pages upon which the events are mentioned.

1607. Jamestown was founded in Virginia, the first permanent English settlement in America, 23.
1609. Hudson discovered the Hudson River, 41.
Champlain discovered Lake Champlain, 54.
1614. Captain Smith explored the coast of New England, 28.
1619. The first Legislative Assembly in America was convened in Virginia, 25.
Negro slavery was introduced into Virginia, 26.
1620. Plymouth was settled by the Puritans, the first permanent English settlement in New England, 30.
1622. Opechancanough's war broke out in Virginia, 26.
1623. Portsmouth and Dover, in New Hampshire, were settled, 36.
The permanent colonization of New York was begun by the Dutch, 41.
1630. Boston was founded by Governor Winthrop, 31.
1634. The colonization of Maryland was begun at St. Mary's, 47.
1635. Wethersfield, Windsor, and Hartford, in Connecticut, were settled by emigrants from Massachusetts, 38.
1636. Roger Williams founded Providence, 40.
1637. The Pequot War occurred in Connecticut, 38.
1638. Delaware was settled by the Swedes and Finns, 46.
New Haven was founded by Eaton and Davenport, 39.
1639. The first printing-press in America was set up at Cambridge, Massachusetts, 70.
1643. The confederacy styled the United Colonies of New England was formed, 33.
1656. Quakers began to come to Massachusetts, 33.
1663. The Rhode Island and Providence Plantations received a royal charter, 41.
The Albemarle colony was established in North Carolina, 51.
1664. New Netherland was taken by the English, and named New York, 43.
Elizabethtown (now Elizabeth), in New Jersey, was settled, 45.
1665. Connecticut and New Haven were united, under the name of Connecticut, 39.

CHRONOLOGY. 73

1670. The Carteret colony was established in South Carolina, 51.
1673. Marquette explored the Mississippi, 54.
1675. King Philip's War began, 34.
1676. Bacon's rebellion broke out in Virginia, 27.
1680. Charleston, South Carolina, was founded, 52.
1682. La Salle explored the Mississippi to its mouth, 54.
Philadelphia was founded by William Penn, 50.
1686. Sir Edmund Andros was appointed governor of New England, 35.
1689. Andros was seized and imprisoned, 35.
King William's War began. The Treaty of Ryswick, in 1697, closed King William's War, 58.
1692. Governor Phipps arrived in Massachusetts with a new charter, extending her territory, but abridging her privileges, 35.
The delusion known as the Salem Witchcraft prevailed in Massachusetts, 35.
1702. Queen Anne's War began. The Treaty of Utrecht closed Queen Anne's War in 1713, 59.
1704. First permanent newspaper in America was printed at Boston, 70.
1710. Port Royal was taken from the French and named Annapolis, 59.
1718. New Orleans was founded by the French, 55.
1729. Carolina was divided into two distinct royal provinces — North Carolina and South Carolina, 52.
1733. The colonization of Georgia was begun at Savannah, by the English under Oglethorpe, 53.
1739. The Spanish intercolonial war began, 60.
1744. King George's War began. The treaty of Aix-la-Chapelle, in 1748, closed King George's War, 60, 61.
1752. Georgia became a royal province, 54.
1755. Defeat and death of Braddock, 63.
The country east of the Penobscot fell under British authority, 63.
1756. The French and Indian War, which had been raging two years, was formally proclaimed, 64.
1758. Louisburg and Fort Duquesne were taken by the English, 65.
1759. Quebec was taken by Wolfe, 68.
1760. Montreal and all Canada fell into the power of the English, 68.
1763. The Treaty of Paris was signed — England making peace with France and Spain, 68.
Pontiac's War broke out, 68.

CHASING THE BRITISH BACK FROM CONCORD.

PERIOD III.—THE REVOLUTION.

FROM THE DECLARATION BY PARLIAMENT THAT A REVENUE SHOULD BE RAISED FROM AMERICA, 1764, TO THE INAUGURATION OF WASHINGTON, 1789.

I. CAUSES OF THE REVOLUTION.

1. At the close of the French and Indian War, the British people found themselves burdened with a heavy **national debt**, much of it incurred in the contest just ended. Although the colonists had borne their share in this war, yet very soon after the declaration of peace the British ministry determined to lighten the burden of taxation at home by raising a revenue from America.

2. For a long period of years, Parliament had regulated the **trade and commerce** of the colonies, by the Navigation Acts and other laws, so as to benefit the merchants and manufacturers of England, at the expense of the colonists. In truth, the interest which the English rulers had shown towards their colonial subjects was almost wholly one of selfish gain. While the last war was going on, they attempted to carry out the oppressive **laws of trade** with greater rigor than had yet been exercised, and the colonists were thus made to feel, more deeply than ever before, the injury done them by such a commercial policy.

3. **Englishmen** were, for the most part, ignorant of the character of their kindred in America. They looked upon the colonists as an inferior class, and had but little true sympathy with them. Yet these causes of alienation were not sufficient, at this time, to make the **Americans** desire a separation from the mother country. They regarded the land of their forefathers with filial affection, and in American families it was common to speak of England as "home."

QUESTIONS.— 1. What is said of the English national debt at the close of the French and Indian war? What did the British ministry determine to do?
2. In what manner had Parliament regulated the trade and commerce of the colonies? During the last war, what had been done by the English authorities? Effect of this course upon the colonists?
3. How did most Englishmen look upon the colonists? How did Americans regard England?

4. The **attempt** of Great Britain **to impose taxes** upon her colonies in America, without their consent, brought on the war of the Revolution, which resulted in the independence of the thirteen colonies planted on the Atlantic coast, and the establishment of a republic, under the name of the *United States of America.*

5. The year after the treaty of peace had been signed at Paris, the British Parliament made known its intention of raising a **revenue from America**, and passed an act laying duties upon certain colonial imports. The next year, namely, 1765, the famous **Stamp Act** was passed, which ordained that stamps should be fixed upon all bills, bonds, notes, and other legal instruments executed in the colonies, as well as upon newspapers, pamphlets, and other printed matter. These stamps were to be bought of the English government.

6. The **Americans** were very indignant when news came of the passage of this act. It seemed to them very unjust that their money should be taken from them by a body of Englishmen three thousand miles away. The colonists were not represented in Parliament, and they maintained that *taxation and representation are inseparable.*

7. The Assembly of **Virginia** was the first to send forth resolutions against the Stamp Act. They were introduced by Patrick Henry, and his wonderful eloquence secured their adoption. The Assembly of **Massachusetts** recommended that a congress be held, to consult for the common welfare; and for this purpose the delegates from nine colonies assembled in New York, October 7, 1765. This body, known as the **Colonial Congress**, drew up a Declaration of Rights, asserting that no taxes could justly be imposed upon the people of the colonies but by their own

---

4. What brought on the Revolution? Result of the Revolution?
5. What did the British Parliament do the year after peace was made? When was the Stamp Act passed, and what did it ordain?
6. With what feelings did the Americans regard this act? What did they maintain?
7. What course was taken by the Assembly of Virginia, and what by that of Massachusetts? When and where did the delegates of the Colonial Congress assemble? What was done by this Congress?

legislatures. A petition to the king, George III., and memorials to Parliament, were also adopted.

8. When the day arrived on which the hated **Stamp Act** was to go into operation, there were no stamps to be found in the colonies. The bales sent from England had been destroyed, hidden away, or returned. At first, no business was done which required the use of stamps; but in a short time it was determined wholly to disregard the act. The principal **merchants** agreed to import no more goods from England while it remained a law.

9. In the spring of the next year, after a warm discussion, **Parliament** repealed the Stamp Act. William Pitt and Edmund Burke, with others less famous, eloquently advocated in Parliament the cause of the colonies. At home the people had bold and able **leaders**. The names of Patrick Henry, of Virginia, James Otis, Samuel Adams, and John Adams, of Massachusetts, and of other patriotic men, will always be remembered and honored throughout our land for their wise words and deeds in those times. But no name is more cherished than that of Benjamin Franklin, who lived during those years in London, and was untiring in his efforts to maintain his country's rights.

10. The project of obtaining money from America was not relinquished by the king's ministers. Another scheme was devised. By their advice, Parliament, in 1767, imposed **duties to be paid** by the colonists on tea, glass, paper, and other articles of import. Other acts were also passed, which were odious to the American people. The same strong feeling of **opposition** that had been aroused by the stamp tax, was again excited throughout the colonies. Associations were again formed to abstain from importing and using, not only the taxed articles, but, as much as possible, all British merchandise.

---

8. What is said of stamps when the day on which the act was to go into operation arrived? What of business? What of the principal merchants?
9. When did Parliament repeal the Stamp Act? What is said of William Pitt (afterwards Lord Chatham) and Edmund Burke? What of patriotic leaders in America? Of Benjamin Franklin?
10. What did Parliament do in 1767? Effect in America of the acts passed by Parliament?

11. The Assembly and people of Massachusetts being regarded by the authorities of England as most active in rebellion, two regiments were sent to Boston. The **troops arrived** in the autumn of 1768, and landing, marched with offensive parade into the town. The sight of armed men sent to overawe the people and reduce them to subjection, aroused the deepest feelings of indignation.

12. The British troops had remained in Boston nearly a year and a half, when an event occurred which produced great excitement. During all this time, there had been much bad feeling between the soldiers and the populace, and quarrels had taken place; but on the 5th of March, 1770, blood was shed. In the evening of that day, a crowd of men and boys assaulted a small guard of soldiers. Provoked by words and blows, the soldiers fired into the crowd, killing three persons and wounding several others. The story of the **Boston Massacre**, as it was called, served still more to inflame the passions of the people.

13. Parliament this year took off the duties from all the articles except tea. A very **small duty** was retained **on tea**, in order to establish the principle of the right to tax the colonists. But this proceeding did not allay the discontent of the Americans. They denied the right of Parliament to tax them at all.

14. As no tea was imported by the colonists, the British East India Company, in 1773, resolved to send cargoes of it to the principal ports of the provinces. Both the Company and the ministry thought that, if the tea could be landed, it would be purchased, especially as an act had been passed which enabled the Company to sell tea cheaper in America than in England. But the people were on the alert to thwart this plan. The **tea ships which arrived** at New York and Philadelphia were sent quickly back to

---

11. Why were British troops sent to Boston? and what is said of their arrival?
12. Give an account of the Boston massacre.
13. What was done by Parliament in 1770? Why was the small duty retained on tea? How did the Americans regard this proceeding?
14. What plan was formed to introduce tea into the colonies? What was done with the tea sent to New York and Philadelphia? With that sent to Charleston?

England with their cargoes. At Charleston the tea was stored in damp cellars, where it soon spoiled.

15. The patriots of Boston demanded that the ships which came there should return with their cargoes, to England; but the governor and other officials of the crown refused to permit them to leave the port. Upon this a party of men, disguised as Indians, — since popularly called the **Boston Tea Party**, — on the evening of the 16th of December, 1773, boarded the vessels and emptied the tea — three hundred and forty-two chests — into the harbor.

16. As a punishment for this bold act, Parliament, the next year, passed the **Boston Port Bill**, which closed the harbor of Boston to commerce and navigation, and removed the custom-house to Salem. About the same time other unjust measures were adopted. More soldiers were sent to General Thomas Gage, the commander-in-chief of the British forces in America, now also appointed royal governor of Massachusetts. Salem refused to profit by the ruin of her sister city, and freely offered her wharves to Boston merchants.

17. Throughout **all the colonies** there now prevailed a determination to make common cause against the oppressive measures of Great Britain. The great body of the people resisted the aggressions of England, and were called *Whigs;* those who favored the British were called *Tories.*

18. In September, 1774, a general congress convened at Philadelphia. This is known as the **First Continental Congress.** All the colonies were represented but Georgia. This Congress sent forth a second Declaration of Rights, and recommended an American Association pledged to hold no commercial intercourse with Great Britain. It also voted a new petition to the king, as well as addresses to the people of Great Britain and Canada.

15. What was done with the tea sent to Boston?
16. In what way did Parliament retaliate?
17. What feeling prevailed throughout the colonies? Who were called Whigs, and who Tories?
18. When and where did the First Continental Congress convene? How many colonies were represented? What was done by this Congress?

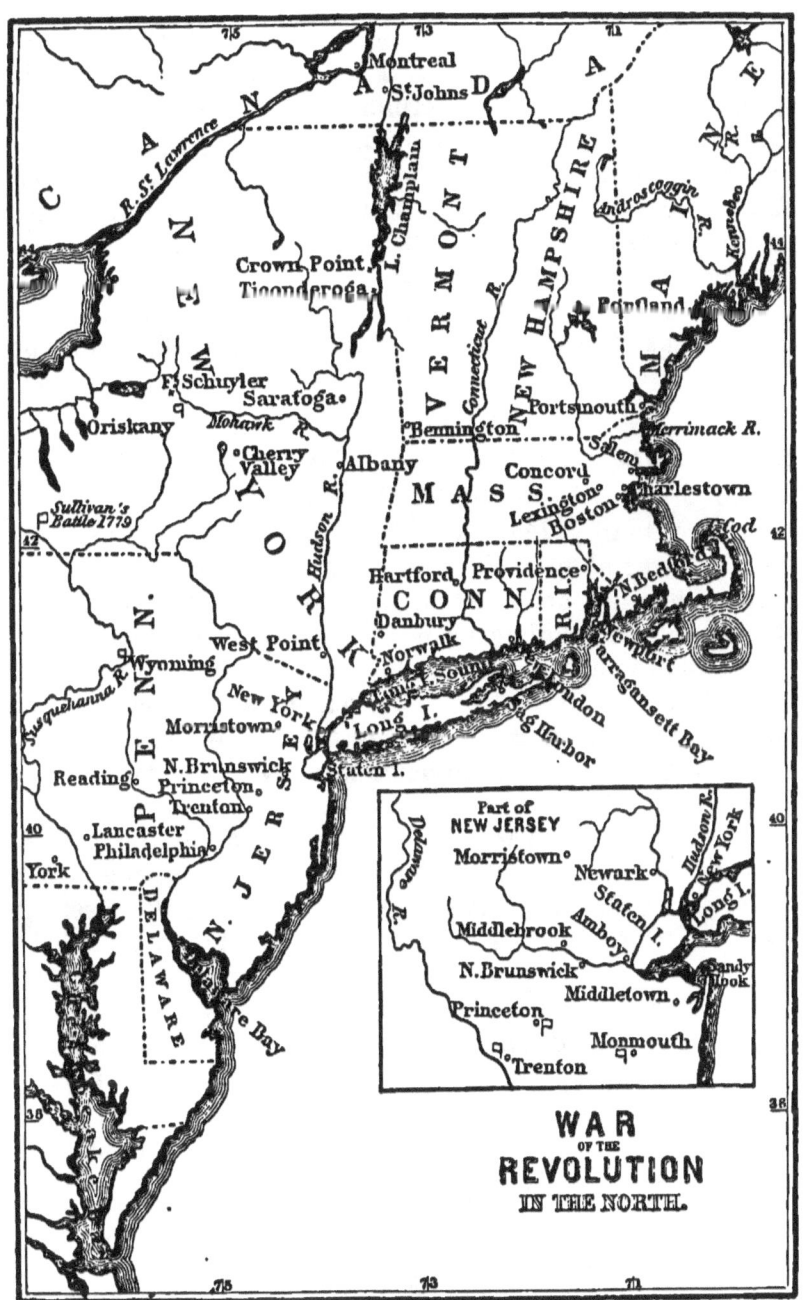

19. But no petition could change the inflexible will of George III. The king, the Parliament, and the people of England were now determined to make the colonists submit. Meanwhile these colonists were arming themselves for the conflict. In Massachusetts, a *Committee of Safety*, with John Hancock as chairman, was formed, with power to call out the militia of the province. A large force was organized as *minute men*, being ready to take up arms at a minute's warning. Such was the condition of things that it needed but a single spark to light up the flames of war.

II. THE WAR.

1. *From the Opening of the War to the Declaration of Independence.*

1. **Events of 1775.** — The first blood of the Revolutionary War was shed at Lexington, Massachusetts, April 19, 1775. The night before, General Gage sent a detachment of eight hundred soldiers from Boston to destroy some military stores which the Americans had collected at Concord. It was intended to make the movement a surprise; but the patriots of Boston gave the alarm as soon as the troops had started, and the intelligence was swiftly borne into the country.

2. Early the next morning, the *red-coats*, as the English soldiers were often called, reached **Lexington**, where they found about seventy men assembled in front of the meeting-house. Major Pitcairn (*pit'kārn*), one of the British officers, rode up to them, and cried out, "Disperse, you rebels! Throw down your arms, and disperse." Not being obeyed, he ordered his soldiers to fire. They did so, killing eight of the minute men, and wounding others. The rest dispersed.

3. The king's troops then marched on to **Concord**, where they destroyed such of the stores as had not been removed,

---

19. What feeling now prevailed in England? Meanwhile what were the colonists doing? What is said of a Committee of Safety? Of minute men? Of the condition of affairs?
1. When and where was the first blood of the Revolutionary war shed? For what purpose were British troops sent from Boston?
2. Give an account of the affair at Lexington.
3. What is said of the British at Concord?

and after a skirmish with the militia there assembled, began a hasty retreat; and none too soon, for the enraged country-people were hurrying up from all sides. From behind trees, stone walls, and houses they fired upon the enemy. On the way back, reënforcements met the British, but the pursuit and firing were kept up till the troops reached Charlestown. The Americans lost about ninety men; the loss of the British, in killed, wounded, and missing, was three times as many.

4. News that the blood of Americans had been spilled at Lexington and Concord by British soldiers, ran with hot haste through the land, and everywhere caused intense **excitement**. From all parts of New England, volunteers hastened to Boston, and within a few days thousands of the militia had assembled, and were holding the enemy shut up in the town.

5. It was decided by some of the patriots to secure **Ticonderoga and Crown Point**, then held by a few British soldiers. Accordingly, in May, a small band of volunteers from Vermont and Connecticut, led by Ethan Allen and Benedict Arnold, captured these forts, and thus obtained a large amount of military stores, of which the Americans stood in great need.

6. The **Second Continental Congress** met at Philadelphia, May 10, but a few hours, as it happened, after the capture of Ticonderoga. This Congress assumed the authority of a general government of the colonies. The army about Boston was adopted as the Continental Army, and **George Washington** was appointed commander-in-chief.

7. While Washington was on his way to take command of the army, news met him that an important battle had been fought. At the time of this conflict the **British army**

---

3. What of the retreat of the British? Loss on each side?
4. What was the effect of news of the affair at Lexington and Concord? Where is Lexington? (See Map, p. 81.) Where is Concord?
5. Give an account of the capture of Ticonderoga and Crown Point.
6. Where and when did the Second Continental Congress meet? What was done by this Congress?
7. What news met Washington while he was on his way to the American army? What is said of the British army at this time?

in Boston, having lately been increased by reënforcements under the distinguished Generals Howe, Clinton, and Burgoyne', numbered more than ten thousand men.

8. The battle of **Bunker Hill**, as it is called, occurred on the 17th of June. The preceding night, Colonel Prescott, with about a thousand men, was sent from the American camp to get the start of the British, by being the first to occupy the heights of Charlestown. He was ordered to take possession of Bunker Hill, which is the highest eminence; but Breed's Hill, being nearer to Boston, was finally selected as a better position for investing the town. Late in the night the Americans began to construct a small redoubt on the summit where the monument now stands to commemorate the battle.

Boston and Vicinity.

9. In the morning **the British** opened fire upon the redoubt from ships in the harbor and from a battery in Boston; but **the Americans** kept steadily at their work. Before the battle began they received reënforcements. In the afternoon three thousand regulars, under command of General Howe, advanced to dislodge them. Twice, the assailants, when near the works, were repulsed by a fire which swept down whole ranks of them. Being reënforced, they were a third time led to the charge, and with better success. The provincials, having now used up their ammunition, slowly and reluctantly retreated. While the battle was raging, **Charlestown** was set on fire by the enemy.

10. **The loss** of the British was more than a thousand men, that of the Americans not half so many; but among their

---

8. When did the battle of Bunker Hill occur? Give an account of operations the night before. In what direction from Boston is Charlestown? Cambridge! See Map above.
9. Give an account of the battle of Bunker Hill.
10 What was the loss on each side?

killed was General Joseph Warren, one of the most active and distinguished patriots of Boston. The **result** was very encouraging to the Americans, while it mortified and dispirited the British, who had often boasted that a few regiments could conquer the whole country.

11. **Washington** reached Cambridge, the headquarters of the American army, about a fortnight after the battle of Bunker Hill. He found there a large body of provincials, ignorant of regular warfare, and deficient in arms, ammunition, and other military stores. He at once set about organizing and disciplining his soldiers, and, while using every effort to obtain supplies, kept the enemy penned up in Boston and Charlestown.

12. At the same time two **expeditions** were sent **against Canada**. Their object was not to molest the inhabitants, but to deprive the British of the province. One army went by the way of Lake Champlain. The command of this expedition was given to General Philip Schuyler (*ski'ler*), but by his illness it soon devolved upon **General Richard Montgomery** (*mont-gum'er-ĭ*), a gallant and able officer, who had served with Wolfe at the taking of Quebec. Montgomery, after capturing some British forts, took possession of Montreal and advanced down the St. Lawrence.

13. Meanwhile, the other invading force, led by **Colonel Benedict Arnold**, ascended the Kennebec River, and, after great suffering from hunger and fatigue in the wilderness, approached Quebec. The forces of Montgomery and Arnold were united, and an unsuccessful assault was made upon **Quebec** on the last day of the year. In the conflict Montgomery was killed and Arnold wounded. After this repulse, the Americans went into camp for the rest of the winter. Early the next summer (1776) they were forced to abandon the country.

---

10. What distinguished patriot was killed in the battle? Result of the battle?
11. When did Washington reach Cambridge? What did he find there, and what did he set about doing?
12. What two expeditions were sent out? What can you tell of the expedition which went by the way of Lake Champlain?
13. What can you tell of the other invading army? Of the attack upon Quebec! What befell the invaders the next summer?

14. During the first year of the war, **royal authority** in the colonies came to an end, most of the king's governors taking refuge on board English ships. Lord Dunmore, the royal governor of Virginia, was particularly active in the king's cause. Fearing Patrick Henry and other Whigs, at length he fled to a British man-of-war. Afterwards, on New Year's Day, 1776, he attacked and burned **Norfolk**, the largest and richest town in Virginia. The same fate had already fallen upon Falmouth (*fal'muth*), now **Portland**, Maine, which was wantonly bombarded and burned by one of the British naval officers who were threatening the coast of New England.

15. **Events of 1776.** — The condition of his army prevented Washington from beginning active operations against the enemy in Boston till the spring of 1776. On the night of March 4, he sent a body of troops to take possession of **Dorchester** (now South Boston) **Heights**. By morning, fortifications had been thrown up, which threatened the harbor and the town.

16. Sir William Howe, who had succeeded General Gage, being unwilling to learn again the lesson of Bunker Hill, finally concluded to give up **Boston** to the Americans. Accordingly, on the 17th of March, he **evacuated** the town, his army and more than a thousand Tories embarking on board ships for Halifax. The British were permitted to retire unmolested, it being understood that, in this case, they would not destroy the town.

17. Fearing that the British fleet, on leaving Boston, would sail for **New York**, Washington moved most of his army to that city. Part of his forces he placed at Brooklyn, on Long Island, to defend the approach from that direction; the rest he stationed in New York. It was supposed that the enemy would endeavor to capture this place, as it was a central position for operating against the colonies.

---

14. What is said of royal authority in the colonies, and of the king's governors? Of Lord Dunmore and the destruction of Norfolk? Of Portland?
15. What steps did Washington take to dislodge the enemy from Boston?
16. When did the British evacuate Boston? What of Tories?
17. Where did Washington next move his army? Where did he place his forces? Why was it supposed the British would endeavor to capture New York?

18. In the winter, Sir Henry Clinton, with British troops, had sailed southward from Boston. Having been joined by a powerful squadron from Great Britain, under Sir Peter Parker, he appeared early in June before **Charleston**, South Carolina. The harbor was guarded by a rude fort on Sullivan's Island, held by Colonel Moultrie (*mole'tri*) with a few hundred men.

19. On the 28th of June the British attacked the fort both by sea and land, and were repulsed with the loss of many men, and with much damage to their ships. The fort was afterwards named Fort Moultrie, in honor of its brave defender. In a few days the British sailed for New York, and for two years and a half the southern colonies had a respite from the calamities of war.

2. *From the Declaration of Independence to the Invasion of Georgia. War chiefly in the North.*

20. **Events of 1776, continued.**—**England** had declared the colonists rebels, and, to subdue them, she determined to increase her army in America by sending over, not only British soldiers, but also seventeen thousand German troops hired of their rulers. Most of these mercenaries were Hessians, from Hesse Cassel (*hess kas'sel*). So far the **colonies** had been struggling for a redress of grievances; but the war was now to be carried on for independence.

21. Early in June, Richard Henry Lee, of Virginia, introduced into Congress, then sitting in the State House at Philadelphia, a resolution, declaring that *These United Colonies are, and of right ought to be, free and independent States.* After much deliberation, Congress agreed to this resolution, and July 4, 1776, adopted a **Declaration of Independence** drawn up by Thomas Jefferson. The date of its adoption is recognized as the birthday of the nation.

---

18. Give an account of the expedition which went against Charleston. How was the harbor guarded?
19. What can you tell of the attack upon the fort? What name was given the fort? How long before war was again carried on in the southern colonies?
20. In what way did England determine to increase her army in America?
21. What resolution did Richard Henry Lee introduce into Congress? Who drew up the Declaration of Independence, and when was it adopted? What further is said of this Declaration?

Throughout the land, now first named the *United States of America*, the declaration was received with great joy.

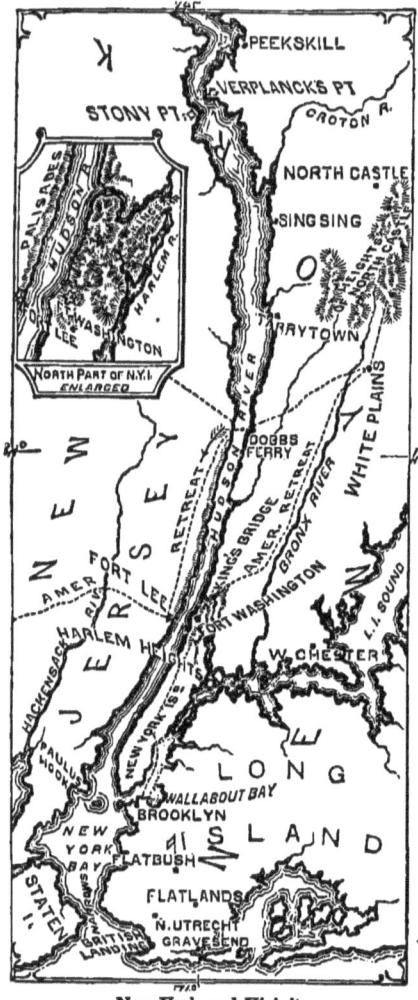

New York and Vicinity.

22. Just before this time, **General Howe** had arrived in New York harbor, from Halifax, with the garrison he had taken from Boston, and with other soldiers. He was soon joined by his brother, Admiral Lord Howe, from England, who brought large reënforcements, and by Clinton, with the troops lately repulsed at Sullivan's Island. The British commander now had an army of near thirty thousand veteran troops; Washington's army was much smaller, and was, besides, poorly armed and disciplined.

23. General Howe first moved against the American troops on **Long Island**, who only four days before this attack had been placed under the command of General Israel Putnam, a brave old soldier, who had served in the French and Indian War. The battle occurred August 27, and resulted in a victory for the British. On the second night after this defeat Washington secretly and skilfully withdrew his troops from Long Island to New York.

---

22. What British forces arrived in New York harbor? What is said of the opposing armies?
23. Give an account of the battle of Long Island. What did Washington do after this defeat?

24. Soon afterwards he removed his army to **Harlem Heights**, in the northern part of New York Island, and the British took possession of the city, September 15. To prevent the enemy from gaining the rear of his camp, the American commander was next compelled to retire to **White Plains**, where a partial action took place near the end of October, in which the British had the advantage. Washington then retired a few miles farther north, to a strong position on the heights of North Castle.

25. The British general now began to retrace his steps, and on the 16th of November attacked **Fort Washington**, a post on the Hudson, in the northern part of New York Island. After a brave defence, the garrison of nearly three thousand men was forced to surrender. Seeing that the British intended to enter New Jersey, Washington crossed over into that state with the main body of his army. A stronger force under Lord Cornwallis (*korn-wol'lis*) followed, and closely pursuing the patriot troops, obliged them to **retreat through New Jersey** to Trenton, where they crossed the Delaware, near the end of the year.

26. This was the gloomiest period of the war. Since the landing of the enemy on Long Island, there had been for the Americans little else than **disasters** and retreats. The city of New York was in the hands of the British; they had overrun New Jersey. Washington's soldiers, now a feeble remnant of an army, were poorly clad, poorly armed, and disheartened. A fleet from New York had just taken possession of Newport, then the second town in New England. To add to these and other discouragements, many persons of wealth and influence, believing the cause to be lost, were going over to the enemy.

27. Having received some reënforcements, Washington, by a bold stroke, revived the spirits of his countrymen. At

---

24. Give an account of the operations of the opposing armies, including the battle of White Plains, and the retreat of the Americans to North Castle.
25. Give an account of the capture of Fort Washington. Of the retreat and pursuit through New Jersey. Where is Trenton? (See Map, p. 81.)
26. What is said about this period of the war? What of New York and New Jersey? Of Washington's army? Of Newport? What other injury to the American cause is mentioned? Where is Newport? (See Map, p. 81.)

the head of twenty-four hundred men he recrossed the Delaware on the stormy night of Christmas, while the river was full of floating ice, and in the morning of December 26, suddenly fell upon a body of Hessians at **Trenton**, and took nearly a thousand prisoners. The Americans lost only four men — two killed, and two frozen to death.

28. **Events of 1777.** — Late in the afternoon, a week later, Lord Cornwallis reached Trenton with a large force. The hostile armies were separated by a small stream when the British general encamped for the night, intending to crush his adversary in the morning. Being too weak to risk an engagement, Washington, by a circuitous route, made a rapid night-march to **Princeton**, where, early in the morning, January 3, he surprised a detachment which was on the way to join Cornwallis, routed it, and took about three hundred prisoners.

29. As soon as Cornwallis heard the firing at Princeton, and saw the deserted camp, he turned in pursuit; but he was unable to overtake the patriot army. Washington encamped in a region difficult of access for an enemy, his headquarters being at **Morristown**. By sending out detachments to harass the British, he soon cleared New Jersey of hostile troops, excepting at New Brunswick and Amboy'. The brilliant exploits at Trenton and Princeton gained for Washington, both at home and abroad, great glory as a prudent, daring, and skilful commander.

30. No very important enterprises were undertaken by either army for about six months. Washington, meanwhile, was reorganizing and disciplining his forces. The chief expedition sent out by the British commander during this time was led by General Tryon, late royal governor of New York. This officer, near the end of April, went up Long Island Sound with two thousand men, and landed in Con-

---

27. Give an account of Washington's victory at Trenton.
28. What can you tell of the hostile armies a week later, and of Washington's success at Princeton? Where is Princeton? (See Map, p. 81.)
29. What can you tell of the pursuit of Washington by Cornwallis? How was most of New Jersey recovered from the British? Where is Morristown? (See Map, p. 81.) New Brunswick? Amboy?
30. How was Washington employed for some months? What can you tell of Tryon's expedition into Connecticut?

necticut. Marching into the country, he destroyed the public stores at **Danbury**, and set fire to the town. The militia and a few continental troops bravely attacked the invaders, and pursued them back to their boats.

31. In the spring of this year, the **Marquis de Lafayette** (*lah-fā-et'*), a wealthy French nobleman, not yet twenty years old, fitted out a vessel and crossed the ocean to fight for American freedom. While many officers from Europe sought for high rank in the patriot forces, and for money, this gallant Frenchman offered to serve as a volunteer, and without pay. Congress, however, soon appointed him a major-general. He proved to be an able officer, and became the trusted friend of Washington. He won the hearts of the people whom he came to aid, and no native of a foreign land has ever been held by the Americans in so high honor. Lafayette brought with him the Baron de Kalb, a German veteran, and several other officers.

32. Two brave and distinguished Poles, **Thaddeus Kos-ci-us'ko** and Count Pulaski (*pu-las'ki*), served in the patriot army, and left honored names in American history. The German, De Kalb, and the Pole, **Pulaski**, both gave their lives for the cause they had embraced. But perhaps no one who came from abroad to help us gain our independence, Lafayette excepted, did so important service as the **Baron Steuben** (*stu'ben*)*, a Prussian, who arrived in the country near the close of this year. After he was appointed inspector-general, he thoroughly trained the American army, and by his rare skill and untiring efforts, soon made its soldiers worthy to be ranked with veterans.

33. Near the end of May, **Washington** placed his main army in a strong position so as to be ready to oppose the British, should they attempt to advance towards Philadelphia. **General Howe**, after unsuccessfully manœuvring to entice the Americans from their strong post, suddenly

---

* German pronunciation *stoi'ben*.

31. What did the Marquis de Lafayette do in the spring of this year? What offer did he make, and what did Congress do? What more can you tell of Lafayette?
32. What can you tell of Kosciusko, Pulaski, and De Kalb? Of Baron Steuben?
33. What did Washington do near the end of May? What did Howe do?

crossed over to Stat'en Island, and put to sea with his brother's fleet and about eighteen thousand men.

PHILADELPHIA AND VICINITY.

34. After a period of suspense, news came that the British fleet was ascending Chesapeake Bay, and it was then certain that the enemy intended to march upon Philadelphia. Washington was ready, though with but eleven thousand effective men, to oppose the invading forces. The armies met at Chad's Ford, on the **Brandywine**, September 11, and after an engagement that lasted nearly all day, the Americans retreated. Congress adjourned, first to Lancaster, and then to York, Pennsylvania, where it remained while the British held Philadelphia.

35. Near the end of September the British entered Philadelphia. Their fleet now went out of the Chesapeake and came round into the Delaware. Howe sent a detachment of his troops to aid in reducing two forts which commanded the river below the city. The main body of the royal army was encamped at **Germantown**, and here Washington attacked it by surprise early in the morning of October 4. It seemed at first as if the enterprise would be successful; but after a severe action the Americans were repulsed with the loss of over a thousand men, being double that of the British.

---

34. What can you tell of the battle of Brandywine? What of Congress?
35. When did the British take possession of Philadelphia? What did the British next do? Give an account of the battle of Germantown. In what direction is Chad's Ford from Philadelphia? Germantown from Philadelphia? (See Map above.)

36. **Forts Mercer and Mifflin**, on the Delaware, bravely withstood the assaults of the land force and the ships sent against them. An attack in October was repulsed with great loss to the assailants; but before the close of autumn the garrisons were compelled to abandon these defences, and the Delaware was thus opened to the British fleet.

37. In December, the troops under Washington went into winter quarters at **Valley Forge**. While the British were enjoying their comfortable quarters in Philadelphia, the patriots at Valley Forge were crouching in their log huts, where they suffered terribly from cold, disease, and the want of food and clothing.

38. The success of the British in Pennsylvania this year was more than balanced by disasters which befell them in the north, through **Burgoyne's invasion**. A plan had been formed to cut off New England from the other states by means of an army from Canada, which should move up Lake Champlain and down the Hudson. To execute this plan, General Burgoyne had in all near ten thousand men, regulars, Tories, Canadians, and Indians.

39. Passing up the lake, he invested **Fort Ticonderoga**, July 1. General St. Clair, who was holding this post with three thousand men, abandoned it, and, after suffering much loss in the retreat, joined General Schuyler, the commander of the northern army, who was then at Fort Edward.

40. **Schuyler** retired on the approach of Burgoyne, and finally took post at the mouth of the Mohawk. By felling trees and demolishing bridges, he had obstructed the route of the invaders, and made their advance extremely slow and difficult. It was the end of the month before **Burgoyne** reached Fort Edward, whence, after stopping some days, he advanced along the east bank of the Hudson. Difficulties soon began to thicken around him.

---

36. What is said of Forts Mercer and Mifflin?
37. Where did Washington go into winter quarters, and what is said of the patriot troops? Where is Valley Forge? (See Map, p. 92.)
38. What plan was Burgoyne to try to execute? How large was his army?
39. What fort did he invest? What is said of St. Clair?
40. Who was the commander of the northern army, and where did he finally take post? What is said of the advance of Burgoyne?

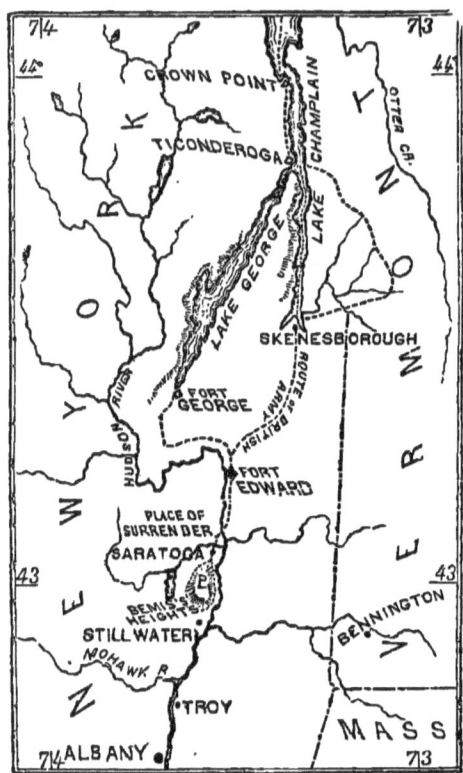

Burgoyne's Expedition. Saratoga and Vicinity.

41. Just before moving forward from Fort Edward, Burgoyne despatched Colonel Baum (*bowm*), with five hundred men, to seize some stores collected at Bennington, Vermont. This detachment and another sent to reënforce it were totally defeated. August 16, by Colonel John Stark, with New England militia. Victory or death was the resolve of Stark, as he led on his men. "There they are," he exclaimed; "we beat to-day, or Molly Stark's a widow!"

42. The invasion received another check. Colonel St. Leger had been sent with a detachment to sweep through the Mohawk Valley, from the west, and join the main army at Albany. With a large force of regulars, Canadians, Tories, and Indians, he laid siege to Fort Schuyler, where Rome now is. General Herkimer hastened with a body of militia to the relief of the garrison, but was stopped at Oris′kany, where he fell into an ambuscade. In this bloody conflict Herkimer was mortally wounded. General Arnold then marched to the assistance of the besieged. Hearing that Arnold was approaching, the Indians fled, and St. Leger gave up the siege.

43. Reënforcements were pouring into the American

---

41. Give an account of the battle of Bennington. Where is Bennington?
42. For what purpose had an expedition been sent under St. Leger? What of the siege of Fort Schuyler, and the battle of Oris′kany? How was the garrison relieved? Where was Ft. Schuyler? (See Map, p. 81.) Oriskany?

camp. Just as General Schuyler was in condition to confront the invaders with a good prospect of success, he was superseded by General Gates. At length Burgoyne crossed the Hudson and advanced down the river. On the 19th of September the armies met at Be'mis's Heights, near **Saratoga**, and an indecisive battle was fought. On the 7th of the next month a second battle occurred near the same place, resulting in a decided advantage to the Americans. In these battles Colonel Daniel Morgan so skilfully led his riflemen as greatly to increase his fame. General Arnold, though without any regular command, was the animating spirit in the last conflict, and displayed reckless daring.

44. The situation of the royal army had now become nearly hopeless; the troops were exhausted with toil and watching; they attempted to retreat, but found that all avenues of escape had been closed; their provisions were almost gone. On the 17th of October **Burgoyne surrendered**, at Saratoga, his whole army of near six thousand men.

45. Clinton had led a strong force some distance up the Hudson to assist the army from Canada. But these troops were too late to aid Burgoyne, and after his surrender they returned to New York. They had captured two forts in the Highlands, burned houses, and plundered property.

46. In November, 1777, Congress agreed upon **Articles of Confederation**, which should form the constitution of the new nation, after they had been approved by all the states In the spring of 1781 all the states had adopted these Articles.

47. **Events of 1778.** — The loss of Burgoyne's army, and fear that France was about to take part in the contest, caused the **British government**, early in 1778, to offer to concede all that the colonies had asked for at the beginning of the controversy. Commissioners were sent over from England to bring about a reconciliation, but the

---

43. By whom was Schuyler superseded, and under what circumstances? What is said of the two battles near Saratoga? Of Morgan and Arnold?
44. What can you tell of Burgoyne's situation, and of his surrender?
45. What is said of a force sent from New York to relieve Burgoyne?
46. What is said of Articles of Confederation?
47. What offer was made by the British government early in 1778?

offers came too late. **Congress** refused to treat unless the independence of the states should be first acknowledged, or the British forces withdrawn.

Benjamin Franklin.

48. Another event which resulted from Burgoyne's surrender produced great joy in America. Early in February **France** acknowledged the independence of the United States, and made treaties of friendship, commerce, and alliance with the infant republic. Before this the French government had secretly aided the Americans with arms and supplies. The distinguished **Dr. Franklin**, then over seventy years old, was the leading commissioner for the United States at the French court. He managed affairs so wisely, and was held in so high regard at the French capital, that we may well believe no other American could have done so much there for his country as he did.

49. Early in the summer, a French fleet was on its way to the assistance of the Americans. As Philadelphia could not safely be held after the arrival of this fleet, **Sir Henry Clinton**, who had lately superseded General Howe, evacuated the city, June 18, and crossed over into New Jersey, intending to concentrate the royal forces in New York.

50. Washington immediately followed, and on the morning of June 28, overtook the enemy at **Monmouth** (*mon'-muth*) Court House, where a battle was fought. At first the Americans came near meeting with serious disaster through the misconduct of General Charles Lee, who led

---

47. What reply did Congress make to the offers?
48. What step did Burgoyne's surrender cause France to take? What is said of Dr. Franklin at the French court?
49. Why did the British evacuate Philadelphia, and when? Where was it intended to concentrate the royal troops?
50. Give an account of the battle of Monmouth. Where was Monmouth? (See Map, "Part of New Jersey," p. 81.)

the van of the pursuing army. But Washington arrived at the critical moment, checked the retreat of Lee's troops, and restored the order of battle. Night put an end to the action, and, under cover of darkness, Clinton silently withdrew his troops and marched for New York.

51. **Washington** crossed the Hudson, and encamped at White Plains. The main army remained several months on the east side of the river, not far from New York; but, during the winter, the troops were cantoned on both sides of the Hudson, the headquarters being at Middlebrook, in New Jersey.

52. In the summer of this year, the lovely valley of **Wyo'ming** (*wi-o'ming*), in Pennsylvania, was the scene of a horrid massacre. A large body of Tories and Indians, led by Colonel John Butler, made a descent into the valley, from Western New York, butchered the inhabitants, and laid waste the settlement. In the fall, **Cherry Valley**, in New York, suffered almost a like fate from Tories and Indians.

53. Early in July, the **French fleet**, under Count D'Estaing (*des-tan[g']*),* sent to aid the Americans, appeared in Delaware Bay. D'Estaing soon afterwards sailed for **Newport**, then held by six thousand British troops. It having been decided to make an attack upon the enemy here, General Sullivan landed on the Island of Rhode Island, with militia and continental troops, to coöperate with the French ships off Newport. Just before the land and naval forces were ready to begin the attack, the British fleet, under Lord Howe, was seen coming to relieve the town.

54. **D'Estaing** sailed out to give battle, but a furious storm prevented an engagement, and so crippled his ships that he afterwards put into the harbor of Boston to refit.

* See note, p. 55.

---

51. Where was Washington's main army for several months? During the winter? Where is Middlebrook? (See Map, "Part of New Jersey." p. 80.)
52. Give an account of the attack upon the valley of Wyoming. The attack upon Cherry Valley. Where is the Wyoming Valley? (See Map, p. 81.) Where is Cherry Valley?
53. When and where did the French fleet arrive, and under whom? What place did the French intend to attack, and who coöperated? What happened just before the attack was to be made?
54. What caused the attack upon Newport to be given up?

The enterprise had now to be abandoned. Although Sullivan was obliged to retreat, he was able to check the pursuit of the enemy, in a sharp action which occurred in the northern end of the island.

3. *From the Invasion of Georgia to the Close of the War. War chiefly in the South.*

55. Events of 1778, continued. — Towards the close of 1778, the south began to be the principal theatre of the war, and **Georgia**, the weakest of the southern states, was the first to be attacked. Late in December, Colonel Campbell,* with thirty-five hundred troops from New York, landed near **Savannah**. They found there only about a thousand men, under General Robert Howe, to oppose them. These were surprised and completely routed, and the town fell into the hands of the English, December 29.

56. Events of 1779. — The year 1779 is distinguished for nothing very decisive in the war of the Revolution. A few days after the fall of Savannah, General Prevost (*pre-vost'*) arrived with royal troops that had been stationed in Florida, and assumed the chief command. A detachment which he sent out, captured Augusta, and soon the **subjugation of Georgia** was completed, in spite of the efforts of General Lincoln (*ling'kun*), the American commander at the south.

57. Two encounters are worthy of mention. In the first, a body of militia, led by Colonel Pickens, defeated seven hundred **Tories**, as they were on their way to the British camp; in the second, a detachment of Americans. under General Ashe (*ash*), was routed at **Brier Creek**. Having conquered Georgia, Prevost marched against **Charleston**, South Carolina; but, as the town was prepared to make a stout resistance and General Lincoln was coming

---
* Pronounced *kam'bel* or *kam'el*.

54. What did Sullivan do?
55. When did the South begin to be the principal theatre of the war? What state was first attacked? Give an account of the fall of Savannah.
56. What is said of the year 1779? Of General Prevost? Of the subjugation of Georgia?
57. What is said of a victory gained by Colonel Pickens? Of the engagement at Brier Creek? Of the attempt of Prevost to capture Charleston?

with his army to its relief, the British general quickly gave up his design. After some fighting the main body of the enemy returned to Georgia.

58. When **D'Estaing** had repaired his ships in Boston, he sailed for the West Indies, to operate against the English there. In September of this year, he appeared with a large fleet before **Savannah**, and laid siege to the town, General Lincoln coöperating. On the 9th of October, the combined forces made an assault upon the enemy's works, and were repulsed with great loss. In this assault the gallant Count Pulaski was mortally wounded. The French reëmbarked, and the Americans retired to Charleston.

59. In the mean time **Clinton**, in the north, was mainly employed in holding New York, and sending out expeditions to destroy towns on the coast, and to pillage the country. One body of marauders invaded Virginia, another, led by the infamous Tryon, burned and plundered towns in Connecticut.

60. About the beginning of summer, Clinton went up the Hudson, and captured Stony Point and Verplanck's Point, where he left strong garrisons. The **American forces** were so small that Washington could only act on the defensive; but his vigilance prevented the British from gaining command of the Hudson above these works, and thus severing New England from the other states.

61. One of the most brilliant achievements of the Revolution was the storming of **Stony Point**, and its recapture from the British by General Anthony Wayne, with troops from Washington's army. Near midnight, July 15, the assault was made, and the garrison forced to surrender at the point of the bayonet. About a month later, Major Henry Lee, with similar daring, surprised and captured a British garrison at **Paulus Hook**, now Jersey City.

---

58. Where did D'Estaing sail after repairing his ships at Boston? What can you tell of the attempt to recover Savannah?
59. Meanwhile how was Clinton employed? What is said of two marauding expeditions?
60. What posts had Clinton captured? What is said of the American forces?
61. What can you tell of the storming of Stony Point? Of the capture of the British garrison at Paulus Hook?

62. Late in the summer of this year, General Sullivan led an army of about five thousand men to chastise the **Indians** of Western New York for their atrocious deeds at Wyoming, Cherry Valley, and other places. Sullivan routed a body of Indians and Tories where Elmira now is, and then, proceeding northward and westward, burned the Indian villages, destroyed the fields of corn and the orchards, laying waste the country to the Genesee (*jen-e-see'*) River.

63. The Americans had made **war on the sea** as well as on the land. In the first year of the contest, 1775, steps were taken by Congress to create a little navy. Many privateers were afterwards sent out; and these took hundreds of English merchant vessels as prizes.

64. The most celebrated of the naval commanders in the service of the United States was **John Paul Jones.** In September, 1779, while cruising near the coast of England with the Bon Homme Richard (*bo-nom're-shar'*), and other ships fitted out in France, he captured two British vessels of war, after one of the most desperate naval combats on record. In the summer of this year **Spain** allied herself with France in the war against England.

65. In the autumn, **Clinton** withdrew the troops from Newport, which the British had held nearly three years. The outposts on the Hudson were also given up, and their garrisons called to New York. Leaving a strong force to hold that place, Clinton, near the end of December, sailed south with seven thousand troops and a large fleet.

66. **Events of 1780.** — Georgia having been subdued, the war was now to be carried into the Carolinas. In the spring, the land force under Clinton, aided by the fleet, laid siege to **Charleston.** After a gallant defence of several weeks, General Lincoln, still the commander at the south,

---

62. Give an account of Sullivan's expedition against the Indians of Western New York.
63. What is said of war on the sea? Of the American navy, and of privateers?
64. What is said of John Paul Jones, and a naval victory which he gained? What did Spain do in the summer of 1779?
65. What posts did Clinton give up in the autumn? After this, what did he do?
66. Where was the war to be carried in 1780? What can you tell of the siege of Charleston?

was compelled, May 12, to surrender the town, with its defenders, to the enemy.

67. Clinton next sent **expeditions** into the interior. A detachment of mounted men, under Colonel Tarleton, overtook and defeated a body of American troops at **Waxhaw Creek**. This was one of Tarleton's bloody exploits. Most of the Americans were killed or maimed after they had begged for quarter. Having overrun South Carolina, and stationed garrisons in various parts of the state, Clinton returned to New York with a large body of his troops, leaving Lord Cornwallis in command at the south.

68. Congress gave General Gates command of the southern department. He hastily marched against the enemy in the Carolinas, and, August 16, met Cornwallis in the battle of **Sanders' Creek**, near Camden. It ended in the complete rout of the Americans. At the first onset, the militia threw down their arms and fled. The regular troops, whom Washington had sent from his army, fought bravely, but they, too, at length gave way. The brave Baron de Kalb was mortally wounded. Two days after this defeat, a body of American troops, under Colonel Sumter, was surprised and scattered by Tarleton's cavalry.

69. Cornwallis was now master of South Carolina, and he treated the Whigs with great severity. But his harsh and cruel measures could not crush out all resistance. The daring leaders, **Francis Marion** (*măr'e-un*) and **Thomas Sumter**, with such irregular troops as they could collect, were always on the watch to injure the enemy. They struck the invaders and the Tories many a sudden blow.

70. Not long after his victory over Gates, Cornwallis moved his army into North Carolina, to attempt the conquest of that state. He had detached Major Ferguson with troops to crush opposition and rouse the Tories in the

---

67. What is said of expeditions? The affair at Waxhaw Creek? Where is Waxhaw Creek? (See Map, p. 80.) What of Clinton?
68. Whom did Congress appoint to command in the south? Give an account of the battle of Sanders' Creek. Where is Camden? (See Map, p. 80.) What befell Sumter's troops?
69. What is said of Cornwallis's course in S. Carolina? Of Marion and Sumter?
70. What did Cornwallis attempt not long after defeating Gates?

western part of the Carolinas. The Tories and regulars, under Ferguson, met with a total defeat, October 7, at **King's Mountain**, at the hands of about a thousand mounted backwoodsmen. Alarmed by this disaster, Cornwallis marched back into South Carolina. In December, **General Nathanael Greene**, one of Washington's best generals, took command in the south in the place of Gates.

71. No important enterprise was undertaken in the Northern States this year. The **troops of Washington**, in huts near Morristown, suffered extremely from the severe cold of the "hard winter" of 1779-80, and from the want of provisions. Owing to the state of the finances it was difficult to obtain supplies for the army. Congress had to depend almost wholly upon **paper money** to carry on the war; and so enormous an amount of it had been issued, that in the spring of this year forty paper dollars were worth only a single dollar in specie. The people feared that the bills would never be paid. In after years this *continental money*, as it was called, became almost worthless.

72. Lafayette had spent the winter in France, and, mainly by his efforts, King Louis XVI. was induced to send another **French fleet and army** to aid the Americans. In July, the fleet, under Admiral de Ternay,* arrived at Newport, bringing more than five thousand soldiers, commanded by Count de Rochambeau.† These troops remained at Newport for some months to protect their ships from an expected attack by a superior British fleet.

73. It was in September, 1780, that the **treason of Arnold** was brought to light. This officer had been one of the bravest and most active defenders of the patriot cause; but now his feelings had become embittered against the government, and he was distressed by his debts. To

---

* *de (e* like *e* in *matter*) *tĕr-nā'*.   † *ro-shŏn[g]-bo'*.

70. What can you tell of the defeat of the enemy at King's Mountain? What did Cornwallis then do? By whom was Gates superseded, and when?
71. What is said of Washington's troops? Of the finances and paper money?
72. What is said of Lafayette? When and where did a French fleet and army arrive, and under whom? Why did the French troops remain at Newport?
73. When was the treason of Arnold brought to light? What is said of Arnold's services, and of his feelings at this time?

gratify his personal enmity, and to obtain money, this selfish and wayward man resolved to turn traitor to his country. He obtained command of the important fortress of West Point, which guarded the Hudson, and offered to deliver it into the hands of the enemy.

74. **Major André** (*an'drā*), a young and accomplished British officer, was sent to meet Arnold below West Point to make the final arrangements. The interview took place, and André, in disguise, set out to return to New York on horseback. While on the road he was stopped by three armed militia-men. They searched him, and found papers in his boots, which revealed the plot. Arnold, hearing of André's capture, fled to the British, who gave him the price of his infamy — a large sum of money, and the rank of brigadier general. André was tried, and hanged as a spy.

75. **Events of 1781.** — The very first day of 1781 — the decisive year of the war — was marked by an event which threatened serious danger to the American cause. This was the revolt of the **Pennsylvania troops**, who, to the number of thirteen hundred, marched from their camp near Morristown, declaring that they would appear before Congress to demand a redress of grievances. The soldiers had not been paid for months, and had suffered severely from the want of food and clothing. The Pennsylvania troops complained of still another hardship — that they were held after their term of service had expired.

76. When **the revolters** had marched as far as Princeton, proposals for satisfying their demands were made to them by a committee from Congress, and being accepted, the mutiny came to an end. A revolt of some of the **New Jersey troops** broke out soon afterwards, but this Washington quickly suppressed by military power. Later in the year, Congress appointed **Robert Morris** to be superintendent of finance for the government. The money

---

73. Why did he turn traitor, and what offer did he make to the British?
74. Give an account of André's connection with this affair, and of his seizure. What further is said of Arnold? Fate of André?
75, 76. Give an account of the revolt of the Pennsylvania troops.
76. What is said of the revolt of the New Jersey troops? What office was conferred upon Robert Morris, and what is said of his efforts?

affairs of the United States were placed by him upon a better basis, and were most skilfully managed. His spirited exertions greatly relieved the wants of the army.

77. When **General Greene** took command at the south, he found an army of only two thousand poorly-clad and half-starved men. But small as his force was, he thought best to divide it. The main body he placed in camp on the Great Pedee', near the northern border of South Carolina, while a detachment, under General Morgan, went into the western part of the state, to annoy the enemy there.

78. The English general, Cornwallis, despatched his favorite officer, Tarleton, to pursue and crush Morgan; but the latter, retreating to a place called **the Cowpens**, made a stand, January 17, and routed his pursuers. Tarleton fled to Cornwallis, who started in hot pursuit of the victors, eager to punish them, and release the five hundred prisoners they had taken. But Morgan was too nimble for his foe. He quickly retreated into North Carolina, and crossed the Catawba River just before the British came in sight. Fortunately a heavy fall of rain raised the waters of the river, and kept back the pursuers.

79. Here Greene reached Morgan's camp, and put himself at the head of the victorious troops. Closely pursued by the superior forces of Cornwallis, the American commander made a **masterly retreat** across North Carolina, and having united the two divisions of his army while on the march, placed his troops in safety on the north bank of the Dan, in Virginia.

80. Cornwallis now gave over the pursuit, and turned southward. In a few days Greene, having been strengthened by a body of militia, followed his adversary, and, March 15, met him at **Guilford** Court House, where a battle

---

77. What is said of the southern army when Greene took command of it? What disposition did he make of his main force and of a detachment?
78. Give an account of Morgan's victory at the Cowpens. What did Cornwallis now do? What did Morgan do? Where is the place called "the Cowpens"? (See Map, p. 80.) The Catawba River?
79. What is said of Greene's masterly retreat across North Carolina?
80. Give an account of what was afterwards done by Cornwallis and Greene, including the battle of Guilford. Where was Guilford Court House? (See Map, p. 80.) After this battle where did Cornwallis go?

was fought, in which the British remained masters of the field, but at such a cost that Cornwallis withdrew to Wilmington, near the sea.

81. Greene pursued him awhile, and then took the bold step of advancing directly upon the British posts in South Carolina. Near Camden, the enemy's strongest post, was fought the battle of **Hobkirk's Hill**, April 25. Lord Rawdon, the British commander in this action, compelled Greene to give up the field, but gained no advantages of a victory.

82. So vigilant was the American general, so well did he lay his plans, and so efficiently was he aided by his officers, Henry Lee, Marion, Sumter, and others, that before the middle of summer almost all the **British** posts in the interior were in the hands of the Americans. They had been captured, or their garrisons had been forced to evacuate them.

83. In the hot and sickly season Greene gave his soldiers rest awhile on the high hills of San-tee'. After a few weeks, he marched against the British, now commanded by Colonel Stewart, and September 8, the hostile forces met in the bloody battle of **Eutaw Springs**, in which both sides claimed the victory. But the enemy was so crippled, that he retreated as fast as possible towards Charleston. The battle of Eutaw Springs was the last general engagement of the war south of Virginia.

84. In January of this year, the traitor Arnold was sent, with sixteen hundred men, chiefly Tories, to invade **Virginia**. He destroyed or seized a large amount of property at Richmond and other places. Lafayette marched at the head of a detachment from Washington's army to resist the invaders; but the latter soon being strengthened by two thousand British troops, under General Phillips, who took the chief command, were too strong for the Americans, and continued to plunder and lay waste the country.

---

81. Give an account of Greene's movements after the battle of Guilford, and of the action at Hobkirk's Hill.
82. What had been accomplished by Greene and his able officers before the middle of summer?
83. What did Greene do in the hot and sickly season? Give an account of the battle of Eutaw Springs. Where are Eutaw Springs? (See Map, p. 40.)
84. What can you tell of Arnold's invasion of Virginia? Of Lafayette and the invaders?

85. We left **Cornwallis** at Wilmington. He soon moved his army into Virginia, and in May effected a junction with the king's troops already in that state. The forces of Cornwallis being greatly superior to those of Lafayette, the latter prudently avoided an engagement. After destroying a great amount of public and private property, the British general collected his troops at Yorktown, which he strongly fortified. A small force under Tarleton also held Gloucester (*glos'ter*) Point, nearly opposite.

86. Meanwhile **Washington** planned an attack on the British in New York. He moved his own troops towards the city, and called the French under Rochambeau from Newport, to take part in the enterprise. But this plan was suddenly changed when news arrived that the Count de Grasse (*gras*) would soon reach the Chesapeake with a powerful French fleet. To destroy Cornwallis now became the object of the American commander. Carefully keeping up the appearance of a design to attack New York, Washington marched southward with **the allied forces**, and was far on the way to Virginia before Clinton suspected his purpose.

87. Hoping to call back part of Washington's army, Clinton sent the traitor Arnold, with Tories and Hessians, to invade Connecticut. **New London** was plundered and burned, and **Fort Griswold**, on the opposite side of the river, taken by assault. Enraged at the brave defence of the fort, the enemy butchered the commander, Colonel Ledyard, and most of the garrison, after the surrender.

88. The French and American forces appeared before **Yorktown**, September 28. The fleet of De Grasse and that from Newport had already arrived, and blocked up the James and York Rivers. The siege was pressed with vigor by the allied armies, which numbered sixteen thousand

---

85. What did Cornwallis do after leaving Wilmington? Why did Lafayette avoid an engagement? Where did Cornwallis finally collect his forces? Where is Yorktown? (See Map, p. 80.)
86. What plan had Washington formed, and what did he do to carry out this plan? Why was the plan changed? What now became Washington's object, and what did he do?
87. Why did Clinton send Arnold to invade Connecticut? What was done by Arnold's troops? Where is New London? (See Map, p. 81.)
88. What can you tell of the investment of Yorktown by the land and naval forces? What was the number of the troops in the opposing armies?

troops. There was no escape, by land or sea, for Cornwallis and his garrison of less than eight thousand. But for three weeks they held out, and then, October 19, **Cornwallis surrendered** his army to Washington, his ships and seamen to De Grasse.

Map of Yorktown.

89. The people shouted for joy when intelligence that Cornwallis had been taken was heralded throughout the country. They believed that the end of the long struggle was near. The **capture of Cornwallis** may be regarded as substantially closing the war, which had now lasted six years and six months. New York, Charleston, and Savannah were the only important places still held by the enemy.

90. **Events of 1782 and 1783.** — The people of England had grown tired of the war. They had gained no glory by it, had greatly increased their national debt, and were now convinced that they could never subdue the Americans. Parliament decided to put an end to the contest, and **commissioners** to settle the terms of a peace were appointed by both governments, to meet at Paris. Besides Benjamin Franklin, the United States had John Adams, John Jay, and Henry Laurens, to represent them.

91. The provisional articles were signed on the last day of November, 1782. The final **treaty** was signed September 3, 1783, and at the same time Great Britain concluded treaties with France and Spain. The independence of the United States was acknowledged. The boundaries assigned on the east and on the north were nearly as at present. The Mississippi was made the western limit, and

---

88. When did Cornwallis surrender?
89. What is said of Cornwallis's capture, and of the duration of the war? What of places still held by the enemy?
90. What is said of the people of England and of Parliament? Of commissioners?
91. When were provisional articles signed? When was the final treaty signed, and what other treaties were made at the same time? What was acknowledged, and what boundaries were assigned to the United States?

Florida the southern. Florida, which then extended to the Mississippi, was made over to Spain.

92. The close of the war was formally proclaimed to the army just eight years from the day on which the first blood was shed at Lexington. Our liberties were now secured, but at a cost that never could be calculated. Those killed or maimed in battle were not the only **martyrs** of the Revolution. History must record the revolting cruelty with which the British treated their American prisoners They crowded them into filthy, loathsome prisons, or prison-ships, where thousands died from unwholesome food, foul air, and cruel treatment in other respects.

93. **New York**, which the British had made the centre of their operations for so long a time, was evacuated November 25, 1783, the anniversary of which day is still celebrated in that city as *Evacuation Day*. Savannah and Charleston had been evacuated the previous year.

94. During the summer and autumn the **American army** was quietly disbanded, only a small force being in the service when the British departed from New York. On the 23d of December **Washington** appeared in the Hall of Congress, at Annapolis, and resigned his commission as commander-in-chief. He then hastened to his home at Mount Vernon, bearing with him the gratitude and devotion of his countrymen.

III. ADOPTION OF THE FEDERAL CONSTITUTION.

1. The authority given to Congress by the **Articles of Confederation** was wholly inadequate for carrying on the national government. There was an enormous public debt, and no way by which Congress could obtain money to pay it. That body could neither lay taxes nor regulate com-

---

91. What is said of Florida?
92. When was the end of the war proclaimed to the army? What is said of the treatment of prisoners taken by the British?
93. When was New York evacuated, and what is said of the anniversary of that day? What of Savannah and Charleston?
94. What is said of the American army? Of Washington?
1. What is said of the authority given to Congress by the Articles of Confederation? Of the public debt, and of powers withheld by the states?

merce, for these and other powers properly belonging to the general government had been withheld by the states.

2. Many of the people were extremely poor, and they complained loudly of the hard times. In Massachusetts a formidable insurrection occurred in 1786. It is known as **Shays's Rebellion**, from one of its principal leaders, Daniel Shays, who had been a captain in the Continental army. Large bodies of armed men assembled, and forcibly closed the courts of law, so that taxes and other debts might not be collected. The governor called out an army of the militia, and the insurrection was put down in 1787. This outbreak was another proof of the need of a stronger national government.

3. In May, 1787, a **convention** was held at the State House, in Philadelphia, to form a better government for the nation. All the states, except Rhode Island, sent delegates. This convention was composed of the most illustrious men in the country. Washington was there, as its president; and Franklin, now more than eighty years old, gave it the benefit of his wisdom. After nearly four months spent in earnest deliberation and debate, a **constitution** was agreed upon, which was submitted to the people of the states, to be accepted or rejected.

4. Although the new constitution met with much opposition, yet before the close of the summer of 1788, it had received the assent of all the states but two. The 4th of March, 1789,* was appointed as the day on which the new government should go into operation. **George Washington** was unanimously elected as the first **president**. **John Adams** was chosen **vice-president**.

---

* Congress appointed the first Wednesday in January, 1789, for the people to choose electors, the first Wednesday in February for those electors to choose a president, and the first Wednesday in March for the government to go into operation. The last named day fell on the 4th. Hence the 4th of March following the election of a president is the day appointed for his inauguration.

---

2. What can you tell of Shays's rebellion?
3. When and where was a convention held to form a better national government? What states sent delegates, and what is said of these delegates? Result of the convention?
4. What is said of the assent of the states? What day was appointed for the constitution to go into effect? Who was elected the first president, and who vice-president?

CONDITION, AT THE CLOSE OF THIS PERIOD, OF WHAT IS NOW THE UNITED STATES.

1. The **boundaries** of the United States at the close of this Period have already been given. Massachusetts had jurisdiction over Maine; New York claimed Vermont. The territory **north of the Ohio** had been claimed by different states, but they had ceded it to the United States.* By an act of Congress it was organized, in 1787, as the **Northwest Territory**. This act, or ordinance, is famous as containing a declaration which secured this vast extent of country to freedom, namely: "There shall be neither slavery nor involuntary servitude in the said territory, otherwise than in punishment of crimes."

2. **South of the Ohio**, the present Kentucky was part of Virginia, and the present Tennessee part of North Carolina. Flourishing settlements had been formed in this western region. Georgia claimed territory westward to the Mississippi, and southward to Florida.

3. The **population** of the United States was nearly four millions, about seven hundred thousand being negro slaves. **Slavery** existed in all the colonies at the beginning of the Revolution, but before the close of this Period the New England States and Pennsylvania had adopted measures for doing away with it, and this example was followed, not many years later, by New York and New Jersey.

4. The wisest and best men of this time, both in the north and the south, regarded it as a great evil, and desired that it might come to an end in all the states. Unfortunate-

---

* Except a reservation, made by Connecticut, of a tract now forming the north-eastern part of Ohio.

---

1. Give the boundaries of the United States at the close of this Period. (*See p.* 107, *verse* 90.) What is said of the jurisdiction of Massachusetts, and the claim of New York? What lands had been ceded to the United States? When was the North-west Territory organized? What famous declaration is contained in the ordinance organizing the North-west Territory?
2. What can you tell of the region south of the Ohio?
3. What was the population of the United States at the close of this Period? What is said of the New England states, and of Pennsylvania, as regards slavery? Of New York and New Jersey?
4. How was slavery regarded at this time? What further is said of slavery? What is Mason and Dixon's Line? (*See p.* 51, *verse* 8.)

ly, however, **the system** became more strongly riveted upon the states south of Mason and Dixon's Line and the Ohio. We shall see hereafter, in the history of the republic, that negro slavery was long a fruitful source of strife in the councils of the nation, and at last the cause of a great civil war.

5. The war of the Revolution had made the inhabitants of different parts of the country better acquainted, and diffused a **common sympathy** throughout the whole nation. Every state had furnished troops for a common cause, and in nearly every one the enemy had been met in bloody conflicts. In this way much had been done to wear away local prejudices. The spirit of religious intolerance, which formerly marked certain parts of the country, had now lost its harshness.

6. The vices inseparable from armies, and the fierce passions aroused by deeds of blood, had in some degree injuriously affected the **morals** of the inhabitants. The thrifty and sober habits of earlier days had been broken up. There was an enormous load of public and private debt, while the vast exertions which had been made, and the failure of the national credit, had exhausted the means of the people. This state of things tended to impair that high sense of integrity which formerly prevailed, and to introduce loose and slippery notions of honesty.

7. The greater part of the shipping had been destroyed by the enemy. **Commerce**, thus suppressed during the war, revived on the return of peace. **Manufactures** made considerable progress during this Period. Attention began to be paid to the cultivation of **cotton** in the Southern States about the year in which peace was made, namely, 1783, and it soon became a staple of that part of the country. About the same time **agricultural societies** were first formed in the United States.

---

5. What beneficial effect is mentioned as resulting from the war? What is said of religious intolerance?
6. How had the war affected the morals of the people?
7. What is said of shipping and commerce? Of manufactures? Of cotton? Of agricultural societies?

CHRONOLOGICAL REVIEW.

NOTE. — The figures in the paragraphs and at the end of them refer to the pages upon which the events are mentioned.

1764. Parliament first declared its intention of raising a revenue from America, 76.
1765. The Stamp Act was passed by Parliament, 76.
The Colonial Congress met in New York, 76.
1767. A tax was imposed on tea, and several other articles, 77.
1770. The affray known as the *Boston Massacre* took place, 78.
1773. The tea was thrown into Boston harbor, 79.
1774. The Boston Port Bill was enacted, 79.
The First Continental Congress met at Philadelphia, 79.
1775. (April 19.) The first blood of the Revolutionary War was shed at *Lexington*, 82.
Royal authority teminated throughout the colonies, 86; Congress assumed the authority of a general government, 83; Washington was appointed commander-in-chief, 83.
The battle of *Bunker Hill* was fought, 84.
1776. The British were driven from *Boston*, 86; an attack on *Charleston*, South Carolina, was gallantly repulsed, 87.
Congress adopted the Declaration of Independence (July 4), 87.
The Americans were defeated on *Long Island*, 88; evacuated New York, and were defeated at *White Plains*, 89; Washington retreated through New Jersey, 89; took a thousand prisoners at *Trenton*, 90.
1777. The army with Washington routed the enemy at *Princeton*, 90; was defeated at the *Brandywine;* left Philadelphia to be occupied by the British; was repulsed by them at *Germantown*, and went into winter quarters at Valley Forge, 92, 93.
In the north, the British were defeated near *Bennington*, 94; and the army under Burgoyne surrendered at *Saratoga*, after two severe battles, 95.
Congress sent out for adoption the Articles of Confederation, 95.
1778. France entered into treaties of alliance and commerce with the United States, 96.
The Americans were victorious at *Monmouth Court-House*, 96; the British took *Savannah*, 98.

1779. The Americans were defeated at *Brier Creek*, 98; the British at *Stony Point*, 99; and John Paul Jones captured two English frigates in one of the most desperate naval combats on record, 100.

General Sullivan led an army into Western New York to chastise the Indians, who had joined with the British and Tories, 100.

1780. *Charleston*, South Carolina, surrendered to the British, 101; the Americans were defeated near *Camden*, and the British at *King's Mountain*, 101, 102.

Arnold plotted to betray West Point to the enemy, 102.

1781. General Greene conducted his celebrated campaign in the Carolinas, 104; the Americans gaining a victory at the *Cowpens*, 104; being defeated at *Guilford Court-House*, 104; and engaging the enemy in a hard-fought but indecisive battle at *Eutaw Springs*, 105.

Washington, aided by the French army and fleet, captured the British army and fleet at *Yorktown* (October 19) — the last important event of the war, 107.

1783. The treaty of peace was signed at Paris, 107.

1788. The new Constitution, prepared the year before, received the assent of the number of states required in order to go into effect, 109.

THE CONSTITUTION WAS RATIFIED BY

Delaware,	. . . Dec. 7, 1787.	South Carolina, . May 23, 1788.
Pennsylvania,	. . Dec. 12, 1787.	New Hampshire, . June 21, 1788.
New Jersey,	. . Dec. 18, 1787.	Virginia, . . . June 26, 1788.
Georgia,	. . . Jan. 2, 1788.	New York, . . . July 26, 1788.
Connecticut,	. . Jan. 9, 1788.	[After the government went into operation]
Massachusetts,	. Feb. 6, 1788.	North Carolina, . Nov. 21, 1789.
Maryland,	. . . April 28, 1788.	Rhode Island, . . May 29, 1790.

PERIOD IV. — NATIONAL GROWTH.

FROM THE INAUGURATION OF WASHINGTON, IN 1789, TO THE INAUGURATION OF LINCOLN, IN 1861.

I. WASHINGTON'S ADMINISTRATION. 1789–1797.

1. THE inauguration of Washington as President of the United States took place on the last day of April, 1789, in the city of New York, which was then the capital. There are three great departments of **government**, the legislative, which makes laws, the executive, which enforces them, and the judicial, which interprets them. By our Constitution the legislative power is vested in a Congress, the executive in the President, and the judicial in certain courts.

Washington.

2. Three **departments** belonging to the executive branch of the government were created by Congress, one of State, one of the Treasury, and one of War. The heads of these departments were styled Secretaries, and they formed, with the Attorney-General, a council, called the President's *Cabinet*. Other departments have since been created.

3. Congress quickly set about providing a **revenue** for the support of government. To obtain it, duties were laid upon imported goods and the tonnage of vessels. A plan for maintaining the **public credit** was soon formed by

---

QUESTIONS. — 1. When and where was Washington inaugurated? Describe the three great departments of government. In what does the constitution vest these powers?
2. What executive departments were created? What is said of the chief officers of these departments? What of other departments?
3. How did Congress provide a revenue? What is said of the public credit? What of Hamilton?

Alexander Hamilton, whom the President had appointed Secretary of the Treasury. Hamilton had been Washington's favorite aide-de-camp, and had done his country great service in other ways — especially by his powerful writings in favor of the Federal Constitution.

4. Following Hamilton's recommendation, Congress adopted measures for paying the foreign and domestic debts of the United States, and also assumed the state debts contracted in support of the war. There was much discussion before the whole plan was agreed to; but Hamilton's financial policy proved to be a wise one, and the country soon entered upon a season of great prosperity. A **national bank** was established during Washington's first term of office.

5. In 1790 an act was passed fixing the **seat of government**, for ten years, at Philadelphia, and after that, permanently on the Potomac. The tract of land forming the present *District of Columbia* was afterwards ceded by Maryland, as a site for the nation's capital, and there the city of Washington was laid out.

6. An **Indian war** broke out in 1790, on the northwestern frontier. Two expeditions, the first under General Har'mar, and the second under General St. Clair, met with defeat at the hands of the savages. The force led by St. Clair was surprised in camp in the western part of Ohio, and routed with dreadful slaughter.

7. **General Wayne**, the hero of Stony Point, next led an army against the hostile tribes. He encountered them in August, 1794, on the Maumee (*maw-mee'*), not many miles from its mouth, and gained a complete victory. After this decisive blow the Indians consented to make peace; and from that time the settlements in the west had a most marvellous growth.

---

4. What did Congress do in regard to the debts of the United States and the war debts of the states? What is said of a national bank?
5. Where was the seat of government fixed? What is said of the District of Columbia?
6. Where did an Indian war break out? What is said of the first two expeditions against the Indians?
7. What can you tell of a victory gained over the Indians? What followed! Where does the Maumee River empty? (See Map, p. 124.)

8. During Washington's first term **Vermont** and **Kentucky** were admitted into the Union as states, the former in 1791, the latter in the next year.*

Washington wished to retire from public life at the close of his term of four years; but he finally consented to hold the office for another term, **and in the autumn of 1792 was unanimously re-elected.**

9. In the summer of 1794 an outbreak, known as the **Whiskey Insurrection**, occurred in the western counties of Pennsylvania. Armed men prevented the collection of the tax which Congress had imposed upon spirits distilled in the United States. The revenue officers were harshly treated and driven away. The president issued a proclamation, commanding the insurgents to desist, and afterwards sent a large force of the militia against them. This ended the insurrection. The insurgents submitted without resistance.

10. The people became much excited on account of the **relations** of the United States **with foreign countries.** The French revolution was in progress, and **France**, then a republic, was again waging war with Great Britain. A large party in America was eager for the nation to become an ally of France; but Washington wisely proclaimed a strict neutrality. This policy of our government was not at all relished by the French republic.

11. A bitter feeling of **hostility to Great Britain** had prevailed for some time in the United States. On each side there were complaints that the other government had

---
* The oldest English settlement in Vermont was made at Brattleboro', where a fort was built in 1724. Fifty years later, in 1774, the first settlement was made in Kentucky by James Harrod, who built a log cabin where Harrodsburg now is. Daniel Boone, the famous pioneer of Kentucky, had already explored this region.

Vermont gets its name from the Green Mountains, its principal range. The name is formed of the French words *vert*, green, and *mont*, mountain.

The name *Kentucky* means, in the Indian tongue, *the dark and bloody ground.* The region was so named by the Indians, on account of the savage warfare of which it was the scene.

---

8. When were Vermont and Kentucky admitted as states? What is said of Washington's reëlection?
9. Give an account of the Whiskey Insurrection.
10. What is said of foreign relations, and the policy of our government towards France?
11. What were the relations of the United States and Great Britain?

violated the treaty which closed the revolution. The Americans also complained of the injuries British policy was inflicting on their commerce. War was imminent; but this calamity was averted by the prudent course of the government.

12. The president appointed Chief Justice John Jay — one of our great statesmen — envoy to England, to arrange the matters in dispute. The **treaty which Jay negotiated** was fiercely denounced by a strong party in the United States; but the government regarded it as better than war, and ratified it in 1795. In the same year, a **treaty was made with Spain**. It defined the boundary of Florida, and gave to the United States the free navigation of the Mississippi. **Tennessee** was admitted to the Union in 1796, making the number of states sixteen.*

13. On various questions which came before Congress, there were long and **exciting discussions**. One of these questions, which came up in the second year of the government, related to slavery. Thus early occurred the first angry debate upon this subject. Through a long series of years, from time to time, many more were to follow.

14. During Washington's administration the people were divided into two great **political parties**, one called the *Federal*, the other the *Republican* party. The adherents of the latter fiercely opposed many of the measures of the administration. This was not the party which existed under the same name many years later.

15. A few months before the end of his second term Washington sent forth his famous "Farewell Address," containing the wisest political precepts. **John Adams**, the

---

* The first permanent settlement within the limits of Tennessee was made in 1768, on the Watau'ga River, in the north-eastern part of the state. In 1756, the English built Fort Loudon, at the confluence of the Little Tennessee and Tellico (*tel'li-co*) Rivers, about thirty miles south-west of Knoxville. The Indians, four years afterwards, massacred the garrison, and broke up the few white settlements which had been made.

Tennessee takes its name from the river so called, the word signifying the *river of the big bend.*

---

12. What can you tell of Jay's treaty with England? Of a treaty with Spain? When was Tennessee admitted to the Union?
13. What is said of a debate in Congress in regard to slavery?
14. Name the political parties at this time. What position did the Republicans take?
15. What is said of Washington's Farewell Address? Who were elected president and vice-president?

candidate of the Federalists, was elected to succeed Washington. Jefferson, a Republican, was chosen vice-president.

II. ADAMS'S ADMINISTRATION. 1797-1801.

1. The **difficulty with France**, which began in Washington's administration, came near ending in a war with that country soon after the accession of Adams. France was displeased because our government had refused to side with her in the war she had declared against Great Britain, and the treaty lately negotiated by Jay with the latter power was the cause of bitter complaint. The authorities of France, disregarding our rights, kept issuing decrees which inflicted immense injury upon American commerce. A great many American merchant vessels were captured by French cruisers and held as prizes.

2. **Envoys** sent to France to settle the difficulties were treated with insults and neglect, and could accomplish nothing. They were given to understand that a bribe was required by those who controlled French affairs. When this became known in America, the people indignantly responded, as had Mr. Pinckney, one of the envoys, "Millions for defence, but not one cent for tribute."

3. Finally, **Congress** authorized the president to raise an army, and put the country in a state of defence. Washington was appointed commander-in-chief. In the same year, 1798, a *Department of the Navy* was created to manage naval affairs, which, heretofore, had been intrusted to the secretary of war. War was not declared, but **hostilities** began on the ocean. Authority was given to capture armed vessels of the French, and a number of such vessels were captured.

4. The resolute stand taken by the United States caused the authorities of France to favor **negotiations**. Accord-

---

1. What caused the unfriendly feeling of France towards the United States? What course was adopted by France?
2. How were our envoys treated by the French government? What is said of a bribe, and what saying expressed the feelings of the American people?
3. What finally was done by Congress? What department was created the same year? To what extent were hostilities carried on?
4. When and with whom was a treaty made?

ingly, President Adams again sent envoys to that country. They found Napoleon Bonaparte at the head of affairs, and with him they negotiated a treaty in 1800. In the summer of the same year the seat of government was transferred from Philadelphia to Washington.

5. An intensely bitter **party spirit** prevailed during this administration. The president's policy met with fierce opposition from the Republicans, with Jefferson at their head. But no acts were more loudly condemned by this party than the **Alien and Sedition Laws**, passed at the time when war with France seemed impending. Under the "alien law," the president could expel from the country any alien whom he should judge dangerous to the United States. Under the "sedition law," any person libelling the government, Congress, or the president, might be fined or imprisoned.

6. Near the close of the century the nation was plunged into grief by the **death of Washington**, the "Father of his Country." He died at Mount Vernon, on the 14th of December, 1799. The whole nation mourned the loss of this great and good man, who was "first in war, first in peace, and first in the hearts of his countrymen." The result of the presidential election, in the following year, was favorable to the Republicans, or Democrats, as they were sometimes called. **Thomas Jefferson**, their leader, was elected president.

III. JEFFERSON'S ADMINISTRATION. 1801–1809.

1. Jefferson, the third president of the United States, served two terms. The admission of Ohio into the Union, the purchase of Louisiana, a war with Tripoli, and the death of Hamilton, were **memorable events** of his first term. Ohio became a state in 1802.* It was the first one carved

---

* The first English settlement within the bounds of Ohio was made in 1788, at Marietta, by emigrants from New England.

Ohio, the Indian name of the river which washes the southern border of the state, signifies the *beautiful river*.

---

4. When did Washington become the capital?
5. What is said of party spirit and the Republicans? What can you tell of the alien and sedition laws?
6. When and where did Washington die? What was the result of the presidential election in the next year?
1. Name four memorable events of Jefferson's first term. When did Ohio become a state?

out of the great North-west Territory. In 1803 the United States purchased **Louisiana** of France for fifteen millions of dollars. This vast region, chiefly west of the Mississippi, reached northward to the British possessions, and westward to the Rocky Mountains. It had but a short time before been ceded to France by Spain.

2. The **war with Tripoli** (*trip'o-li*) began in 1801, and lasted four years. The Bar'bary States, in the north of Africa, of which Tripoli is one, sent out cruisers in those days to seize the merchant vessels of Christian nations, and the captives which these pirates took were held as slaves till a ransom was paid. Strange as it seems to us now, it was the custom of Christian nations to pay tribute to these piratical powers. Our government had already given large sums of money and rich presents to secure American commerce from their attacks. But now the greedy Bashaw of Tripoli wanted more money or presents, and declared war against the United States.

3. The president sent a **naval force** into the Mediterranean, and several actions, gallant on the part of the Americans, took place. Commodore Preble, Captain Bainbridge, and Lieutenant Deca'tur greatly distinguished themselves. The city of Tripoli was blockaded and bombarded by the fleet. Early in 1805, William Eaton, an adventurous American, led a few hundred men, mostly Arabs, from Egypt, across a wide desert, and with the help of an American squadron captured the Tripolitan city of Der'ne. Soon afterwards peace was made.

4. In July, 1804, **Aaron Burr**, then vice-president, fastened a political quarrel upon Alexander Hamilton, and killed him in a duel. Burr, after the expiration of his term as vice-president, organized an expedition, with the design, it was believed, to conquer the Spanish province of Mexico, and also to separate the country west of the

---

1. What can you tell of the purchase of Louisiana? Extent of the purchase?
2. When did the war with Tripoli begin, and how long did it last? What was the practice of the Barbary States? What the custom of Christian nations? Course of our government? Why did the Bashaw of Tripoli declare war?
3. What was done by the navy? What of Eaton's expedition?
4. What is said of the killing of Hamilton? Of Burr's western expedition?

Alleghanies from the Union. His expedition was broken up, and in 1807 he was brought to trial for treason against the United States. There was not sufficient proof, however, to convict him, and he was set at liberty.

5. The same year, 1807, witnessed the success of the famous inventor, **Robert Fulton,*** in applying steam for propelling vessels through water. The first voyage of Fulton's steamboat was from New York to Albany. Twenty years before this, John Fitch had made a boat which he moved in the Delaware River by steam; but Fulton's invention first made steam navigation a source of profit.

6. At this time England and France were engaged in a furious struggle with each other, and neither power respected **American rights on the ocean.** On the one hand the British government issued "Orders in Council,"† for the purpose of restricting or destroying the commerce of neutral nations with France and her allies; and on the other hand, Napoleon Bonaparte, Emperor of the French, issued his "Decrees" against commercial intercourse with the British Islands. The principal sufferer was the United States, whose merchant vessels became the prey of both the hostile parties.

7. The British government also claimed the "right of search," as it was called. Under this pretended right, American vessels were stopped on the high seas, and searched for seamen of British birth; and if any such were found, they were taken away for service in the British navy. Worse than this, many **American vessels were robbed of seamen** who were natives of the United States.

8. The bitter feeling in America against Great Britain was changed to one of deep indignation by an event which occurred in June, 1807. The British frigate **Leopard** fired into the American frigate **Chesapeake**, while off the coast

---
* The *u* in Fulton is sounded as *oo* in *foot.*
† Orders proclaimed by the advice of the Privy Council, a body of men selected by the English king as his advisers in matters of state.

---
5. What successful application of steam was made in 1807? What of John Fitch?
6. What is said of English "Orders in Council," and French "Decrees," and their effect upon American commerce?
7. What was done by the British under their claim of "the right of search"?
8. Give an account of the affair of the Chesapeake and the Leopard.

of Virginia. The American commander, being wholly unprepared for action, struck his colors, after having three of his men killed and eighteen wounded. The British then took from the Chesapeake four of her crew, claiming them as deserters. Three of these were Americans by birth. The president, by a proclamation, ordered all British armed vessels immediately to leave the waters of the United States. Although the English government did not defend the outrage upon the Chesapeake, yet reparation was withheld for more than four years.

9. The course of England and France inflicted so much injury upon American commerce, that near the end of the year 1807 Congress decreed an **embargo**, to keep at home all American vessels, and to prevent foreign vessels from taking cargoes from our ports to foreign ports. This policy proving to be unwise, the act was repealed in the spring of 1809, and in its place a **non-intercourse act** was passed, forbidding all commerce of the United States with Great Britain and France. Such was the condition of affairs when Jefferson retired from office. **James Madison**, of Virginia, was chosen to succeed him as president.

IV. MADISON'S ADMINISTRATION. 1809-1817.

1. For some time **the Indians** on the north-western frontier had shown a hostile spirit. Tecum'seh, a famous chief of the Shawnees (*shaw-neez'*), and his brother, "the Prophet," had persuaded many tribes to unite in a league against the whites. General William Henry Harrison led a small army against the savages, and in November, 1811, defeated them near the mouth of the **Tippecanoe** (*tip-pe-kan-oo'*), in Indiana. The Indians tried their favorite plan of creeping up stealthily, and falling upon the whites in the early morning; but Harrison was not to be thus surprised. When this battle was fought, Tecumseh was absent, persuading distant tribes to join the league.

---

8. What was done by the president and the English government?
9. What is said of an embargo? A non-intercourse act? Who succeeded Jefferson?
1. What is said of the Indians on the north-western frontier? When and by whom was the battle of Tippecanoe gained?

2. **Louisiana*** was admitted into the Union in 1812. The state was formed from part of the Louisiana Purchase.†

3. English cruisers continued to prey upon the commerce of the United States. The war spirit already existing between the two nations was increased by the affair of the **President and the Little Belt.** In May, 1811, Commodore Rodgers, sailing in the American frigate President, off our coast, hailed a British sloop of war, and received a shot in reply. The fire was returned, and in a few minutes the sloop was disabled. The commodore now hailed again, and this time got a civil answer.

THE SECOND WAR WITH GREAT BRITAIN, OR THE WAR OF 1812.

1. From the Declaration of War to the Beginning of the Year 1814.

1. **Events of 1812.** — The wrongs inflicted by England, in harassing the commerce of the United States, and the impressment of seamen from American vessels, at last becoming too hard to bear, our government decided to make war upon the tyrant of the ocean. An act, declaring **war against Great Britain**, was passed June 18, 1812. Steps were taken to increase the army; and General Henry Dearborn (*deer'burn*) was appointed commander-in-chief.

2. It was determined to invade **Canada**. About the middle of summer, **General Hull** crossed from Detroit, with a small army, and encamped on Canadian soil. While he was preparing to attack Fort Malden (*mawl'den*), not many miles south of his camp, a party of the enemy cap-

---

* The French were the earliest settlers in Louisiana. In 1700 they built a fort on the Mississippi, about fifty miles from its mouth — the first European establishment within the present limits of the state. (See p. 55, ¶ 4.)

† The strip east of the Mississippi, and north of the Iberville and the lakes, was claimed by Spain, as part of Florida. The United States, on the other hand, claiming that the Louisiana Purchase extended to what is now the present western boundary of Florida, annexed the strip to the State of Louisiana.

Louisiana was named in honor of the French king, Louis XIV. (See p. 54, ¶ 3.)

---

2. When was Louisiana made a state? From what was it formed?
3. Give an account of the affair of the President and the Little Belt.
1. What caused the government of the United States to declare war against Great Britain? When was war declared, and who was commander-in-chief?
2. State what you can of Hull's invasion of Canada. What American post was captured? Where is Detroit? (See Map, p. 124.) Mackinaw?

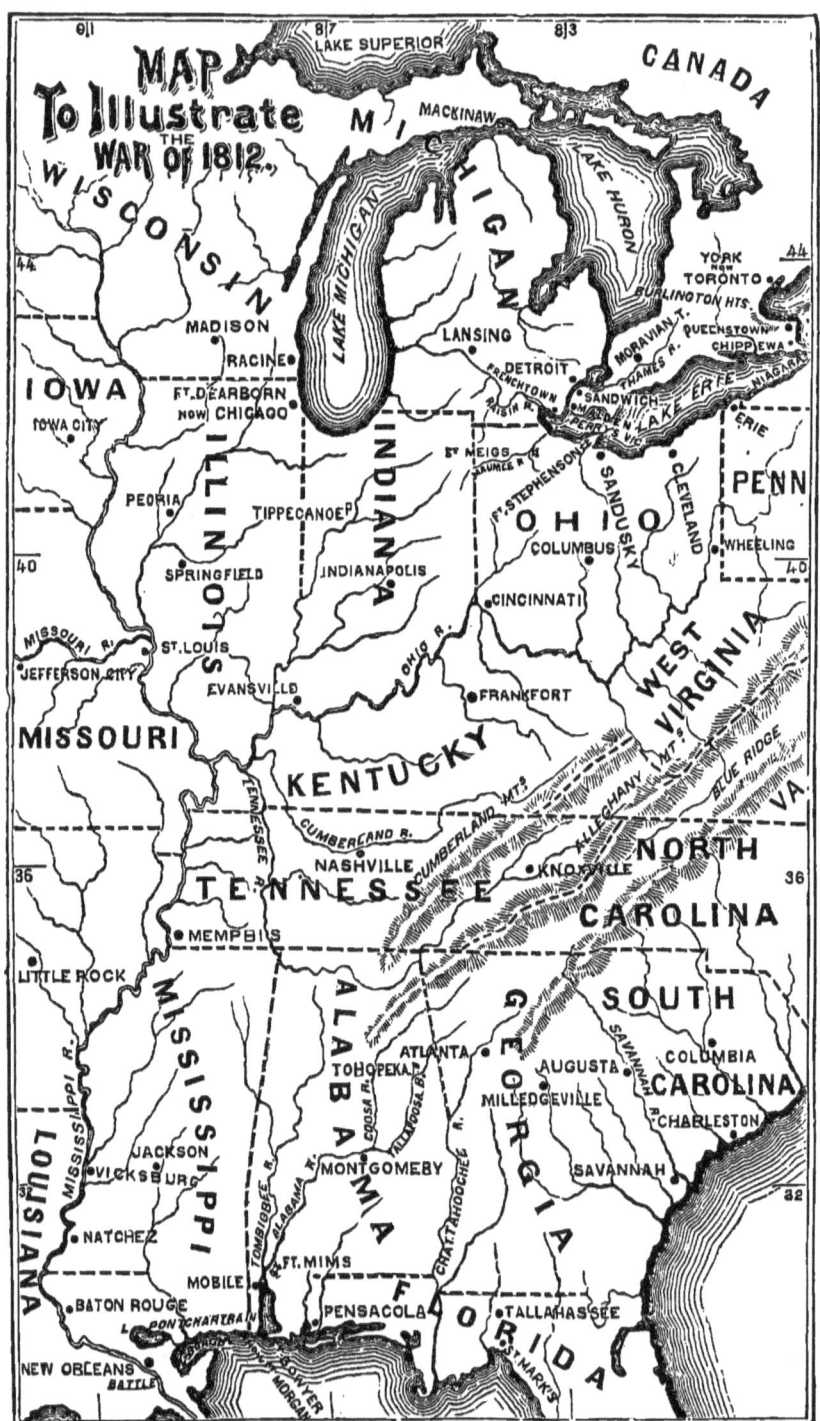

tured the American post at Mack'inaw, an important stronghold for keeping the northern Indians in check.

3. Without making an attack upon Fort Malden, Hull recrossed the river, and took shelter within the defences of **Detroit**. General Brock followed him, with British and Indians. When the enemy advanced to assault the works on the 16th of August, Hull would not permit his men to fire, but, to their great indignation, ordered a white flag to be hung out, in token of submission. He surrendered his army, and the whole territory of Mich'igan, to the British. Such was the issue of Hull's campaign near the western end of Lake Erie.

4. Late in the year **another attempt** was made upon Canada. This time the country bordering on the Niagara River, which flows from the eastern end of Lake Erie into Lake Ontario, was the scene of operations. General Van Rensselaer (*ren'se-lur*), who was in command of an American army at Lewiston, sent a detachment across the river, October 13, to attack the British at Queenstown.

5. An obstinate battle ensued on **Queenstown Heights**, in which victory, at first, inclined to the invaders; but at last they were overpowered, and compelled to surrender. While the conflict was going on, a large body of the American militia remained on this side of the river, refusing to cross and aid their countrymen. Lieut. Colonel Winfield Scott and Captain John E. Wool, who afterwards became famous generals, took a gallant part in this action.

6. The Americans, mortified by disasters on the land, found encouragement in the brilliant exploits of their little **navy** on the ocean. We can here name only the most important actions. In August, the frigate *Constitution*, Captain Isaac Hull, won a victory over the British frigate *Guerriere*.* The Constitution was a favorite vessel of the Americans, and was popularly called *Old Ironsides*.

* Pronounced *gĕr-re-ĕre'*, the *g* sounded as in *get*.

3. Tell what you can of Hull's retreat to Detroit, and of his surrender.
4. Where and when was another attempt made upon Canada?
5. What can you tell of the battle of Queenstown Heights? What is said of Scott and Wool? Where is Queenstown? (See Map, p. 125.)
6. What is said of naval exploits? What victory was won in August?

7. In October, two naval triumphs were gained by the Americans. The sloop of war *Wasp*, Captain Jones, after a desperate fight, captured the English brig *Frolic*. The same day both vessels were taken by an English ship of seventy-four guns. It would have been useless for the sloop to resist a ship of such force. Just a week later, in the same month, the frigate *United States*, commanded by Commodore Decatur, captured the English frigate *Macedonian*. Near the end of December the *Constitution*, then commanded by Commodore Bainbridge, won another victory, in the capture of the British frigate *Java*.

8. These and other **naval combats** caused the Americans to exult in the prowess of their seamen, while the British, who had boasted that they would quickly drive our "bits of striped bunting" from the ocean, were filled with surprise and mortification. Immense loss was inflicted upon their commerce by **American privateers**, which cruised in every direction, capturing English merchantmen. Before the end of the year our national ships of war and private armed vessels had taken about three hundred prizes.

9. Most of the Federalists were opposed to the war; but a majority of the people favored its prosecution, as was shown by the reëlection of Madison, in the autumn of 1812.

10. **Events of 1813.**—The Americans planned to invade Canada with **three armies** in 1813. The Army of the West, commanded by General William Henry Harrison, was collected near the western end of Lake Erie; the Army of the Centre, under General Dearborn, was at Sackett's Harbor and on the Niagara frontier; the Army of the North, assembled on the shores of Lake Champlain, with General Wade Hampton as its commander.

11. In January, General Winchester, who commanded a division of the **Army of the West**, sent forward a detach-

---

7. Give an account of two victories gained by the American war-vessels Wasp and United States. Of another victory by the Constitution.
8. Effect of our naval triumphs? What of American privateers?
9. How was the war regarded by the people of the United States?
10. What was planned for 1813? Where, and under whom, was the Army of the West? Army of the Centre? Army of the North? Where is Sackett's Harbor? (See Map, p. 125.)
11. Give an account of the advance of Winchester's detachment to Frenchtown?

ment, which routed the British and Indians at **Frenchtown**, near the mouth of the River Raisin ($rā'zn$), and then moved the rest of his force to that place. These troops were chiefly Kentuckians.

12. There, January 22, they were attacked by a large body of British and Indians, under Colonel Proctor. After a brave defence, they surrendered, on condition of being protected from the Indians. Proctor violated his pledge. The wounded **prisoners were massacred** by the savages.

13. The disaster at Frenchtown compelled Harrison to delay his advance. Near the Maumee Rapids he built **Fort Meigs** ($megz$), where, about the 1st of May, he was besieged by Proctor, with white troops and Indians. After a few days the arrival of a body of Kentuckians caused the siege to be given up, although the enemy captured or killed a large part of the relieving force.

14. Nearly three months later Proctor advanced against **Fort Stephenson**, at Lower Sandus'ky. A small garrison, under the gallant young Major Croghan ($kro'gan$), held the fort, and signally repulsed a storming party of the British. The enemy then made a hasty retreat.

15. **Perry's victory**, on Lake Erie, turned the tide of affairs in the north-west wholly in our favor. Each of the hostile parties had fitted out a few vessels to contend for the mastery of this lake. On the 10th of September, the American squadron, commanded by Captain Oliver Hazard Perry, encountered, in the western part of the lake, the British squadron, commanded by Captain Barclay. The battle raged for three hours, and then Perry had won a glorious victory. All the British vessels were captured. "We have met the enemy, and they are ours," Perry wrote to Harrison, in a despatch announcing the victory.

16. **Harrison** hastened to profit by this success. Embarking his troops on board of Perry's fleet, he crossed to Canada, and advanced upon the enemy's post at Malden,

---

12. What is said of the surrender and massacre at Frenchtown?
13. What occurred at Fort Meigs? Where was Fort Meigs? (See Map, p. 124.)
14. What can you tell of the attack upon Fort Stephenson?
15. Tell what you can of Perry's victory on Lake Erie.
16. What did Harrison do after Perry's victory?

only to find that Proctor had fled. Harrison pursued him up the **Thames** (*temz*), and overtook him, October 5, waiting to give battle. The mounted backwoodsmen charged upon the English, broke their ranks, and made them surrender. The savages made a braver stand, but soon their leader, Tecumseh, was slain, and they were put to flight. This celebrated warrior had taken part against the Americans in many conflicts, and for years had been the chief instigator of Indian hostilities in the west.

The victories of Perry and Harrison brought the war to an end on the north-western frontier.

17. Events in which the **Army of the Centre** took part are now to be related. Commodore Chauncey (*chahn'se*) had command of a small American fleet on Lake Ontario. Late in April General Dearborn embarked at Sackett's Harbor, with sixteen hundred men, and crossed the lake to attack **York** (now Toronto), where a large amount of military stores was deposited. The town was captured, but not before the enemy had blown up his magazine, killing or wounding more than two hundred of the assailants. General Pike, the gallant leader of the Americans in the attack, was mortally wounded by the explosion.

18. The troops were soon conveyed by the fleet to the **Niagara frontier**. Here Dearborn collected a considerable army, and a month after the capture of York forced the British to give up Fort George. The whole country along the Canada side of the Niagara River then fell into our possession. But our success was followed by reverses, and late in the year most of the troops were withdrawn from this quarter to operate elsewhere. Then the enemy not only recovered the posts on the Canada side of the river, but crossed over and captured Fort Niagara, which he held till the end of the war.

19. Almost at the very time that the enemy was forced to abandon Fort George, the British fleet crossed the lake

---

16. Give an account of the battle of the Thames. What is said of Tecumseh? Result of the victories?
17. What can you tell of the capture of York?
18. What successes were gained on the Niagara frontier? What of reverses?

with about a thousand troops, under General Pre-vost', to attack **Sackett's Harbor**, the chief naval station of the Americans. They were repulsed by General Brown, at the head of a few regular troops and a body of militia.

20. It was planned by the Americans to move against **Montreal** with the Army of the Centre and the army assembled near Lake Champlain. Early in November General Wilkinson, who had succeeded General Dearborn, having collected the Army of the Centre, began the descent of the St. Lawrence.

21. While on the way down the river, the flotilla was followed and annoyed by the enemy. Some American troops having landed, an indecisive action, called the battle of **Chrysler's Field** (*kris'lerz*), was fought. According to the plan of the expedition, General Hampton was to push forward to the St. Lawrence, with his forces from Lake Champlain, and join Wilkinson. Hampton refusing to do this, the expedition against Montreal was given up.

The campaigns of the Armies of the Centre and the North were failures, caused chiefly by the want of skill and energy in the generals, and by personal jealousies.

22. Near the end of December there was dreadful work on the **Niagara frontier.** When the Americans deserted Fort George, their commander ordered the Canadian village of Newark to be burned. The inhabitants were left shelterless in the wintry air. It was an act which deserves our severest censure, and most cruelly did the enemy retaliate, laying waste the New York border with fire and sword. Buffalo and several other villages were burned.

23. The British blockaded the **Atlantic coast**, and kept some of our national vessels from getting to sea. One of the British admirals, Cockburn (*ko'burn*), spent some time in the spring plundering and burning villages and farm-

---

19. Give an account of the enemy's attempt upon Sackett's Harbor.
20. What plan was made, and what did Wilkinson do early in November?
21. What more can you tell of the expedition against Montreal?
22. What can you tell of the burning of a Canadian village, and of the retaliation of the British?
23. What is said of a blockade? Of the plundering and burning of villages and farm-houses?

houses on the shores of Chesapeake Bay. This was congenial occupation for Admiral Cockburn.

24. There were **conflicts on the ocean**. Off the coast of Guiana,* early in the year, the sloop-of-war *Hornet*, Captain James Lawrence, compelled the British brig *Peacock* to strike her colors after an action lasting but fifteen minutes. The conquered ship was already sinking. On his return to the United States, Lawrence was promoted to the command of the frigate *Chesapeake* — the same ill-starred vessel that had struck her flag to the Leopard six years before.

25. On the 1st of June, Lawrence, with his vessel ill-equipped and ill-manned, put to sea from Boston, to engage the British frigate *Shannon*, which, with a well-disciplined crew, was lying off the harbor inviting an attack. **The action was short, but very furious.** Fortune favored the Shannon. In a few minutes the Chesapeake became exposed to a raking fire, and her chief officers were killed or wounded. Then the enemy boarded her, and hauled down the colors. Lawrence, after he was mortally wounded, gave his last heroic order: " Don't give up the ship." This was the most memorable sea-fight of the year.

26. **A war with the Creeks**, an Indian nation in Alabama, began in 1813. Tecumseh had been among them exciting them to take up arms. Part of the nation, however, remained friendly. The beginning of hostilities was marked, near the end of August, by a horrible massacre at **Fort Mims**, in Southern Alabama. The fort was surprised by the savages, and hundreds of men, women, and children were butchered in cold blood. Volunteers, chiefly from Tennessee and Georgia, with General Andrew Jackson as their leader, hastened to avenge this massacre. A number of **battles** took place, in which the savages were beaten, and, March 27, 1814, at To-ho-pe'ka, or Horse-shoe Bend, on the Tal-la-poo'sa River, Jackson gave them a terrible defeat, which brought the war to an end.

* *ge-ah'nah* — *g* as in *get*.

24. Give an account of a sea-fight won early in the year by Captain Lawrence.
25. Give an account of the fight of the Chesapeake and the Shannon.
26. Who had excited the Creeks to take up arms? What can you tell of the massacre at Fort Mims? Who went against the savages? Result?

2. From the Beginning of the Year 1814 to the End of the War.

27. Events of 1814. — General Wilkinson having been relieved of his command in the spring of this year, and Hampton, another incompetent general, having resigned, the war on the **northern borders** was henceforth conducted with more credit to the American arms.

28. In July two memorable battles were fought on the **Niagara frontier**. Early in this month, an American army, under General Brown, crossed the river near **Fort Erie**, which post the enemy surrendered without resistance. The Americans then marched down the river, General Winfield Scott leading the advance, and, July 5, gained a brilliant victory over the British under General Riall (*ri'al*), who, leaving his intrenchments beyond the **Chippewa** (*chip'pe-waw*), crossed the creek and gave battle.

29. Riall retreated down the river, and after some time was reënforced by General Drummond, his superior in command. The British then advanced, and on the 25th of July the hostile armies met at **Lundy's Lane**, close by the great Falls of Niagara. This was the most fiercely contested battle of the war. General Scott's troops began the conflict, which raged from near sunset till near midnight.

30. The enemy's battery had been placed upon a hill, and to secure the victory the Americans had to capture these guns. Colonel Miller, being ordered by General Brown to carry the height and take the cannon, said, "I'll try, sir." His perilous charge was successful. Three times the British, advancing to retake their battery, were hurled back. After the close of the action our troops held the field awhile, and then retired to their camp. Generals Brown and Scott were severely wounded in this battle.

31. The American army fell back to **Fort Erie**. Gen-

---

27. What is said of the war on the northern borders after the spring of 1814?
28. Give an account of operations early in July, including the battle of Chippewa. Where was Fort Erie? (See Map, "Niagara Frontier," p. 125.) Where is Chippewa Creek?
29. What is said of the battle of Lundy's Lane?
30. What more can you tell of this battle?
31. What fort was afterwards occupied by the American army?

eral Drummond followed, and besieged the fort with a superior force of veteran soldiers. In an attempt to take the works by storm, he was repulsed with the loss of nine hundred men. A few weeks afterwards the besieged made a sortie, and inflicted so great a loss upon Drummond that he raised the siege. In November, it being too late in the season to make offensive movements, the Americans blew up Fort Erie, and withdrew from the Canada shore.

32. The close of the war in Europe, by the overthrow of Napoleon, had enabled the British government to send to Canada a large army of **veteran soldiers**, who had served under the Duke of Wellington. Early in September, General Prevost, at the head of fourteen thousand troops, mostly veterans, appeared before **Plattsburg**, the principal American post on Lake Champlain, at this time held by General Macomb (*ma-koom'*), with a force hardly one third as large.

33. The American squadron, under Commodore Macdonough (*mak-don'ŭh*), was anchored off Plattsburg. On the 11th of September, the British squadron, under Captain Downie, bore down upon the American vessels, and the severe **battle of Lake Champlain** was fought. Although the enemy excelled in the number of his men and cannon, yet Macdonough won a decisive victory. At the same time Prevost, attacking Macomb's position on shore, was vigorously resisted. He gave up the assault when the British fleet surrendered on the lake, and that night began a hasty and disorderly retreat towards Canada.

34. This year the British kept up a stricter blockade of the **Atlantic coast**. Several towns on the seaboard, in the eastern part of Maine, were captured, and the whole district, as far west as the Penobscot, was claimed by the enemy as a subdued country. In August a British fleet entered the Pa-tux'ent from Chesapeake Bay, and landed about five thousand men, under the command of General

---
31. What can you tell of the siege of Fort Erie? What was done in November?
32. What is said of British soldiers sent to Canada? What of the hostile land forces at Plattsburg? Where is Plattsburg? (See Map, p. 125.)
33. Give an account of the naval battle on Lake Champlain. Of the battle on land.
34. What is said of the blockade in 1814? Of operations in Eastern Maine?

Ross, who marched upon Washington, then a straggling town of fewer than nine thousand inhabitants. The American forces, mostly raw militia, were posted at **Bla'densburg**, where they were routed by the invaders on the 24th.

35. The British then marched on, and in the evening of the same day reached **Washington**. They burned the Capitol, the president's house, and other public buildings, and, on the following night, stole away, returning to their ships. Part of their fleet, having sailed up the Potomac, compelled the town of Alexan'dria to purchase safety by the payment of a heavy ransom.

36. The British next sailed up the Chesapeake to attack **Baltimore**. On the 12th of September, about nine thousand troops landed at North Point, some miles below the city. Marching towards Baltimore, they were opposed, and General Ross, their commander, was killed. A spirited action followed, and the American detachment was forced to retire. The invaders the next day approached the works defending the city, but not daring to risk an attack, turned back in the early morning of the 14th. The fleet, which meanwhile had moved up the Pataps'co, and bombarded Fort McHenry with very little effect, also turned back. Thus failed the attempt to capture Baltimore.

37. The United States had very few regular war-vessels at sea in 1814, and for a while none. The blockade and losses by captures had well nigh exhausted our little **navy**; but American privateers were still scouring the seas and taking many rich prizes. The remarkable cruise of Captain Porter, in the national frigate *Essex*, should be mentioned. This frigate entered the Pacific early in 1813, and besides protecting American ships in that ocean, made great havoc among British whalemen. In March, 1814,

---

34. What movement was made against Washington? What occurred at Bladensburg? In what direction is Bladensburg from Washington? (See Map, "Baltimore and Vicinity," p. 125.)
35. What was done at Washington by the British? What occurred at Alexandria?
36. What city did the British next go against, and where did they land? What took place while the British were on the march for Baltimore? Give an account of land and naval operations on the second day after the landing, and on the morning of the 14th.
37. What was the condition of the navy of the United States in 1814? What is said about the cruise of the Essex in the South Pacific, and her fate?

the Essex fell a prey to two of the enemy's war-vessels off Valparaiso (*vahl-pah-rī'so*).

38. Opposition to the war, or to the way it was managed, was strongest in New England. The legislatures of Massachusetts, Connecticut, and Rhode Island appointed delegates, who, with others from some counties in New Hampshire and Vermont, met at Hartford, in December, to consider the condition of the New England States, and also certain measures of the national government. The **Hartford Convention** was in secret session three weeks, but nothing of importance resulted from its deliberations. The friends of the administration called it a dangerous and treasonable body, while, on the other hand, the peace party considered it a patriotic council.

39. The course of our narrative now leads us to the most southern part of the country. Late in the summer a British squadron arrived at **Pensacola**, which then belonged to Spain, and, with the consent of the Spanish commander, made that place the headquarters for sending out expeditions. **Fort Bowyer** (*bō'yer*), now Fort Morgan, defending the approach to Mobile, was attacked by war-vessels and a land-party, but the garrison repelled the assailants. Finally, General Jackson, the commander in the south, seized Pensacola and drove away the English.

40. **Close of the war.** — In December a powerful fleet, with over ten thousand troops, the flower of England's army, came to anchor near the entrance to Lake Borgne (*born*). The design was to capture **New Orleans.** The American gunboats on the lake were overpowered after a gallant combat. General Jackson was then in New Orleans, providing for its defence. As soon as he learned that British troops (who crossed the shallow lake in small craft) had landed and taken post below the city, he made a night-attack upon their camp, and struck them a blow which kept them back for a while. He then threw up

---

38. What of opposition to the war? How, and for what purpose, were delegates appointed? What can you tell of the Hartford Convention?
39. What can you tell of events which happened at Pensacola and Fort Bowyer? Where is Pensacola? (See Map, p. 124.)
40. What force threatened New Orleans? when and how? Where is New Orleans? (See Map, p. 136.) What is said of a naval action and a night-attack?

New Orleans and Vicinity.

intrenchments a few miles below New Orleans, and behind them repelled the enemy who confronted the defences on the 28th of December, and furiously cannonaded them on New Year's Day.

41. On the 8th of January, 1815, the British, under Sir Edward Pakenham (*pak'n-am*), advanced to storm the intrenchments, which were defended by fewer than six thousand men. So deadly a fire did the American marksmen pour into the assailants, that they gave way, and fled in horror and dismay. Jackson that day won a **great victory**, killing and wounding two thousand of the British, with the loss of eight of his own men killed and thirteen wounded. Pakenham was killed, and the two generals next in command wounded, one of them mortally. The British army, not long afterwards, stole away in the night-time towards their ships. The battle of New Orleans was the last important engagement of the war on the land, which had lasted a little over two years and a half.

42. A **treaty of peace** was signed at Ghent,* in Belgium, December 24, 1814, by American and British commissioners. Tidings of this treaty reached the United States little more than a month after the battle of New Orleans, and were everywhere hailed with joy. The treaty said nothing about the two chief causes of the war — aggressions upon American commerce and the impressment of seamen. Peace between the powers of Europe had removed these abuses.

43. Several **sea-fights** took place in the early part of the

* Pronounced *gent* — *g* as in *get*.

---

40. What of two repulses of the enemy before the grand assault?
41. Give an account of the battle of New Orleans. How many were killed and wounded on each side? What else is stated concerning this battle?
42. When was a treaty of peace made, and what is said about this treaty? Was the treaty of peace signed before or after the battle of New Orleans?
43. What is said about sea-fights early in 1815?

year 1815, before it was known that a treaty of peace had been made. In one, the frigate *Constitution*, then commanded by Captain Charles Stewart, engaged two small English vessels of war, the *Cyane* (si-an') and the *Levant* (le-vant'), and took both of them.

44. **War with Algiers.** — From 1795 to 1812 an annual tribute had been paid the **Dey of Algiers** (ăl-jeerz') to secure American vessels from seizure by the Algerines. But the same year in which war began with Great Britain the Dey became hostile. One of his cruisers captured an American vessel, and her captain and crew were held as captives, the Dey refusing a high ransom offered by our government.

45. After peace had been made with Great Britain, **Commodore Decatur** was sent to Algiers with a squadron. On the way he captured two Algerine ships of war, and soon afterwards appeared in the harbor of Algiers. The frightened Dey quickly agreed to the terms of peace which the American commander dictated. Decatur then proceeded to **Tunis and Tripoli**, and compelled their rulers to pay for American vessels which they had permitted the English to seize in these ports. No more tribute was paid by our government to the North African sea-robbers.

46. In the year 1816, a new bank, called the **Bank of the United States**, was chartered, to continue twenty years. The presidential election occurred this year, and resulted in the choice of **James Monroe** (mun-ro'), of Virginia.

Indiana was admitted as a state in 1816. The French were the discoverers of this region, and the earliest settlers.*

V. MONROE'S ADMINISTRATION. 1817-1825.

1. Monroe was president during two terms. Party spirit subsided to such a degree that when he was chosen for a

---

* Vincennes (vin-senz'), the oldest town in Indiana, was the site of a trading-post of the French early in the preceding century, perhaps as early as 1705. *Indiana* gets its name from the word *Indian*.

---

44. What is said of a tribute to the Dey of Algiers, and of his hostility?
45. Who was sent against Algiers, and with what success? What did the commodore next do?
46. When and for how long was a new Bank of the United States chartered? Who was elected president in 1816? What of a new state?
1. What is said of party spirit during Monroe's two terms?

second term he received the almost unanimous vote of the electors. The period of Monroe's administration is known as the "era of good feeling."

2. During Monroe's presidency five states were added to the Union, namely, Mississippi, in 1817, Illinois, in 1818, Alabama, in 1819, Maine, in 1820, and Missouri, in 1821. In all these states, excepting Maine, whose early history has already been given, the first settlements were made by the French.*

3. When the admission of Missouri was proposed, a violent debate arose on the question, whether it should be a slave or or a free state. It was finally arranged, in 1820, by an agreement, known as the **Missouri Compromise**, that Missouri might come in as a slave state, but that slavery should be prohibited in all other territory belonging to the United States west of the Mississippi and north of parallel 36° 30'.

4. Troubles which arose between the settlers in Southern Georgia and the **Seminole Indians**, ended in a war in the autumn of 1817. General Jackson, at the head of a force of white troops and friendly Creeks, marched into Florida, which then belonged to Spain, and overran the country of the hostile savages. Believing that the Spaniards were giving the Indians protection, Jackson took the Spanish fort at St. Mark's, and seized Pensacola. During this invasion he put to death two British subjects, accused of inciting the Seminoles to war. The course of Jackson in seizing Spanish forts and executing the two British subjects caused hot debates in Congress and much excitement in England and Spain.

---

* The first settlement in Mississippi was made in 1699, at Biloxi. (See p. 55, ¶ 4.) The first in Illinois, at Kaskaskia, as early as 1693, perhaps earlier. The oldest settlement in Alabama was made on Mobile River, in 1702. The oldest town in Missouri is St. Genevieve (*jen-e-rêve'*), founded in 1755. For Maine, See p. 36.

Mississippi, Illinois, Alabama, and Missouri derive their names, which are of Indian origin, from rivers of the same names. *Mississippi,* according to some, means *the father of waters,* according to others, *the great and long river* ; *Alabama, here we rest* ; *Missouri, muddy water* ; *Illinois* is formed from Indian *illini,* men, and the French suffix *ois.*

---

2. What states were formed during Monroe's presidency, and in what years?
3. State what you can about the agreement known as the Missouri Compromise.
4. How and when did a war arise with the Seminoles? What can you tell of Jackson's operations against the savages? Against the Spaniards? Where is St. Mark's? (See Map, p. 124.) What is said of two British subjects? Of Jackson's course?

5. For some time the government had been trying to buy **Florida**. In 1819 a treaty was made, by which Spain ceded the province to the United States. The treaty was finally ratified in 1821, and that year Florida was delivered up to the United States. The price paid was five millions of dollars, besides the giving up by the American government of all claim to Texas.

6. The president, in one of his annual messages, asserted a principle, since known as the Monroe doctrine. He declared, in effect, that the attempt of any European power to gain new dominion in America, by either colonization or conquest, would be regarded by the United States as an unfriendly act.

7. In the summer of 1824, **Lafayette** came to the United States, as "the Nation's Guest." He remained in this country a little more than a year, during which time he visited each of the twenty-four states. His tour was a triumphal progress. Everywhere the people welcomed him with heartfelt joy.

John Quincy Adams, of Massachusetts, son of the second president, was elected to succeed Monroe.

VI. JOHN Q. ADAMS'S ADMINISTRATION. 1825-1829.

1. John Quincy Adams became president on the 4th of March, 1825. His term of four years was a period of great **national prosperity**. Many improvements of the highest importance were going on throughout the country. The building of the first railways in America was in Adams's presidency, but locomotives were not used for travelling till 1830.

2. The 4th of July, 1826, was the fiftieth anniversary of the national independence, and is memorable from the deaths of the famous patriots **John Adams** and **Thomas Jefferson**, which occurred on that day. Both had lived to be very old men.

---
5. State what you can of the purchase of Florida.
6. State what you can of the Monroe doctrine.
7. Give an account of Lafayette's visit. Who succeeded Monroe as president?
1. When did John Quincy Adams become president, and what is said of his term! What of the first railways, and of locomotives used for travelling?
2. What is said of the deaths of John Adams and Thomas Jefferson?

3. The question of a **protective tariff** excited much discussion during part of this administration. Such a tariff law was enacted in 1828, with the view of protecting home manufactures, by imposing heavy duties upon articles of the same kind brought to this country from abroad. This policy, which was called the *American system*, has been a fruitful cause of contention between political parties. We shall see that in the next administration South Carolina came near taking up arms against the national government on account of the tariff question.

4. When the time again came around for a presidential **canvass, the most** bitter **party spirit** burst forth. President Adams was a candidate for a second term; but the result of the contest was the election of **Andrew Jackson**, of Tennessee, the "Hero of New Orleans."

VII. JACKSON'S ADMINISTRATION. 1829-1837.

1. Jackson, the seventh president, held his office during two terms. The same decision and vigor which had marked his military operations were shown in his control of civil affairs. One of his first steps was to make numerous **removals from office** of those who had opposed his election, and to appoint to office his political friends. This policy, though injurious to the public welfare, has been continued by succeeding administrations.

2. The year 1832 is memorable in the history of our country for important events, namely, the Black Hawk war, nullification in South Carolina, the president's veto of the bill rechartering the United States Bank. In the spring of this year, a war, known as the **Black Hawk war**, broke out with some tribes of the north-west, led by Black Hawk, a chief of the Sacs. The scene of hostilities was in Northern Illinois and Southern Wisconsin. The war was soon ended, and the usual results followed — the Indians ceded large tracts of land to the government, and removed farther westward.

---

3. What kind of a tariff law was enacted in 1828, and for what purpose?
4. How was the campaign of 1828 conducted, and who was elected president?
1. What is said of Jackson's control of civil affairs? Of removals from office?
2. What important events of 1832 are mentioned? State what you can of the Black Hawk war.

3. The tariff of 1828 caused loud and bitter complaint in the south, where there were no great manufacturing interests to encourage. Congress modified the law, but failed to satisfy its opposers. Late in 1832 South Carolina, by a state convention, issued an ordinance of **nullification**, declaring the tariff laws null and void. The ordinance also declared that the state would secede from the Union if the federal government employed force to execute those laws in South Carolina.

4. **John C. Calhoun**, of South Carolina, was the foremost advocate of this false doctrine of state rights, namely, that a state has the right to set aside a law of the national government. He resigned the vice-presidency, and boldly upheld the doctrine in the senate-chamber. Among the senators of great ability who opposed it, **Daniel Webster**, of Massachusetts, was most conspicuous.

5. The authorities of South Carolina threatened armed resistance; but **President Jackson** did not hesitate a moment. He was ready to enforce the laws by the army and the navy, if things should come to such a pass. Finally, **Henry Clay**, senator from Kentucky, brought forward a bill for a compromise tariff. It became a law, and provided for a gradual reduction of duties. South Carolina then returned to her allegiance.

6. Jackson's financial policy formed a prominent feature of his administration. In 1832 he vetoed a bill passed by Congress to renew the charter of the **United States Bank**. As the bill failed to become a law, the bank ceased to be a national institution when its charter expired, four years afterwards. The excitement and discussion which followed the veto were greatly increased the next year, in 1833, by a new proceeding of the president against the bank. He ordered the secretary of the treasury to cease depositing the public moneys in that institution. This was done, and

---

3. What is said about the tariff of 1828? What can you state concerning nullification in South Carolina?
4. What is said of the course of Calhoun? Of Webster?
5. What of Jackson's course? What of Clay and a compromise tariff?
6. What bill relating to the United States Bank did the president veto? What change in keeping the public moneys was made by Jackson's direction?

they were placed in certain state banks. **Thomas H. Benton**, senator from Missouri, was a powerful helper of Jackson in his war upon the bank.

7. At the close of 1835 the **Florida war** began. This contest with the Seminoles and other Indians lasted seven years before they were subdued. It was caused by an attempt, on the part of the government of the United States, to remove the Indians to lands west of the Mississippi. A treaty for their removal had been made; but their ablest warrior, Os-ce-o'la, and the greater part of the Seminoles, declared that the treaty was not a valid one.

8. The **opening of the war** was signalized by a dreadful massacre. Major Dade and more than a hundred men, while on a march, were waylaid near Wahoo (*wah-hoo'*) Swamp and all but three killed.

9. There had been considerable fighting with the Seminoles, when, in October, 1837, **Osceola** entered the American camp under the protection of a flag of truce. General Jes'up, the American commander, detained him as a captive. This has been regarded as a base action; but General Jesup pleaded in excuse for it the treachery of the savage chieftain. Osceola was sent to Fort Moultrie, at Charleston, where, a few months afterwards, he died.

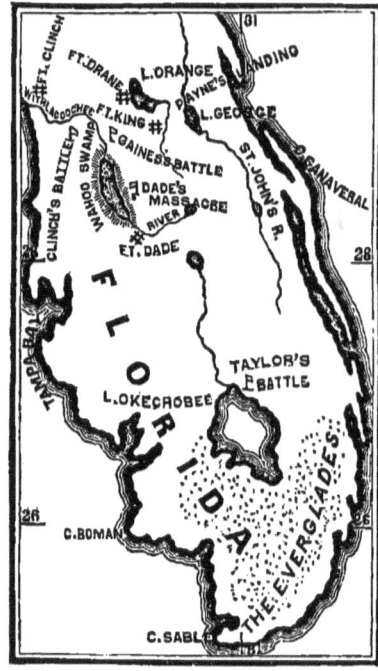
Map of Part of Florida.

10. But the capture of this famous warrior did not end

---

6. What is said of Benton?
7. When did the Florida war begin, and how long did it last? State the cause of the war. What of a treaty?
8. What signalized the opening of the war?
9. What is said of Osceola — his seizure and fate?

the contest. After striking a blow, the savages would scatter to their lurking-places in swamps and thickets which well defended them from pursuit. Colonel Zachary Taylor marched far into their country, and beat them in a hard-fought battle near **Lake O-ke-cho'bee**, in December, 1837. The war, however, lingered till 1842, when a peace was made.

11. **Arkan'sas** entered the Union in 1836, and **Mich'igan**, in 1837, both while Jackson was president. The admission of Michigan made the number of states twenty-six,—double the original number.*

12. **Party lines** were distinctly drawn on the bank and the tariff questions. Those who supported the administration, and opposed the United States Bank and a protective tariff, were called *Democrats*. Those who opposed the administration, and advocated a bank and protective duties, were called *Whigs*. At the election in the autumn of 1836, the democrats made their candidate, **Martin Van Buren**, of New York, president.

VIII. VAN BUREN'S ADMINISTRATION. 1837–1841.

1. Very soon after Van Buren took the helm of state, a **commercial crisis** occurred. Hundreds of mercantile houses became bankrupt, and there was wide-spread distress, affecting all branches of industry. The banks, which by freely lending their notes had encouraged speculation, for a while ceased to redeem them in hard money. The United States have never since experienced so disastrous a financial storm as swept over the country in 1837.

2. In the same year a **rebellion** broke out **in Canada**.

---

* The French made the first settlement in Arkansas, at Arkansas Post, in 1685. Detroit, the oldest permanent European settlement in Michigan, was founded by the French, in 1701.

Arkansas takes its name from a tribe of Indians now extinct.

The name *Michigan*, it is said, is derived from an Indian word meaning *the lake country*.

---

10. What course did the savages adopt? What is said of a hard-fought battle?
11. When did Arkansas and Michigan become states? What is remarked concerning the admission of Michigan?
12. What is said of Democrats and Whigs? Who was elected to succeed Jackson?
1. Give an account of the great commercial crisis of 1837.
2. What can you tell of the breaking out of a rebellion in Canada?

Many adventurers from the United States aided the insurgents, who attempted to overthrow the British government of the colony; and at one time affairs took such a turn that there was danger of another war between our country and Great Britain. The president issued a proclamation forbidding American citizens to aid the disaffected Canadians. After some fighting, British troops and loyal Canadians suppressed the rebellion.

3. In the latter part of Van Buren's administration a change was made in the mode of keeping the **public moneys**. An act was passed, providing that they should be kept in the treasury at Washington, and in sub-treasuries established in some of the chief cities of the republic. At the election in 1840, after a most exciting canvass, **William Henry Harrison**, of Ohio, the candidate of the Whigs, was chosen president, with John Tyler, of Virginia, as vice-president. Harrison was the successful general in the battles of Tippecanoe and the Thames.

IX. HARRISON'S AND TYLER'S ADMINISTRATIONS.
1841-1845.

1. **Harrison died** just one month after his inauguration. The vice-president, **John Tyler, became president.** The Whigs, being in power, now expected to establish a United States Bank; but **bills passed** by Congress for this purpose **were vetoed** by President Tyler, greatly to the chagrin of the party that had elected him, and to the disgust of his cabinet, every member of which resigned, except Webster, the secretary of state, who held his position awhile longer.

2. In 1842, the people of Rhode Island were greatly agitated by what is called, from its leader, the **Dorr rebellion.** The trouble arose from efforts made to establish a new and more liberal constitution in place of the old charter, granted by Charles II., under which Rhode Island

---

2. What danger was there, and what did the president do?
3. What change was made in the mode of keeping the public moneys? What is said of the canvass and election in 1840?
1. How long was Harrison president, and who became president after Harrison's death? What bills did Tyler veto, and how was his course regarded by his party and cabinet?.
2. In what state did the Dorr rebellion arise, and how?

was still governed. For a short time the strife seemed likely to bring on a bloody struggle ; but Dorr and those of his followers who took up arms to put in force their scheme of reform, soon dispersed without fighting. The people legally adopted a new constitution in the same year.

3. In the latter part of Tyler's presidency the question of the annexation of **Texas** came before the people. The Texans, having thrown off the authority of Mexico, and established a republic of their own, wished to come under the government of the United States ; but the proposition to admit Texas was strongly opposed, in the free states, by those who were unwilling to extend our slave territory. On the other hand, her admission was strongly advocated in the south as favorable to the interests of slavery.

4. In the presidential contest of 1844, the Democratic candidate, **James K. Polk**, of Tennessee, who was pledged to favor the annexation of Texas, was elected president over Henry Clay, the Whig candidate. On the 1st of March, 1845, — three days before the end of the term, — **Tyler** signed resolutions passed by Congress permitting annexation on certain conditions. **Texas** accepted the conditions, and was admitted into the Union in the following December.*

5. On the day before the inauguration of the new president, Tyler signed a bill admitting **Florida** and **I'owa** into the Union.† The former became a state on the passage of the act, in 1845, the latter not till the next year.

* The permanent occupancy of Texas may be dated from the year 1715, when the Spaniards established posts and missions to prevent the region from falling into the hands of the French, who were then colonizing Louisiana. In 1821, Mexico, including Texas, declared herself independent of Spain. In the course of time Santa Anna became president of Mexico. The Texans revolted, and on the 21st of April, 1836, under the command of General Houston (*hews'tun*), totally defeated, in the battle of San Jacinto, an advance division of a large Mexican army under Santa Anna, whom they took prisoner. This decisive battle secured Texan independence.

† The settlement of Iowa was begun in 1833, just after the close of the Black Hawk war. Dubuque (*du-book'*, *oo* as in *food*) and Burlington are the oldest towns. (For FLORIDA, see pp. 12, 13).

Iowa gets its name from that of a tribe of Indians, the Iowas, whose name signifies the *drowsy* or *sleepy ones*.

2. What more can you state concerning this difficulty?
3. What important question came up in the latter part of Tyler's presidency? What had the Texans done, and what did they wish? On what grounds was the annexation of Texas opposed and advocated in the United States?
4. Who was elected president in 1844? When did Tyler sign resolutions permitting the annexation of Texas?
5. When were Florida and Iowa brought into the Union as states?

6. The population of the **north-west** was rapidly increasing, and every year the settlers were advancing farther westward. Towns and cities were now springing up as if by magic. It was common for a number of emigrants to form a company, and with a long train of wagons make their way through the prairies to their new homes.

X. POLK'S ADMINISTRATION. 1845–1849. THE WAR WITH MEXICO.

1. Operations of the Army under Taylor.

1. Polk's administration began on the 4th of March, 1845, and was most marked by the **war with Mexico**, which resulted from the annexation of Texas. The Texans, most of whom were emigrants from the United States, had waged a successful war with the Mexicans, and established a republic, whose independence had been recognized by the United States and by the principal European powers; but Mexico still claimed the country as part of her domain.

2. The passage of the resolutions permitting Texas to join the Union was considered by the Mexicans as an act of hostility. Moreover the western **boundary of Texas** was in dispute. The Texans claimed the country as far as the Rio Grande, while, on the other hand, the Mexicans contended that the revolted province had never spread farther westward than the River Nueces (*nwā'sĕs*).

3. While war was impending, **General Taylor**, in obedience to orders from his government, advanced into Texas with a body of American troops to repel a threatened invasion of the Mexicans. In August, 1845, he formed his camp at Corpus Christi (*kris'te*), just within the disputed territory; and in the early part of the next year, having received positive orders to advance, he **moved to the Rio Grande**, opposite Matamoras (*mat-a-mō'ras*). Here, on the east bank

---

6. What is said of the north-west region?
1. What caused the war with Mexico? Who were most of the Texans, and what had they done?
2. How did the Mexicans regard the passage of the resolutions permitting annexation? What dispute was there as to boundary?
3. What movement was made while war was impending? Where did Taylor form his camp in August, 1845, and what did he do early the next year? Where is Matamoras? (See Map, p. 149.) The River Nueces? The Rio Grande?

A COMPANY OF EMIGRANTS CROSSING THE PRAIRIES.

of the river, he began to build a fort — afterwards called Fort Brown. Before arriving at the Rio Grande, he established a depot of supplies at Point Isabel.

4. The Mexican forces were on the opposite side of the river, about Matamoras. On the 25th of April, 1846, a small **reconnoitring party** of American dragoons, led by Captain Thornton, was surprised on the east side of the Rio Grande, and, after losing sixteen men, killed and wounded, was forced to surrender.

5. A few days later, having learned that the Mexicans were crossing the river in great force, Taylor marched his main army back to Point Isabel to obtain supplies and make his depot there secure. Having done these things, he set out to return, with about twenty-three hundred men, to the fort opposite Matamoras. On the way he met General Arista (*ah-rees'tah*), May 8, with a Mexican army greatly superior in numbers, and beat him in a battle on the plain of **Palo Alto.***

6. The next day, May 9, Taylor, advancing, met the Mexicans again, strongly posted at **Resaca de la Palma,**† and totally defeated them. They fled beyond the Rio Grande. On the 18th of May, Taylor crossed that river, and took possession of Matamoras, where he waited awhile for reënforcements.

7. Intelligence of the capture of Captain Thornton's party produced intense **excitement** throughout the United States. The whole nation was aroused. Many more men than the government needed were eager to volunteer for the rescue of Taylor's little army, which was supposed to be in great danger. **Congress** took measures to prosecute the war with vigor.

8. After about three months General Taylor was in a condition to carry the war still farther into the enemy's

---

* *pah'lo ahl'to.* † *rā-sah'kah dā lah-pahl'mah.*

4. Where were the Mexican forces? Give an account of the surprise and capture of a small party of American dragoons.
5. Give an account of a movement of Taylor's army before the battle of Palo Alto. Give an account of the battle of Palo Alto.
6. Give an account of the battle of Resaca de la Palma. What did Taylor next do?
7. What took place in the United States when the capture of Captain Thornton's party became known?
8. When did Taylor advance still farther into the enemy's country?

country. He moved his army of about six thousand six hundred men against **Monterey** (*mon-te-rā'*), a strongly fortified city, defended by General Ampudia (*ahm-poo'de-ah*), with ten thousand Mexican troops. On the 24th of September, after a siege of four days and a series of assaults, the city was surrendered to the Americans.

9. Before this time the American government had prepared **two expeditions** to penetrate Mexico north of Taylor's line of operations. One of these was to invade and conquer New Mexico and California. The conquest of these countries will be related hereafter. The other was to move against Chihuahua (*che-wah'wah*).

10. The expedition against **Chihuahua** was commanded by General Wool. About the time of the fall of Monterey he marched from San Anto'nio, in Texas, with near three thousand men. The route was long and wearisome, but after some weeks he reached Monclo'va, where he received orders to give up the expedition. He afterwards marched southward, and joined General Taylor.

11. Some weeks after the taking of Monterey, Taylor advanced a division of his army, and occupied **Saltillo** (*sahl-teel'yo*). About the same time a naval force from the American fleet in the Gulf took possession of the city and port of **Tampico** (*tahm-pe'ko*). In January, 1847, a large part of Taylor's best troops was withdrawn to aid General Scott, who had been ordered to invade Mexico, by way of Vera Cruz (*vā'rah-kroos*).

12. Meanwhile Santa Anna, general-in-chief of the Mexican forces, had collected twenty thousand troops, and with these he marched northward, hoping now to gain a victory over Taylor's diminished army. The Americans, hardly five thousand men, under Taylor and Wool, awaited

---

8. Give an account of the taking of Monterey. Where is Monterey? (See Map.)
9. What is said of two expeditions?
10. Who led the expedition which set out for Chihuahua? Give an account of this expedition. Where is San Antonio? (See Map, p. 149.) Monclova? Chihuahua?
11. What can you tell of the taking of Saltillo and Tampico? Where is Saltillo? (See Map.) Tampico? How was Taylor's army weakened in January, 1847?
12 Who was Santa Anna, and what did he do? Where were the Americans posted?

the attack in a narrow mountain-pass near the plantation of **Buena Vista** (*bwa'nah vees'tah*). The battle began with skirmishing in the afternoon of the 22d of February, 1847. It opened anew early the next morning, and raged with great fury till night, when Santa Anna retreated, leaving his killed and wounded on the battle-field. This victory put an end to the war in the region held by Taylor's forces. From this time the chief efforts of Mexico were to resist the invasion which Scott was about to make to the very centre of her power.

2. *Conquest of New Mexico and California.*

13. Very soon after the beginning of the war the conquest of **New Mexico** was planned at Washington. A small army, collected for this purpose at Fort Leavenworth, set out in June, 1846, under the command of General Stephen W. Kearny (*kar'ni*). After a march of nine hundred miles, through a wild and uninhabited region, the invaders, in August, entered Santa Fé, the capital of New Mexico. Kearny took possession of this vast province without opposition, and set up a new government. He then, with a squadron of cavalry, pushed on for California. His design was to coöperate with the Pacific fleet in the conquest of that Mexican state.

14. Part of the Americans who entered Santa Fé marched southward, near the end of the year, against **Chihuahua**. Colonel Doniphan led the expedition. It was a long and adventurous march. On the way the little army, numbering about eight hundred men, defeated the enemy in two battles, in which American bravery and Mexican cowardice were signally displayed. The last victory, gained at the pass of the Sacramento, February 28, 1847, gave Doniphan possession of the city of Chihuahua.

---

12. Give an account of the battle of Buena Vista. What is said of this victory and of Mexican efforts afterwards?
13. Where, when, and under whom was an army collected to march against New Mexico? Where is Fort Leavenworth? (See Map, p. 149.) Santa Fé? What can you tell of Kearny's march and of operations in New Mexico?
14. What expedition went southward from Santa Fé? What was accomplished by this expedition?

15. A few months before the opening of the Mexican war, Captain John C. Frémont entered California, with a small exploring party. He was seeking a new route to Oregon, farther south than the one usually travelled by emigrants. After some time, learning that the Mexican commandant was about to expel the American settlers in California, he espoused their cause, and after some conflicts with the Mexicans, called the Americans together at a town near San Francisco, where, by his advice, July 5, 1846, they declared their independence. Frémont as yet did not know that we were at war with Mexico.

16. Only two days later Commodore Sloat, who had been cruising off the Pacific coast, and had lately learned that war existed between the United States and Mexico, seized Monterey, and proclaimed that the Americans would henceforth hold the country. **Commodore Stockton** shortly afterwards took the command in place of Sloat, and aided by **Frémont**, continued the work of overturning Mexican authority. This was fully completed early in January, 1847. General Kearny, with his small party, arrived a little while before the struggle was over, and took part in the last battle. On his march from Santa Fé he had experienced great hardships, and had narrowly escaped being cut off by the enemy.

3. *Operations of the Army under Scott.*

17. Mexico was now threatened with an invasion more dangerous than she had yet experienced. **General Scott** had collected an army of over twelve thousand men, with the design of marching upon the capital. He landed his army near Vera Cruz, March 9, 1847, and soon had completely invested the city. After a furious bombardment,

---

15. When and why had Frémont entered California with an exploring party? What cause did Frémont espouse, and what was done July 5, 1846?
16. What happened only two days later? What is said of Commodore Stockton and Frémont? Where is Monterey in California? (See Map, p. 149.) When had Mexican authority in California been completely overturned? What is said of Kearny's arrival, and of his march?
17. How many men had Scott collected, and for what purpose? Where and when did he land his army? Give an account of the capture of Vera Cruz and the castle. Where is Vera Cruz? (See Map, p. 149.) In what direction is the city of Mexico from Vera Cruz?

of four days, from the army and fleet, **Vera Cruz**, and the strong castle of San Juan de Ulloa,* surrendered, March 29.

18. A few days afterwards Scott began his march towards the city of Mexico. At the mountain-pass of **Cer′ro Gor′do**, he met Santa Anna, who, since his defeat at Buena Vista, had collected another army, with which he was guarding the pass. The Americans stormed the works on the 18th of April, and totally routed the Mexicans.

19. The victors continued their march to **Puebla** (*pwä′-blah*), which important city was given up by the Mexicans without a struggle. Here Scott waited nearly three months for reënforcements. Santa Anna, meanwhile, was planning new means for the defence of the capital. He organized bands of guerrillas, and with surprising energy raised another army to resist the invaders.

20. Scott's reënforcements arrived, and in the early days of August he resumed his march. The invading army now numbered somewhat over ten thousand men. Thirty thousand Mexican soldiers, within the fortifications which guarded the approaches to the capital, awaited them.

21. On the 19th of August the Americans, who had turned to the left from the direct road in order to avoid the strongest fortification, found their advance impeded by the fortified camp of **Contreras**,† about twelve miles south of the city of Mexico. The next morning the camp was assaulted and carried. This success was followed the same day by the brilliant victory of **Churubusco**.‡ The Mexicans fell back upon the city.

22. Scott might now have taken the city, but hoping that the Mexicans would be willing to negotiate a peace, he granted Santa Anna an **armistice**. After a little while it was seen that the terms of peace could not be agreed upon, and hostilities were resumed.

* *sahn hwahn′ dä oo-lo′ah.* † *kon-trä′rahs.* ‡ *choo-roo-boos′ko.*

18. Give an account of the battle of Cerro Gordo.
19. What is said of Puebla and the stay there? Of Santa Anna?
20. When did Scott take up the march again? State the strength of the hostile forces.
21. What occurred on the 19th of August? What the next day?
22. Why did Scott grant an armistice, and with what result?

23. On the 8th of September General Worth led his column against the forces of the enemy in a strong stone building, called the **Molino del Rey**.* The battle fought on that day was the most bloody of the war, but at last the position was won. Five days later the Americans stormed the rock and castle of **Chapultepec**,† the last strong defence of the capital, and routed the whole Mexican army. On the following day, September 14, the victorious Americans entered the **city of Mexico,** and raised the "stars and stripes" over the national palace. Mexico was conquered. Santa Anna and the miserable remnant of his army had fled in the night.

24. Among the **American officers** who bravely fought in the battles won by Taylor and Scott, were many who, fourteen or fifteen years afterwards, became leaders on each side in the great civil war which put an end to slavery.

25. The fall of the capital may be considered as closing the war. There was very little fighting afterwards. A **treaty** was concluded, February 2, 1848, and peace was proclaimed by President Polk on the 4th of July following. By this treaty the United States gained a vast territory, stretching north-west of Texas, to the Pacific. They agreed to pay Mexico fifteen millions of dollars, and to assume her debts to American citizens to the amount of over three millions more.

4. Other Events in this Administration.

26. For a long time before Polk became president both the United States and Great Britain had conflicting claims to the region then known as **Oregon**. In the early part of the administration, it seemed as if war might come from

* *mo-le'no del rā.*   † *chah-pool-ta-pek'.*

---

23. What is said of the taking of the Molino del Rey? Of the storming of the last defence of the capital? When did the victors enter the city of Mexico? What had become of Santa Anna?
24. What statement is made as to officers who fought under Taylor and Scott in the Mexican war?
25. What may the fall of the city of Mexico be considered? When was a treaty of peace concluded? What was obtained on each side?
26. What can you tell about conflicting claims to Oregon at the beginning of Polk's administration?

these rival claims; but peaceful counsels prevailed. The long controversy was settled in 1846, by a treaty establishing the present boundary of the United States from the Rocky Mountains to the Pacific.*

27. Just before the conclusion of the treaty with Mexico, **gold** was discovered **in California**. News of this discovery caused a wonderful tide of emigration from all parts of the civilized world to set towards the land of gold.

In 1848 **Wisconsin** became a state. There were now fifteen free states and fifteen slave states in the Union.

28. As a result of the acquisition of territory from Mexico an important and exciting **question** arose: Shall slaveholding be allowed in this vast region, or in any part of it? Violent debates took place in Congress. In the south deep feeling was aroused, and in the north the anti-slavery sentiment became stronger than ever.

29. A new party, called the *Free Soil party*, opposed to the extension of slave territory, sprang up. But it was by no means so strong as either the Whig or the Democratic party. General Taylor's services in Mexico were soon rewarded by the highest honors in the gift of the nation. At the election in 1848, the Whig candidates were successful. **Zachary Taylor**, of Louisiana, was chosen president, and **Millard Fillmore**, of New York, vice-president.

* The claim of the United States to Oregon was based on several grounds — on American discovery, exploration, and occupation of the region, and on the cession made by Spain in the Florida treaty (1821) of whatever rights she had through her early navigators who reached those parts. In 1792 Captain Gray, of the ship Columbia, from Boston, discovered and entered the great river of the north-west, and named it after his vessel. In 1804-5 Lewis and Clark, officers of the American army, led an exploring expedition, which traced the Missouri towards its source, and descended the Columbia to the Pacific. The discovery and first exploration of this river gave our government, according to the law of nations, a right to the country drained by its waters. In 1811 the Pacific Fur Company, which had been formed by John Jacob Astor, of New York, set up, at the mouth of the Columbia, an establishment known as Astoria.

† The oldest town in the state is Green Bay, which was permanently settled in 1745 by the French. But many years before that time they had explored the country, and established missions and trading-posts in Wisconsin.

Wisconsin takes its name from the Wisconsin River, whose Indian name means *the gathering of the waters.*

26. How, and when was the controversy settled?
27. When was gold discovered in California, and what followed? When was Wisconsin admitted into the Union? What of slave and free states?
28. What great question arose? What of public feeling?
29. What new party sprang up? Who were elected president and vice-president in 1848?

XI. TAYLOR'S AND FILLMORE'S ADMINISTRATIONS.
1849-1853.

1. Questions relating to **slavery** were the subject of exciting debates in Congress during Taylor's short administration. It was necessary to provide governments for the territories ceded by Mexico. The region thus acquired had, under Mexican rule, been free from slavery. But a great majority in **the south** now contended that slave-owners should not be forbidden to migrate to these territories with their slaves and hold them there.

2. In **the free states** there was a large and growing party opposed to extending the area of slavery. The members of this party believed it to be the duty and right of Congress to prohibit slaveholding in all the territories.

3. Besides this great question, there were others connected with slavery — one, whether slavery, or at least the slave-trade, should be abolished in the **District of Columbia**. For many years petitions praying that this might be done had been received by Congress. Another related to **fugitive slaves**, and still another to the **boundary of Texas** — this slave state having set up a claim to a large part of New Mexico. The leading champion of the slave-power was **John C. Calhoun**, whose life was now near its close. He died on the last day of March, 1850.

4. **California** formed a constitution, and applied to Congress for admission into the Union as a free state. Her admission was opposed by the southern leaders, and for several months a hot discussion was carried on within the walls of Congress.

5. At length **Henry Clay**, himself a slaveholder, but opposed to the extension of slavery, brought forward a plan of a compromise which he believed would settle the difficulties. This plan was in discussion when the nation

---

1. What topic agitated Congress during Taylor's presidency? What is said about the territories obtained from Mexico? For what did the south contend?
2. What was the belief of a large party in the north?
3. Name three other questions connected with slavery. What is said of John C. Calhoun?
4. What did California do, and what followed in Congress?
5. What did Henry Clay bring forward in the Senate?

was called to mourn the death of its chief magistrate. **President Taylor died July 9, 1850.** His administration had lasted but little more than sixteen months. The vice-president, **Millard Fillmore, became president.**

6. The measures devised by Clay, known as the **Compromise of 1850**, passed Congress in September of that year. They provided, 1st. For the *admission of California**** as a free state. 2d. For organizing territorial governments in *Utah and New Mexico*, without any provision for or against slavery. These two territories embraced the remainder of the country acquired from Mexico. 3d. For establishing the *boundary of Texas*, as at present, and paying that state ten millions of dollars to relinquish all claim to additional territory. 4th. For prohibiting, not slavery, but the *slave-trade in the District of Columbia.* 5th. For the enactment of a *Fugitive Slave Law*, to enable masters to recover their slaves escaping to a free state.

7. The **Fugitive Slave Law** was designed to carry out more effectually a provision of the Constitution. Runaway slaves were caught in the north and returned to bondage. But it is not too much to say that the enforcement of this law violated the moral feelings of the great body of the people in the free states, and greatly aided to bring on the final conflict.

8. Two remarkable men, and leading statesmen, died in 1852 — **Henry Clay** and **Daniel Webster.** In the same year the presidential election took place, and **Franklin Pierce,** of New Hampshire, the candidate of the Democratic party, was chosen.

---

* The first white settlement within the limits of the present State of California was a Catholic mission, established under Spanish authority, at San Diego (*de-ä'go*), in 1769. During the fifty years following, other missions were established all along the coast as far north as San Francisco.

The name *California* is first met with in a Spanish romance published in or about the year 1510, being given, in that book, to an imaginary island "on the right hand of the Indies, very near to the Terrestrial Paradise." It is believed that Cortes, twenty-five years later, sailing up the west side of Mexico, applied the name to the Peninsula of California.

---

5. When did Taylor die, and who became president?
6. When did compromise measures pass Congress? For what did they provide?
7. What can you say about the fugitive slave law?
8. What leading statesmen died in 1852, and who was elected president in the same year?

XII. PIERCE'S ADMINISTRATION. 1853-1857.

1. In the early part of Pierce's administration a new **boundary treaty** was made with Mexico, the United States purchasing of that republic a considerable strip of land south of the Gila (*he'lah*) River. But by far the **most important events** of this administration were the repeal of the Missouri Compromise by Congress, and the struggle in Kansas.

2. The political calm brought about by the compromise measures of 1850 did not last long. In the beginning of 1854, Stephen A. Douglas (*dug'las*), of Illinois, brought forward in the national Senate a bill, known as the **Kansas-Nebraska Bill**, organizing two vast territories, to be called Kansas and Nebraska, and leaving the people of these territories to decide whether they would have slavery or not. This region was much more extensive than the present states of Kansas and Nebraska.

3. As the passage of the bill would repeal the **Missouri Compromise** of 1820, and permit slavery to enter a region from which it had been excluded by that solemn compact, a large part of the people in the free states vehemently opposed the proposition. Most exciting discussions followed in Congress, and the people in all parts of the country were deeply moved. Notwithstanding all opposition, the bill became a law in May, 1854.

4. The **struggle for Kansas** now began. Settlers soon entered the territory in large numbers. Some of the free-state men who came as colonists were sent by societies formed in the north with the intent of securing Kansas for freedom. Slaveholders and their friends came, intending to secure it for slavery. When elections were held, residents of the neighboring slave state of Missouri swarmed

---

1. What is said of a boundary treaty with Mexico? Name the two most important events of Pierce's administration.
2. When and by whom was the Kansas-Nebraska bill brought forward in the Senate? State the object of this bill.
3. Why did a large part of the people in the free states vehemently oppose the Kansas-Nebraska bill? When did the bill become a law?
4. What can you tell of those who entered Kansas? What happened when an election was held?

over the border to vote, with the design of making Kansas a slave state. After voting they returned to their homes.

5. Hostile **encounters** took place. Armed bands of ruffians, mostly from Missouri, made incursions into the territory, murdered free-state men, and laid waste their settlements. Towns were sacked, houses burned, and farms plundered. Although the free-state settlers were greatly in the majority, yet both President Pierce, and his successor, President Buchanan (*buh an'an*), sided with the pro-slavery party in the territory. But by neither fair means nor foul could Kansas be made a slave state. During some years, however, she was kept waiting for admission into the Union.

6. Public feeling had become so thoroughly aroused in regard to slavery as to cause the **reorganization of parties.** The *Whig party* broke up. The *Democratic party* gained great strength in the Southern States, while in the free states an organization opposed to the extension of slavery became powerful under the name of the *Republican party.* The Democrats carried the election of 1856, and made **James Buchanan,** of Pennsylvania, president.

XIII. BUCHANAN'S ADMINISTRATION. 1857-1861.

1. Buchanan was inaugurated March 4, 1857. Early in his administration trouble arose with the **Mormons,** or "Latter-Day Saints,"—a sect of fanatics who uphold and practise polygamy as part of their religious belief. Under the guidance of Brigham Young they had founded Salt Lake City, in Utah, about ten years before, and they now threatened to resist the national authority by force of arms. The president sent a strong body of troops to that territory; but the difficulty was settled without bloodshed.

In the autumn of 1857 a **commercial crisis** greatly disturbed the business of the country.

J. What can you tell of the civil strife in Kansas? What position did Pierce and Buchanan take?
J. What caused the reorganization of parties? What is said of the Whig party? The Democratic party? The Republican party? Who were successful in the election of 1856?
I. What can you tell of the Mormons and their chief city? What is said about their difficulty with the government? What of a commercial crisis?

2. The slavery question still agitated the people. The anti-slavery feeling of the north was further roused by a decision of the majority of the Supreme Court of the United States in the case of the negro **Dred Scott.** This decision, which was delivered by Chief Justice Taney (*taw'ni*) just after Buchanan took office, declared the Missouri Compromise unconstitutional; that the Constitution gave slave-owners the right to hold their slaves in the territories, and that neither negro slaves nor their descendants, slave or free, could become citizens of the United States.

3. The legislatures of some of the free states passed, or revived enactments, called **Personal Liberty Laws**, which obstructed the execution of the fugitive slave law. These laws gave great offence to the people of the South.

4. In October, 1859, — a few months before the beginning of the presidential canvass of 1860, — an event occurred which roused the southern people to a high pitch of excitement and indignation. This was the **raid of John Brown**, who, with only twenty-one followers, seized the United States arsenal at Harper's Ferry, in Virginia, as a part of his plan for liberating slaves on a large scale. The strange, mad project failed. The insurgents were attacked, and most of them were killed. Brown and six of his associates were tried, convicted, and hanged.

5. The resolute old man who thus violated the law of the land had been a leader of the free-state men in Kansas, where he and his sons had suffered from pro-slavery outrages. Affairs in **Kansas** were in an unsettled condition during nearly the whole time of Buchanan's administration. The efforts made in Congress by the friends of the slave power to force a slave constitution upon the people of that territory, greatly increased the bitterness of sectional feeling.

---

2. How was the anti-slavery feeling in the north further roused? What decision, in the case of Dred Scott, was delivered by Chief Justice Taney?
3. State what you can concerning Personal Liberty Laws.
4. When and where did the raid of John Brown occur? What was Brown's design, and what was his fate?
5. What more is said of Brown? Of affairs in Kansas, and of efforts in Congress, which increased sectional feeling?

6. Such was the state of affairs in 1860, when the presidential canvass took place. The people became divided into four parties. The Republican party was successful, and elected **Abraham Lincoln**, of Illinois, president.

7. As soon as the result of the election was known, the political leaders in several of the Southern States set in motion a plot already formed for withdrawing their states from the Union. South Carolina took the lead, and in December passed an ordinance of **secession,** declaring herself out of the Union. Mississippi, Florida, Alabama, Georgia, and Louisiana followed. These five states passed similar acts in January, 1861, and on the first of February Texas joined them. Seven states had now thrown off their allegiance — all the Gulf States, together with South Carolina and Georgia.

8. Delegates from these states met in **convention at Montgomery,** Alabama, in February, and organized a government under the name of the *Confederate States of America.* They elected Jefferson Davis, of Mississippi, president of their confederacy.

9. The **rebellious states** seized forts, arsenals, custom-houses, ships, and national property of all kinds within their boundaries. There remained in the possession of the United States only Fort Sumter, in Charleston Harbor, Fort Pickens, near Pensacola, and the forts off the southern extremity of Florida. The brave and patriotic commanders of the first two, Major Anderson and Lieutenant Slemmer, gained honor by their conduct in these trying times.

10. Major Anderson, with about eighty men in all, occupied Fort Moultrie. Believing that he could not defend that post, he removed his garrison in the night-time to Fort Sumter, a stronger fort, on an island in Charleston

---

6. Into how many parties were the people divided in 1860, and who was elected president?
7. State what was done by some of the southern leaders. By South Carolina. What six states followed the lead of South Carolina, and when?
8. What was done by delegates from the seven insurgent states, and when?
9. What befell the national property in these states? What forts alone remained in possession of the United States?
10. State what you can concerning the removal of the garrison from Fort Moultrie to Fort Sumter.

Harbor. This act raised the indignation of the South Carolinians beyond all bounds. Early in January, the national government sent an unarmed steamer, the Star of the West, with troops and supplies for Fort Sumter. When within sight of the fort, January 9, the steamer was fired upon by a rebel battery, and compelled to turn back.

11. **Fort Pickens** was saved by Lieutenant Slemmer, who removed his small garrison from an insecure fort to that stronghold just in time to prevent its capture. He was soon besieged by a strong force of insurgent troops, but he determined to hold out to the last.

12. **General Twiggs**, in Texas, committed an act of base treason. He surrendered his command — about twenty-five hundred national troops — and all the national property in his charge to Texan insurgents.

13. **At Washington** but little was done to stem the tide of treason. President Buchanan was weak, and wholly unfit to conduct the nation in such a crisis. Some members of his cabinet were disloyal, and the public offices were full of conspirators. The members of Congress from the seceding states resigned their seats, and defiantly exulted in their treason. They denounced "coercion" by the national government, and would listen to no terms for conciliation.

14. Three new states were added to the Union during the presidency of Buchanan — Minnesota, in 1858; Oregon, in 1859; and Kansas, in 1861.*

---

* St. Paul, the first town founded in Minnesota, was laid out in 1847; but nine or ten years before this time its site had been occupied by a few cabins. The oldest towns in Kansas are Lawrence and Leavenworth, founded in 1854. Only a few hundred American citizens had removed to Oregon before the year 1843. (See note, p. 155.)

Minnesota is named from the principal river which empties into the Mississippi within the boundaries of the state. The word is formed from two Dakota words, *minne*, water, and *sotah*, sky-colored.

Kansas is the name of a river and of a tribe of Indians, and is said to signify *smoky water*.

The name *Oregon* is supposed to be derived from the Spanish word *oregano*, wild marjoram, which grows on the Pacific coast.

---

10. What open act of war was committed at Charleston in January, 1861?
11. How was Fort Pickens saved for the national government?
12. What can you tell of Twiggs's treason?
13. What is said of President Buchanan, part of his cabinet, and the public offices? Of members of Congress from seceding states?
14. How many and what territories became states during Buchanan's term?

CONDITION OF THE UNITED STATES AT THE CLOSE OF THIS PERIOD.

1. During the seventy-two years that had passed since the organization of the government, the United States enjoyed a degree of **prosperity** without a parallel in the history of nations. The number of states had increased from thirteen to thirty-four.

2. The **national domain**, which at the beginning of this period extended only to the Mississippi, at its close reached to the Pacific. Its area had expanded nearly fourfold, while its population had increased eightfold. Our country in 1860 comprised over three millions of square miles, and the number of its **inhabitants** somewhat exceeded thirty-one millions. Nearly four millions of these were negro slaves.

3. West of the Atlantic states vast regions, which in 1789 were almost wholly a wilderness, now had a great population. Every year swarms of **emigrants** had gone out from the old states to the fertile grain-fields of the west. Other swarms had come from the countries of the Old World. These settlers and their descendants had dotted the country with farm-houses, and built up beautiful villages and large cities.

4. In **commerce, manufactures,** and **agriculture** the increase had been in a still greater ratio than that of the population. Vast quantities of wheat, cotton, tobacco, and other domestic products, were exported every year. The various branches of industry had been greatly extended by means of many **inventions** and **discoveries**, some of the most useful and wonderful of which were made by citizens of the United States.

---

1. What is said of the condition of the country from Washington's administration to Lincoln's?
2. How had the area of the national domain been expanded? What was the area of the country, and the number of inhabitants in 1860? Number of slaves?
3. What is said of regions west of the Atlantic states? Of emigrants and their descendants?
4. What of commerce, manufactures, and agriculture? Of exports? Of inventions and discoveries?

5. The **steamboat**, the **railroad**, and the **electric telegraph**, unknown at the beginning of the century, had come into common use before the close of this period. In the year 1860 there were more than thirty-one thousand miles of railroad in the United States, while new roads were fast building. An electric telegraph, invented by Professor Morse, an American, was first put in operation in our country in 1844 — the line extending from Washington to Baltimore. Soon a great network of lines was spread over the country.

6. This period witnessed, too, a wonderful advance in the **intellectual growth** of the people. Education was especially fostered. Most of the states had established the common-school system, in order that every child might receive instruction. The means of moral and **religious culture** were also liberally supplied. Literature, the arts, and the sciences took long strides forward.

7. But this unexampled career of national **prosperity** was now to be rudely shocked. What seemed at the time of Washington's administration but a speck of trouble no bigger than a man's hand, had grown to be a dark and threatening cloud which overshadowed the whole country. The **strength of the government** was to be fully **tested**, by a bloody civil war — a war destined to effect great and lasting changes in the political condition of the fifteen slaveholding states, and indeed of the entire republic.

8. Asserting the interests of slavery to be in danger, and claiming peaceable **secession** as a state right, the seven most southern states declared, before the inauguration of Lincoln, their connection with the Union to be at an end. Four other slave states afterwards joined the confederacy.

---

5. What is said of steamboats, railroads, and the electric telegraph? What can you tell of the invention and first practical use of the electric telegraph?
6. What is stated about education? Moral and religious culture?
7. How was the strength of the government to be fully tested, and with what effect?
8. What position had the seven most southern states taken before the inauguration of Lincoln? How many other states afterwards joined them?

CHRONOLOGICAL REVIEW.

NOTE. — The figures in the paragraphs, and at the end of them, refer to the pages upon which the events are mentioned.

☞ For the admission of the states in chronological order, see p. 219.

1789. Washington became president, 114. He served two terms.
During this administration the government was organized, 114; and the United States came near being involved in a war with Great Britain, as an ally of France, 116.

1790. A war broke out with the Indians north of the Ohio, 115.

1794. The Whiskey Insurrection broke out in Pennsylvania, 116.

1797. Adams became president, 118. He served one term.
During this administration war with France became imminent. Hostilities were in fact begun on the ocean, 116.

1799. Washington died at Mount Vernon, 119.

1801. Jefferson became president, 119. He served two terms.

1803. Louisiana was purchased of France, 120.

1805. A peace, which concluded a war with Tripoli, was negotiated, 120.

1807. Fulton successfully applied steam to navigation, 121.

1809. Madison became president, 122. He served two terms.

1811. General Harrison gained a victory at *Tippecanoe*, 122.

1812. British aggressions on American commerce, begun in Jefferson's administration, led to a war with Great Britain, 123.
The Americans surrendered *Detroit*, 126; and were defeated at *Queenstown*, but were, almost without exception, victorious on the ocean, 126.

1813. The Americans were defeated at *Frenchtown*, 128; took *York*, 129; gained, under Perry, a decisive victory on *Lake Erie*, 128; defeated, under Harrison, the British and Indians on the *Thames*, 129; began an unsuccessful expedition against Montreal, 130; and before the end of the year were driven from their posts on the Niagara, 129.
The British frigate Shannon captured the American frigate Chesapeake, 131.
The Creek war began by a horrible massacre at Fort Mims, 131.

1814. General Jackson broke the power of the *Creeks* in the battle of Tohopeka, 131. The Americans took *Fort Erie*, won the battles of the *Chippewa* and *Lundy's Lane*, 132, and closed the war in the north by the decisive victory on *Lake Champlain* and at *Plattsburg*, 133.
The British blockaded the *Atlantic coast*, 133; captured *Washington*, but were compelled to retire from before *Baltimore*,

1814. 134. The little navy of the United States had become well nigh exhausted, 134.

1815. Jackson gained a decisive victory at *New Orleans*, 136.

News of a treaty of peace, signed at Ghent, in December of the previous year, reached the United States, 136.

The claims of Algiers and other Barbary States to tribute were effectually resisted, 137.

1816. The Bank of the United States was chartered for twenty years, 137.

1817. Monroe became president, 137. He served two terms.

The period of this administration is known as the *era of good feeling*, 138.

1817. A short war with the Seminole Indians broke out, 138.

1820. The Missouri Compromise was adopted, 138.

1821. Florida was delivered up to the United States by Spain, 139.

1825. John Quincy Adams became president, 139. He served one term.

A protective tariff law, which caused much controversy, was enacted, 140.

1829. Jackson became president, 140. He served two terms.

1832. The Black Hawk war broke out, 140. South Carolina opposed the tariff laws, and issued an Ordinance of Nullification, 141.

1835. A war, lasting seven years, arose with the Florida Indians, 142.

During this administration the president inaugurated a new financial policy by his opposition to the United States Bank, 141, and the *Democratic* and *Whig* parties were organized, 143.

1837. Van Buren became president, 143. He served one term.

A financial storm swept over the country, 143, and in 1840 the mode of keeping the public moneys in the treasury and in sub-treasuries was adopted, 144.

1841. Harrison became president. He died one month after his inauguration, and Vice-President **Tyler** became president for the rest of the term, 144.

1842. The Dorr Rebellion occurred in Rhode Island, 144.

1844. Morse's electric telegraph was put in operation between Baltimore and Washington, 164.

1845. Texas was annexed to the United States, 145.

1845. Polk became president, 146. He served one term.

1846. The boundary between the United States and British America, from the Rocky Mts. to the Pacific, was established, 155.

War with Mexico broke out, 146. Taylor gained victories at

1846. *Palo Alto* and *Resaca de la Palma*, 148, and captured *Monterey*, 150.

Kearny took possession of *New Mexico*, and detached a small force under Doniphan, who, early the next year, conquered *Chihuahua*, 151.

1847. Early in the year Mexican authority was completely overturned in California, which had been virtually conquered the year before by Captain Frémont, of the army, and Commodores Sloat and Stockton, of the navy, 152.

Taylor gained a decisive victory at *Buena Vista*, 151.

Scott conducted his victorious campaign, taking *Vera Cruz*, defeating the Mexicans at *Cerro Gordo*, gaining brilliant victories at *Contreras* and *Churubusco*, 153, *Molino del Rey* and *Chapultepec*, and entering in triumph the city of *Mexico*, 154.

1848. A treaty made at Guadalupe Hidalgo (*gaw-dah-loop' he-dal'go*), February 2, ended the war, and gave the United States large accessions of territory, 154; about the same time gold was discovered in California, 155.

During this administration the *Free Soil Party* was organized, 155.

1849. **Taylor** became president, 156. He died in July, 1850, and Vice-President **Fillmore** became president, 157.

1850. The Compromise Measures were passed, 157.

1853. **Pierce** became president, 158. He served one term.

1854. The Kansas-Nebraska Bill was passed, repealing the Missouri Compromise of 1820, 158.

During this administration parties were reorganized, and the *Republican Party* was formed, 159.

1857. **Buchanan** became president, 159. He served one term.

1857. A financial storm swept over the United States, 159.

1859. John Brown made a mad attempt to free slaves in Virginia, 160.

During this administration the Dred Scott Decision, the Personal Liberty Laws, the Struggle for Kansas, and other causes, roused an intense excitement on the subject of slavery, 160. Secession was organized, and treason crept into places of influence, 161, 162.

1860. South Carolina took the lead in secession, 161.

1861. Before March six states had followed the lead of South Carolina, and sent delegates to Montgomery, where a government was organized for the insurgent states under the name of the *Confederate States of America*, 161.

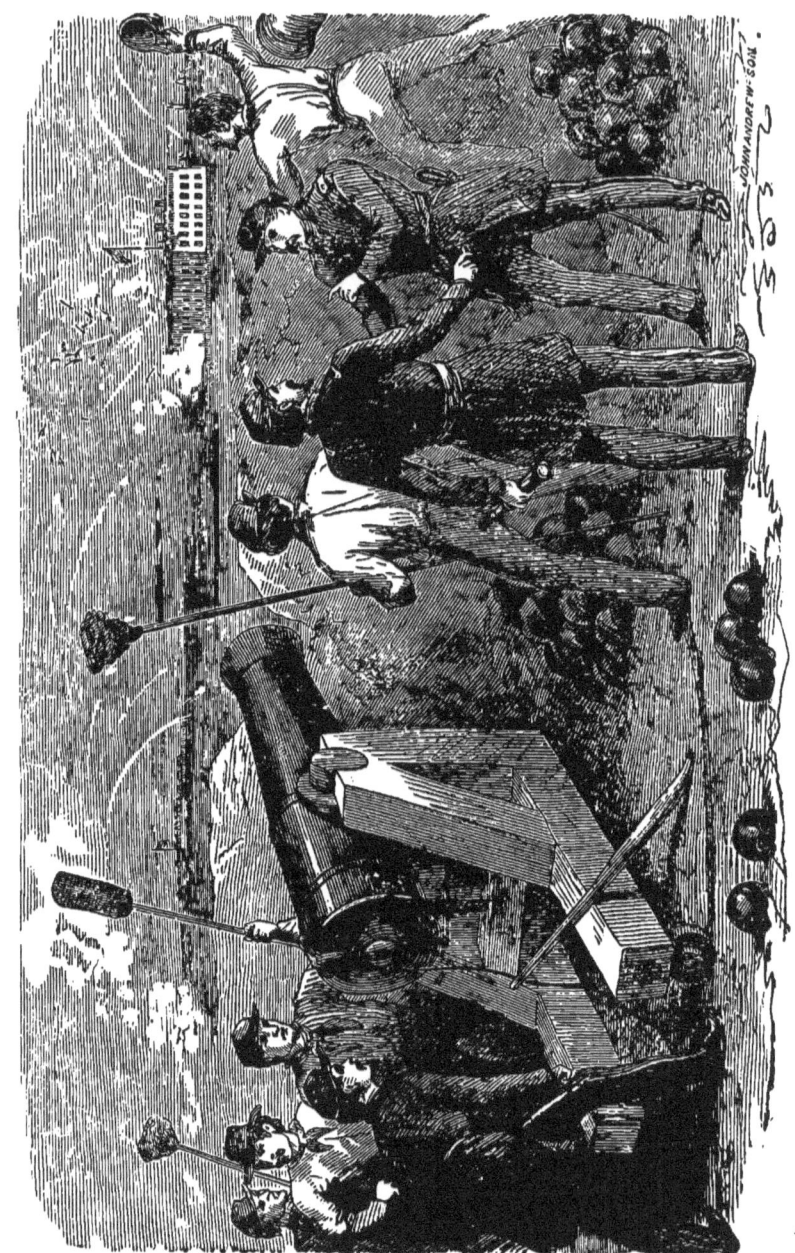

REBELS FIRING UPON FORT SUMTER.

PERIOD V.
DISTINGUISHED FOR THE GREAT REBELLION.
FROM THE INAUGURATION OF LINCOLN, IN 1861, TILL THE YEAR 1879.

I. LINCOLN'S ADMINISTRATION. THE WAR.

1. From the Beginning of Lincoln's Administration to the Close of the Year. Growth of the Rebellion.

1. **Events of 1861.** — When, on the 4th of March, 1861, Abraham Lincoln became president, he found himself beset with many and **great difficulties.** Neither the army nor the navy was then available to aid the republic in its extreme peril. The national troops, only a few thousand in all, were scattered far and wide, chiefly on the remote frontiers, while most of the war-vessels were dispersed in distant seas.

2. **The president** hoped that war might be averted. In his inaugural address he

Lincoln.

declared that he had no right to interfere with slavery in the states where it existed, but that he should take care faithfully to execute the laws in all the states.

3. The pause before the shock was not long. General Beauregard (*bo're-gard*) had command of several thousand insurgent troops at Charleston, South Carolina. Learning that President Lincoln was about to send supplies to **Fort Sumter**, this general, in obedience to orders from the Confederate government, demanded the surrender of the

---
QUESTIONS. — 1. What is said of the difficulties which beset President Lincoln? Where were the national troops and war-vessels?
2. What did the president declare in his inaugural address?
3. Give an account of the attack upon Fort Sumter by Beauregard.

fort. His demand being refused, he opened fire upon it from forts in the harbor and from powerful batteries which the rebels had erected for this purpose.

4. **Major Anderson** made a spirited defence, but after withstanding a furious bombardment for more than thirty hours, his provisions being nearly exhausted, the officers' quarters and the barracks being on fire, he **capitulated,** April 13. Strange to say, no one on either side had been killed or seriously hurt. The next day, April 14, he evacuated the fort. Its defenders embarked for New York.

5. News of the fall of Fort Sumter caused the wildest excitement throughout the **free states,** and was immediately followed by a great uprising of the people. They declared almost with one voice that the Union should be preserved. On the day following the evacuation of Fort Sumter, **President Lincoln** called for seventy-five thousand troops to serve for three months.

6. The national capital was in danger, and volunteers hastened to its defence. A few companies from Pennsylvania were the first to reach **Washington.** On the next day, April 19, a Massachusetts regiment on its way through **Baltimore** was attacked by a mob of secessionists, who killed three soldiers and wounded others. The soldiers fired into the mob, killing and wounding a number of persons.

7. The governors of all the **slave-labor states** which had not decreed secession — excepting Delaware and Maryland — declared, in answer to the president's call, that they would furnish no troops to aid the national government. Four of these states, *Virginia, Arkansas, Tennessee,* and *North Carolina,* soon joined the Confederacy. Four border slave states, *Delaware, Maryland, Kentucky,* and

---
4. Under what circumstances, and when, did Major Anderson capitulate?
5. What effect did news of the fall of Fort Sumter produce in the free states? What did the president now do?
6. What troops first reached Washington for its defence? Give an account of the attack made by a mob in Baltimore on a Massachusetts regiment.
7. What was the reply of most of the governors of those slave states called upon for troops to aid the Union cause? What slave states afterwards joined the Confederacy? What four border slave states were on the side of the Union?

Missouri, did not join it; but some of these states came very near being dragged into disunion by their political leaders.

8. Within a few days after the firing on Fort Sumter, disloyal Virginians seized **Harper's Ferry** and the United States navy yard near **Norfolk**. The national arsenal at the Ferry was burned to prevent its falling into disloyal hands, but at the navy yard the rebels secured a great number of cannons, and other public property of immense value. **Fortress Monroe** was held by its little garrison for the Federal government.

9. The attack upon Fort Sumter also roused to a high pitch of enthusiasm the warlike spirit prevailing in **the insurgent south**. Troops from the southern states were hurried into Virginia, and mostly concentrated near Manas'sas Junction, a point where the railway running from Washington southward is joined by the one leading from the great valley of the Shen-an-do'ah. A smaller rebel army occupied this valley, and finally took post at Winchester. Richmond was made the rebel capital, and there the Confederate Congress assembled in July.

10. Before that time, however, the veteran Winfield Scott, who was the general-in-chief of the Union forces, had ordered **an advance into Virginia**. National troops crossing from Washington on the night of May 23, took possession of Arlington Heights, opposite the city, and of Alexandria, a few miles below. About the same time General Benjamin F. Butler, who had displayed great energy in the Union cause, was placed in command at **Fortress Monroe**, where a national army was assembling. A badly managed expedition, sent out by Butler in June, suffered a mortifying repulse in an attack upon the enemy's works at **Big Bethel**

---

8. What property of the government was seized by Virginians? What great fortress remained in possession of the government? Where is Harper's Ferry? (See Map, p. 172.) Norfolk? Fortress Monroe?
9. What effect did the attack upon Fort Sumter produce in the south? Where in Virginia were southern troops concentrated? What city became the rebel capital? Where is Manassas Junction? (See Map, p. 172.) Winchester? Richmond?
10. What can you tell of the advance of national troops into Virginia? What of Fortress Monroe? Of the affair at Big Bethel?

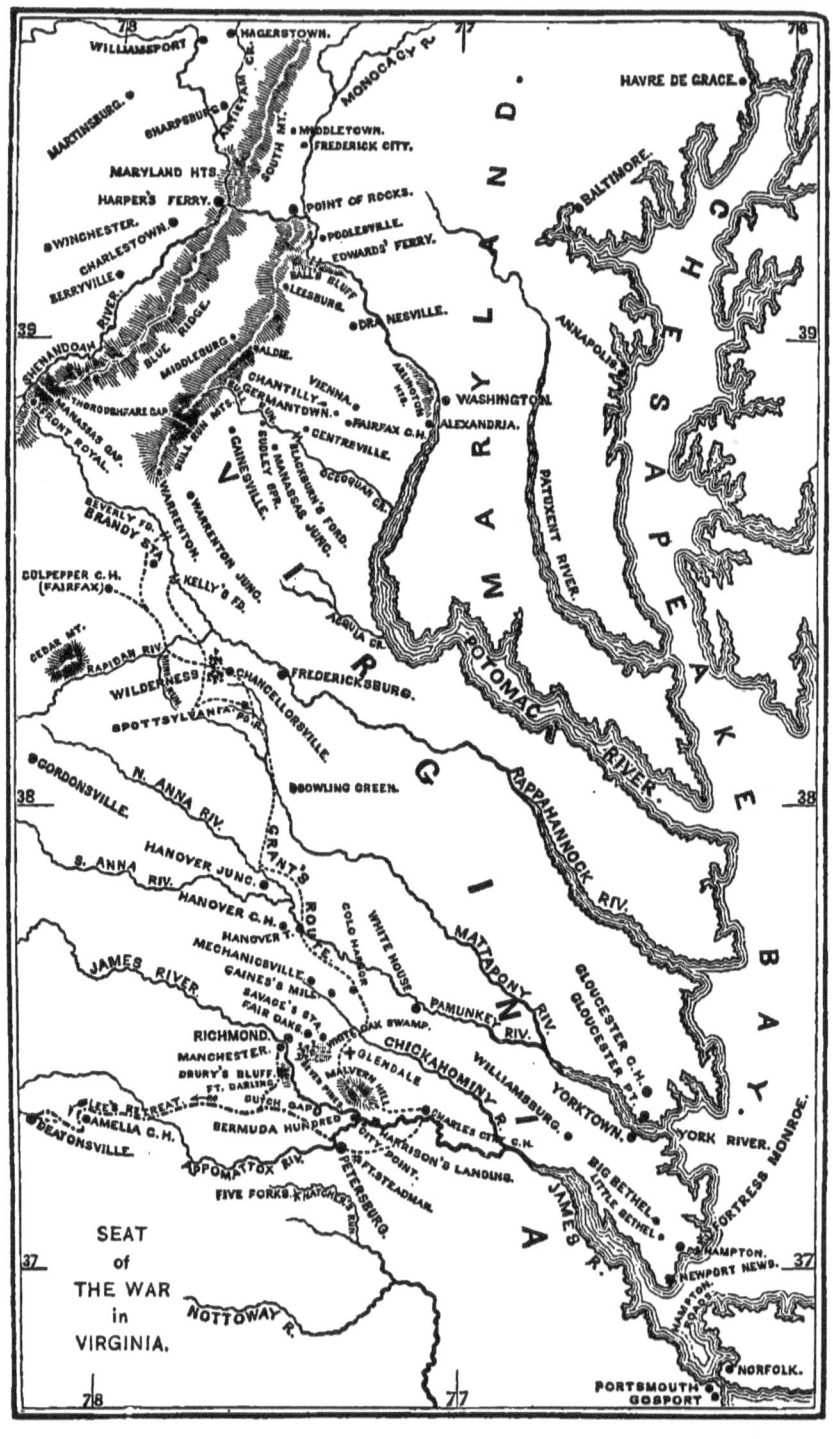

11. About the middle of July the **national army** opposite Washington marched against the Confederates who were encamped under Beauregard near Manassas Junction. Before an engagement took place General Joseph E. Johnston was able to join Beauregard with a great part of the Confederate army of the Shenandoah Valley. General Scott being too infirm to take the field in person, General Irvin McDowell led the Union troops.

12. The Confederates were found beyond a small stream called **Bull Run**, and there the first great battle of the war was fought, Sunday, July 21. It was a struggle in which full forty thousand men were engaged. After hours of hard fighting victory seemed almost within the grasp of the Federals; but just then a strong body of Confederate troops from the Shenandoah Valley reached the field, and turned the tide of battle. The Federal troops gave way; part of them fled panic-stricken, and the rest marched back to the fortifications of Washington. The Union loss in killed, wounded, and prisoners was probably over three thousand men; the Confederate loss was considerably less.

13. The disaster at Bull Run was wholly unexpected by the people of the loyal states. They now saw more clearly the nature of the great conflict, and a sterner determination nerved them to crush out the rebellion. The president in May had called for additional troops; he now called for half a million volunteers.

14. **General George B. McClellan**, who had just conducted a successful campaign in West Virginia, was summoned to Washington to take command of the troops on the Potomac. This army soon became immensely strong, but made no general advance until the next year. Some months were spent in organizing and disciplining the grand

---

11. State what movement of national troops took place in July. What is said of General Johnston? Who led the Union army?
12. When was the battle of Bull Run fought, and how many men struggled on the field? What more can you tell of the battle?
13. How were the loyal people affected by this defeat? What did the president now do?
14. Who was placed in command of the army on the Potomac? What is said of this army?

army. On the 1st of November McClellan succeeded the aged chieftain Scott as **general-in-chief** of the armies of the United States.

15. In the autumn a severe action took place at **Ball's Bluff**, on the Potomac, above Washington. Nearly two thousand Union troops sent across the river from the Maryland side by General Stone, the commander in that vicinity, were defeated in a battle October 21, with heavy loss. Colonel Baker, a national senator from Oregon, and the leader of the expedition, was among the killed.

16. The people of **West Virginia** were strongly loyal. They repudiated the Virginia ordinance of secession, set up a loyal government, and took steps to form a new state from that part of the old one. Congress approved of their proceedings, and admitted West Virginia into the Union as a separate state in 1863.

17. The rebels endeavored to hold West Virginia, and early stained its soil with the blood of civil war. Some time before the battle of Bull Run General McClellan had been appointed to command in that region. About the beginning of July he began a vigorous campaign. A detachment of his army commanded by Colonel (afterwards General) Rosecrans (*rōz'krants*) routed a rebel force July 11, in the battle of **Rich Mountain**, near Bev'erly. The main body of the enemy, posted a few miles distant, then endeavored to escape the Union forces approaching from various directions. McClellan ordered a hot pursuit, and at **Carrick's Ford**, the fugitives, being overtaken, were thoroughly routed in a sharp conflict.

18. Later in the year Confederate troops took positions in and near the Kanawha (*ka-naw'wah*) Valley; but they could gain no firm foothold in that region. Before the end

---

14. What position was given General McClellan?
15. Give an account of the battle of Ball's Bluff.
16. What did the people of West Virginia do? When did Congress admit West Virginia as a state?
17. When and by whom was a vigorous campaign begun in West Virginia? What is said of the battle of Rich Mountain and the pursuit of the Confederates? Where is Rich Mountain? (See Map, p. 185.) Carrick's Ford?
18. What further is said of affairs in West Virginia?

of 1861 Rosecrans, who succeeded McClellan, had nearly cleared West Virginia of armed rebels.

19. Looking farther westward, we shall notice important events in Missouri and Kentucky. In **Missouri** there was a fierce struggle. The loyal citizens were a majority, but the governor, C. F. Jackson, was a persistent rebel, and did all he could to turn the state over to the Southern Confederacy.

20. **Captain Nathaniel Lyon**, an able and loyal officer, had command of the United States arsenal at St. Louis. Aided by patriotic citizens, he foiled the treasonable designs of the governor. A camp of disloyalists was formed in the suburbs of St. Louis to aid the governor in getting military control of the state. Lyon suddenly surrounded the camp, May 10, with a large force of armed Unionists, and took the troops collected there prisoners.

21. The governor soon after called for fifty thousand of the militia to drive the national troops from the state. Lyon was quickly upon him, and near **Booneville** put him and a body of his followers to flight. They were pursued into the south-western part of the state, where, after some encounters, a very severe battle was fought on **Wilson's Creek**, near Springfield, August 10. In this battle Lyon had only about five thousand men, while the Confederates, under Generals McCulloch (*mak-kul'luh*) and Price, numbered three or four times as many — a large part being from the south. The heroic General Lyon was killed, and the Union troops, after a hard-fought conflict, fell back, leaving Southern Missouri under the sway of the Confederates.

22. Another disaster followed in September. Colonel Mulligan, with nearly twenty-eight hundred Union troops, was besieged in an intrenched camp, at **Lexington**, by an overwhelming Confederate army under General Price. The

---

19. What can you say of the people and the governor of Missouri?
20. Who foiled the treasonable designs of the governor of Missouri? What is said of the capture of a disloyal camp?
21. What step did the governor take soon after, and what followed? When was the battle of Wilson's Creek fought, and what is said of the hostile forces? Result? Where is Booneville? (See Map, p. 184.) Wilson's Creek?
22. What Federal disaster followed the battle of Wilson's Creek? Where is Lexington? (See Map, p. 184.)

besieged held out bravely during some days, but were at last obliged to surrender.

23. **General John C. Frémont** at this time and before the battle of Wilson's Creek held the chief command of the *Western Department*. He made his headquarters at St. Louis, and organized a large army, with which he took the field in person soon after the fall of Lexington. But before he reached his foe, who had retreated to the southwestern corner of the state, he received orders to turn over his command to General Hunter. A few days later **General Henry W. Hal'leck** arrived at St. Louis and took the chief command.

24. **Cairo** (*kā'ro*), at the extreme southern point of Illinois, where the Mississippi and the Ohio meet, was at an early day occupied by a Union force. Its situation made it a post of great importance. Early in November, General Ulysses S. Grant, with about three thousand men, went down the river from this place and attacked a fortified camp of the rebels at **Belmont**, on the Missouri shore. At first he had the better of the enemy, but the Confederates, being strongly reënforced, compelled the Union troops to take to their boats and return to Cairo.

25. **Kentucky** was always loyal by a great majority of her inhabitants, but the secessionists within her borders had influence enough to hold her neutral for a time. As was the case with all the border slave states, she had citizens enlisted both in the national and the Confederate armies. Early in September, more than a month before the battle of Belmont, the Confederates, under General Polk, invaded the state. They seized and fortified **Columbus**. General Grant, with national troops from the camp at Cairo, immediately entered the state and took possession of **Paducah** (*pa-doo'kah*), at the mouth of the Tennessee

---

23. Who was in command of the Western Department, and what did he do soon after the fall of Lexington? What is said of Hunter and Halleck?
24. What is said of Cairo? Give an account of the fight at Belmont. Where is Belmont? (See Map, p. 184.)
25. What position did Kentucky at first take? What invasion of the state occurred, and what did Grant then do? Effect of the invasion? Where is Columbus? (See Map, p. 184.) Paducah?

River. After the invasion of her soil by southern forces, Kentucky took a decided stand for the Union.

26. About the same time Confederate troops, coming through Cumberland Gap, invaded Kentucky on the east. Another large Confederate force was speedily concentrated at Bowling Green (*bōl'ing-green*), near the centre of the southern part of the state. The Confederates, by occupying various strong positions, had military control of all Southern Kentucky. But great Union armies were preparing to drive them southward. Such was the state of affairs in this region in the latter part of 1861.

27. In the first year of the war two naval and military expeditions, sent out by the government, gained footholds on the **southern coast**. Commodore Stringham (*string'am*) and General Butler commanded the first one, which near the end of August captured the Confederate forts at **Hatteras Inlet**, off the coast of North Carolina. The second was a far stronger expedition. Commodore Du Pont, commanding a fleet of fifty war-vessels and transports, captured, on the 7th of November, the forts at **Port Royal Entrance**, South Carolina. An army under General Thomas W. Sherman accompanied the fleet, and occupied the forts. The coast islands of lower South Carolina, famous for producing the finest of all cotton, were also taken possession of by the national government.

28. The national navy was rapidly increased by the purchase and construction of numerous vessels. A blockade of the southern ports was established, yet vessels freighted with valuable cargoes frequently succeeded in entering them. After some time the blockade was made much more strict and effective.

29. Two days after President Lincoln's first call for troops, Jefferson Davis sent forth a proclamation offering to commission **privateers**. A few of these vessels got to sea,

---

26. What is said of other Confederate forces in Kentucky? State of affairs in Kentucky late in 1861?
27. How were Union footholds gained on the southern coast? Who led the first expedition, and what was gained by it? The second expedition?
28. What is said of the national navy and of the blockade?
29. What is said of rebel privateers?

and inflicted great injury upon the commerce of the United States. The most noted Confederate cruiser of this year was the steamer Sumter, Captain Semmes (*semz*). After a successful career in capturing merchant vessels, the Sumter ran into the Bay of Gibraltar, where she was closely watched by a United States gunboat. After some time she was sold in port, and her officers went to England, where a better steamer, the Alabama, was built for their service.

30. The **British government**, with unseemly haste, acknowledged the rebellious states as a belligerent power, and thus accorded them the same rights in war as if they were really an established government. A little later the Emperor of the French did the same. Most of the English people showed an unfriendly temper towards the United States. They evidently hoped to see the great republic broken up.

31. In the latter part of this year an occurrence, known as the **Trent affair**, gave the Confederates hopes of aid from England. Captain Wilkes (*wĭlks*), in the United States steamer San Ja-cin'to, stopped the British mail steamer Trent, took from her Mason and Sli-dell', Confederate envoys to England and France, and brought them to the United States as prisoners. The British government at once assumed a warlike attitude, and demanded the envoys. The American policy concerning neutral rights did not warrant the seizure, and Mason and Slidell were handed over to the British. Thus war with the nation which could harm us most was averted.

2. *From the Beginning of the Year 1862 to the Close of the Year 1863. The Rebellion in its Strength.*

32. **Events of 1862.** — We are now to relate how the Confederates were forced to abandon **Kentucky** and most of **Tennessee**. But first we should understand the situation

---

29. Give an account of the career of the Sumter.
30. What course did England and France hasten to adopt ? What is said of the stand taken by most of the English ?
31. What occurrence gave the Confederates hope of aid from England ? State what was done by Captain Wilkes. What more is said of the Trent affair ?

of the opposing forces in this part of the country. At the beginning of 1862, the Confederates held a long line of defences, being strongly posted at Columbus, Forts Henry and Don'elson, Bowling Green, Mill Spring, and Cumberland Gap. Two Union armies confronted this line. One was commanded by General Grant, at Cairo, the other by General Don Carlos Buell, who had placed his troops chiefly in the central portion of Kentucky.

33. General George H. Thomas, who commanded a division of Buell's grand army, won a victory near **Mill Spring**, January 19, and this was the first of a series of brilliant successes. Next followed the capture of **Fort Henry**, on the Tennessee, and of **Fort Donelson**, a much stronger post, on the Cumberland. These forts were in the State of Tennessee, not far from its northern line, where the rivers approach within twelve miles of each other.

34. Both a land force under General Grant, and a small fleet under Commodore Foote, went against these strongholds, but the fleet alone reduced **Fort Henry**, February 6, before the army arrived. Grant next marched to the rear of **Fort Donelson**, while the fleet moved up the Cumberland to join in the attack. The enemy repelled the gunboats, but after stoutly resisting the land force for three days, was forced to surrender, on the 16th of February, to General Grant. About ten thousand prisoners were taken.

While the siege of Fort Donelson was going on, the Confederates evacuated Bowling Green, and shortly afterwards Columbus. Kentucky was thus freed.

35. The capture of Fort Donelson led in a few days to the occupation of **Nashville** by General Buell. Grant's victorious army, increased to about forty thousand men, proceeded up the Tennessee River, and encamped near

---

32. At the beginning of 1862 what posts forming a line of defences were held by the Confederates? Where was each of these posts? (See Maps, pp. 184, 185.) What is said of the Union forces confronting these posts?
33. Give an account of General Thomas's victory. What forts were next taken?
34. How and when was Fort Henry taken? Give an account of the capture of Fort Donelson. What is said of Bowling Green and Columbus?
35. What is said of the fall of Nashville? Where did Grant's victorious army afterwards encamp?

Pittsburg Landing. There the famous battle of **Shi'loh** *, was fought April 6 and 7.

36. The Confederates, over forty thousand strong, under Generals Albert S. Johnston and Beauregard, suddenly attacked the national troops early in the morning of the 6th, and after most desperate fighting, drove them from their camps back to the river. There the Union gunboats helped check the enemy. Thus matters stood at night. At this time General Buell, with his army, was on his way to join Grant. He arrived that night with a large force, and in the morning the battle was resumed. After a terrible struggle the Confederates gave way, and retreated to Corinth, whence they had come. On each side nearly ten thousand men were killed and wounded. The Union loss was also large in prisoners. Among the slain was the Confederate commander-in-chief, General Johnston.

37. After the battle of Shiloh, General Halleck took command in person of the armies at Pittsburg Landing, and, having been reënforced, he very cautiously and slowly advanced, with over one hundred thousand men, against the enemy intrenched at **Corinth**, about sixteen miles southwest of the Landing. Beauregard, being greatly outnumbered, evacuated Corinth on the night of May 29, and on the following day the Union army took possession. The Confederates had escaped.

38. A few days afterwards Halleck detached an army, under Buell, to go eastward against Chattanoo'ga, a place of great importance as a base of operations. **General Bragg**, who succeeded Beauregard, put his army in motion for the same place, and reached it first. Presently he began to

* Three miles south-west of Pittsburg Landing was a meeting-house, called Shiloh, near which some of the severest fighting occurred.

---

35. When was the battle of Shiloh fought?
36. Give an account of the first day's fight at Shiloh. What reënforcements reached Grant's army, and what is said of the second day's fight? State the number of killed and wounded in the battle. Where is Pittsburg Landing? (See Map, p. 184.)
37. What can you tell of Halleck's advance against Corinth? Of its evacuation by Beauregard? Where is Corinth? (See Map, p. 184.)
38. Against what place was Buell sent, and what did Bragg then do? Where is Chattanooga? (See Map, p. 185.) What campaign of invasion was begun by Bragg?

move northward with full forty thousand men to recover Tennessee and Kentucky. General Buell was then compelled to turn about to protect his line of supplies and repel the invaders.

39. Part of Bragg's army, under E. Kirby Smith, moving northward from Knoxville, routed a Federal force near *Richmond*, August 30, and then marching on, threatened Cincinnati, and took possession of *Frankfort*. Meanwhile, Bragg, with the main body, was pressing northward from Chattanooga. At *Munfordville* he captured four thousand Federal troops, and then went on towards Frankfort.

40. Buell failed to strike the invader a blow, but he so handled his army as to guard Nashville and Louisville. Rebel foraging parties overran Central Kentucky, and collected a vast quantity of plunder. Bragg made but a short stay in the vicinity of Frankfort. He turned back, pursued by Buell, and, after fighting a severe battle at Perryville, October 8, made good his escape.

41. About the end of October Buell was superseded by General Rosecrans, who had just won important victories at and near Corinth. These we must now notice. Some weeks after the capture of Corinth, Halleck was called to Washington, to be the general-in-chief of all the armies of the republic. He left Grant in command of a large district in the west.

42. While Bragg was making his gigantic raid towards the Ohio, Generals Van Dorn and Price undertook to aid his enterprise by moving against Corinth. A rebel army led by Price advanced to I-u'ka, where it was attacked and routed, September 19, by the troops of General Rosecrans, who then held a command under Grant. Two weeks later

---

38. What did Buell then do?
39. Give an account of operations by the invaders under E. Kirby Smith. Of the operations of the main army under Bragg. Where is Richmond? (See Map, p. 185.) Cincinnati? Frankfort? Munfordville?
40. What is said of Buell? Where is Nashville? (See Map, p. 185.) Louisville? What of rebel foraging parties? What more can you tell of the invasion? Where is Perryville? (See Map, p. 185.)
41. Who superseded Buell? What is said of Halleck and Grant?
42. How did Van Dorn and Price coöperate with Bragg? What is said of the battle of Iuka? Where is Iuka? (See Map, p. 184.)

the combined forces of Van Dorn and Price attacked the army under Rosecrans in the strong defences of **Corinth**, and on the second day of the fight, October 4, were repulsed with heavy loss.

43. Bragg, some time after his retreat from Kentucky, gathered his forces at **Mur'freesboro'**. Rosecrans marched against him, and near that place, on the west side of Stone River, one of the fiercest conflicts of the war was fought on the last day of 1862. The Confederates nearly won the day, but their tide of victory was stayed, and after another severe encounter on the 2d of January, 1863, they were forced to retreat, yielding the advantages of a great victory to Rosecrans.

44. Far **west of the Mississippi** there was also severe fighting in 1862. About the middle of February, General Curtis, who held command under Halleck, pushed Price across the southern border of Missouri into Arkansas. The Confederates made the most zealous efforts to support Price, and got together, in a short time, full twenty thousand men. General Van Dorn took the chief command of this army. Curtis had but little over half as many men, but he totally defeated Van Dorn in the fierce battle of **Pea Ridge**, which was fought March 7 and 8, in the north-western corner of Arkansas.

45. During the summer, bands of rebel **guerrillas** roamed over much of the State of Missouri, and many combats took place between them and bodies of loyal militia. Later in the year, another large Confederate army was gathered in Arkansas, and in the north-western part of the state, at **Prairie Grove**, December 7, a considerable battle was fought. The poorly-armed and badly-disciplined Confederates were defeated by much fewer Union troops.

---

42. What is said of the battle at Corinth?
43. How was the battle of Murfreesboro' brought on, and what further is said of it? Where is Murfreesboro'? (See Map, p. 185.)
44. What is said of affairs beyond the Mississippi? What of Curtis and Price? What of Confederate efforts in this region? Of the battle of Pea Ridge?
45. What is said of guerrilla bands in Missouri? Of another large Confederate army in Arkansas, and of the battle of Prairie Grove?

46. The rebels had erected forts and placed batteries at commanding positions on **the Mississippi** in order to control that great highway. During the spring of 1862 a number of these posts were gained by the national forces. Columbus being untenable after the capture of Fort Donelson, the Confederates went down the river to Island No. 10 and New Madrid. These posts they fortified.

47. General John Pope, with a Union army, assailed **New Mad'rid**, and drove the rebels out of it. They fled to **Island No. 10**,* which was much more strongly fortified. Commodore Foote attacked the works on this island, and pounded away at them with shot and shell for three weeks, till Pope could cross the river so as to place his army in the rear of the stronghold. On the 7th of April — the last day of the great battle of Shiloh — the army crossed, and Island No. 10 was surrendered. About seven thousand prisoners were taken.

48. The fleet advancing down the river was next stopped at **Fort Pillow**. This fort and rebel gunboats barred the way for some time, but the fall of Corinth exposing the post to capture from the rear, the garrison abandoned it early in June, and the Federal fleet then passed on to **Memphis**. There a naval battle took place, and Captain Davis (successor to the gallant Foote) won a victory which gave the national forces possession of the city.

49. Far below Memphis is **Vicksburg**, which was the strongest Confederate post on the Mississippi. Almost at the very close of the year General William T. Sherman, with a large Union army, made an assault upon the works north of the town, and was repelled with severe loss. They were too strong to be taken by assault.

* The islands in the Mississippi, from the mouth of the Ohio downward, are numbered in their order.

---

46. How did the rebels try to keep control of the Mississippi? What posts did they occupy after they abandoned Columbus?
47. How was New Madrid gained? Give an account of the Union victory at Island No. 10.
48. Give an account of operations at Fort Pillow and of its evacuation. How was Memphis repossessed? Where is Memphis? (See Map, p. 184.) Fort Pillow?
49. What is said of Vicksburg, and of Sherman's attempt to take it?

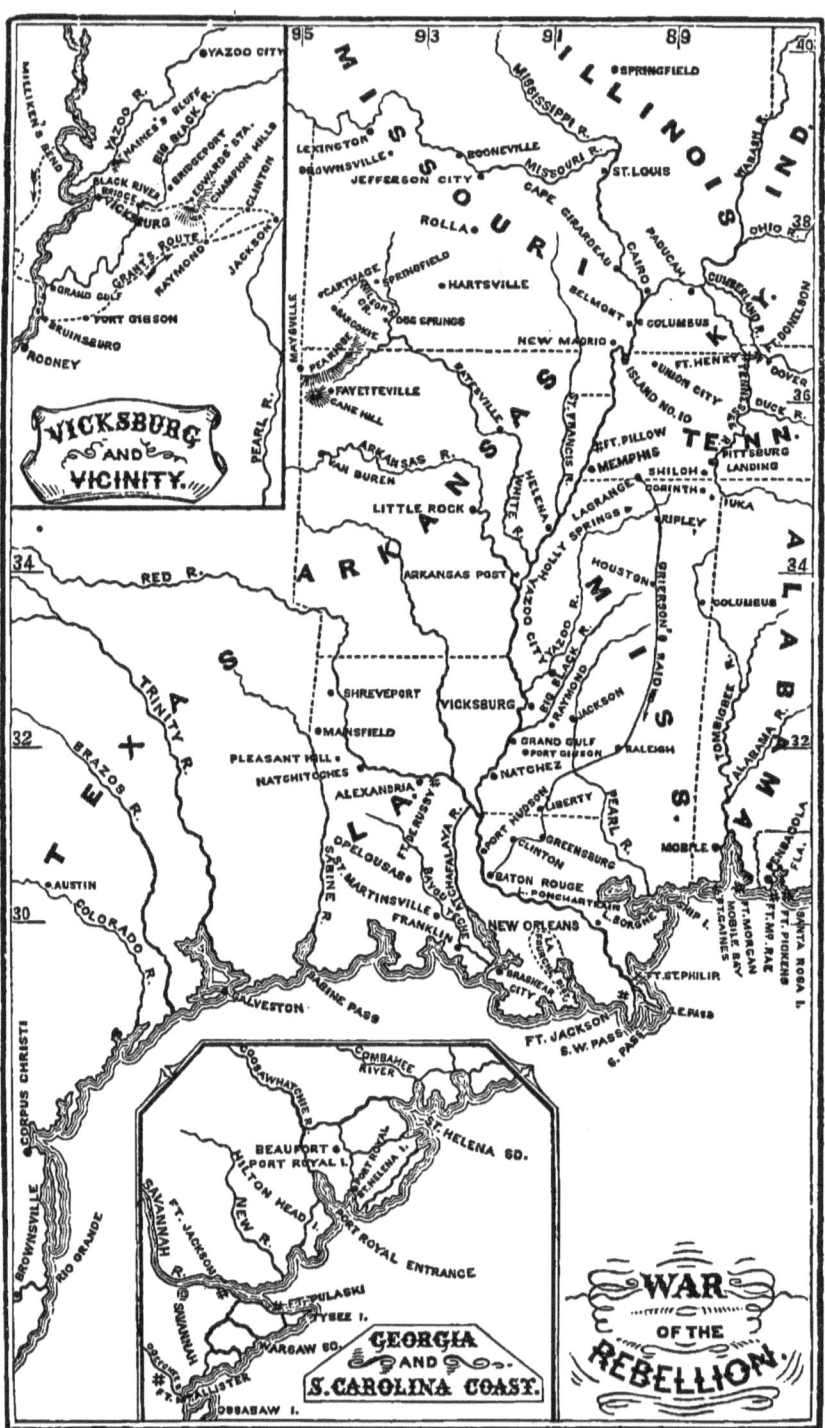

50. Efforts to open the Mississippi were also made by way of its mouth. Early in the year a naval armament, under Commodore David G. Far'ragut, was fitted out to act with an army under General Butler, for the capture of **New Orleans.** About seventy-five miles below the city, two forts, on opposite sides of the river, guarded the approach from the Gulf.

51. **Farragut,** having with little effect bombarded these forts for six days, on the 24th of April ran past them with the principal vessels of his fleet. This he did before the dawn of day, fighting a terrific battle with the forts, rebel gunboats, rams, and fire-rafts. Nearly the whole Confederate fleet was destroyed, and the next day Farragut appeared before the city. The Confederate forces fled, and New Orleans lay at the mercy of the national war-vessels. The forts yielded after two or three days to the mortar boats under Commander Porter. **Butler** took military possession of the city, and held it with a strong hand for the national government. The capture of New Orleans was the severest blow yet inflicted upon the rebellion.

52. Afterwards the fleet went up the river, capturing towns, and, aided by the gunboats from above, tried to batter down the works at **Vicksburg.** This was in the spring and summer before Sherman's repulse.

53. On the **Atlantic coast** new positions were won from the Confederates early in the year. A land and naval expedition, under General Burnside and Commodore Goldsborough (*gōldz'bur-o*), sailing from Annapolis and Fortress Monroe, captured the forts on **Roanoke Island,** by severe fighting, February 7 and 8.

54. A little while afterwards **Newbern,** an important town, was taken, the Confederates who defended it being defeated in a hot engagement; and near the end of April

---

50. What forces were sent against New Orleans? What is said of two forts?
51. Give an account of the naval battle below New Orleans? After this battle what did Farragut do? What did General Butler do?
52. How was Farragut's fleet afterwards employed?
53. What is said of Union successes on the Atlantic coast? How were the forts on Roanoke Island captured? Where is Roanoke Island? (See Map, p. 185.)
54. What important town was shortly afterwards taken?

Fort Macon (*ma'kun*), commanding Beaufort (*bu'furt*) Harbor, surrendered after ten hours' bombardment. Nearly the whole of the North Carolina seaboard then lay at the mercy of the national arms. Meanwhile conquests farther south had been made, the most important being **Fort Pulaski** (*pu-las'ki*), guarding the mouth of the Savannah River. This fort yielded to Union batteries erected by Captain (afterwards General) Gillmore.

55. When the Federals abandoned the navy yard near Norfolk, among the vessels which they sunk was the **frigate Merrimack**. The rebels raised this frigate, and

Fight between the Monitor and the Merrimack.

transformed it into an iron-clad ram, armed with ten heavy guns. On the 8th of March this terrible engine of war, steaming out from Norfolk, made a descent on the national fleet in Hampton Roads, destroyed the sloop-of-war Cum-

---
54. What is said of Fort Macon and its capture? Where was Fort Macon? (See Map, p. 185.) What of the North Carolina seaboard? Of Fort Pulaski and its capture?
55. How did the rebels come by the Merrimack, and what did they make of her? Give an account of the havoc made in Hampton Roads by the Merrimack. Where are Hampton Roads? (See Map, p. 172.)

berland and the frigate Congress, and at evening seemed only to wait for the dawn of another day to complete the destruction of the whole fleet. Then what might not the monster do to northern cities on the coast?

56. But that night the **Monitor** arrived. She was an iron-clad vessel, just constructed on a new plan, and armed with two enormous guns in a turret. The turret could be revolved so as always to point the guns towards an antagonist. In the morning the little Monitor attacked the giant Merrimack, and after a fierce combat, the latter, considerably injured, gave up the fight, and made off towards Norfolk. This success caused the government to construct other vessels of the same kind as the Monitor.

57. The most important events of the year, in the west, on the lower Mississippi, and on the Atlantic coast, have been given. We shall now notice the movements and battles of great armies in **Virginia**, where was the heart of the rebellion.

58. **McClellan** was not ready to advance till early in March; but just before he took the field the Confederates abandoned Manassas, and fell back towards Richmond. After McClellan had personally taken the field, the president relieved him of his duties as general-in-chief, and thus permitted him to give his undivided attention to the army of the Potomac. It being at length decided to go against Richmond by way of Fortress Monroe, the grand army was conveyed down the Potomac River and Chesapeake Bay, and landed at the Fortress.

59. On the 4th of April McClellan began to advance up the peninsula, between the James and York Rivers; but he was very soon stopped by fortifications and a Confederate force at **Yorktown**. After he had spent a month in preparing to reduce these works by a siege, the

---

56. What description can you give of the Monitor? What can you tell of the fight between the Monitor and the Merrimack? Who commanded the Monitor? *Ans.* Lieutenant Worden (*wur'dn*.)
57. What events of the year have been given, and what are we now to notice?
58. What movements were made by the Confederates just before McClellan took the field? What is said of a change in McClellan's official duties? Whither was the army conveyed, and for what purpose?
59. Give an account of operations at Yorktown.

enemy quietly evacuated them, and retreated towards Richmond. A rapid pursuit brought on a sharp fight at **Williamsburg**, May 5, but only a small part of the pursuing army was engaged, and after a spirited defence the Confederates made good their retreat. General Wool, commanding at Fortress Monroe, was now able to take possession of **Norfolk**, and the Confederates destroyed their famous iron-clad ram **Merrimack**.

60. McClellan moved forward towards Richmond, and establishing his base of supplies at White House, on the the Pamunkey, threw the left wing of his army across the Chickahom'iny, a very few miles from the rebel capital. This wing was attacked, May 31, near **Fair Oaks** and **Seven Pines**. The battle lasted part of two days, and at its close the Confederates fell back to Richmond. The loss was very severe on each side. General Joseph E. Johnston, the Confederate commander, was severely wounded, and General Robert E. Lee was afterwards assigned to command in his place.

61. McClellan had been expecting to be reënforced by McDowell, who was at Fredericksburg, in command of over forty thousand men. To keep the way open for McDowell to join him, he had sent forward a column under General Fitz-John Porter, who routed a body of the enemy at Hanover Court House, four days before the battle of Fair Oaks. But a bold enterprise performed by the Confederate General Jackson, popularly known as "Stonewall" Jackson, prevented the junction of McDowell and McClellan.

62. To understand this achievement we must turn to the Shenandoah Valley and the adjacent regions. Besides McDowell's army, two other armies were coöperating with the grand army of the Potomac — one under General

---

59. Give an account of the fight at Williamsburg. Who took Norfolk? Where is Norfolk? (See Map, p. 172.) Fate of the ram Merrimack?
60. Where did McClellan establish his base of supplies, and where did he place his army? Where is the Pamunkey River? (See Map, p. 172.) The Chickahominy? Give an account of the battle of Fair Oaks. What is said of Johnston and Lee?
61. How was McClellan expecting to be reënforced? What is said of the affair at Hanover Court House? Where is Hanover Court House? (See Map, p. 172.) Fredericksburg? What is said of a bold enterprise?
62. What three armies were coöperating with the army of the Potomac?

Banks, in the Shenandoah Valley, the other under General Frémont, who had command in West Virginia.

63. Jackson, who was far up the **Shenandoah Valley**, suddenly struck a blow at Frémont, and then advanced with twenty thousand men to crush Banks at Strasburg. Banks, being vastly outnumbered, rapidly retreated down the valley, pursued by his foe, and reached the Potomac, but not without loss.

64. Jackson's movements startled the north, and produced the wildest excitement in Washington, which was thought to be in great peril. McDowell, then on the point of marching to reënforce McClellan, was **kept back**, and ordered to head off Jackson when he returned up the valley. For this purpose he detached a large force, and Frémont hastened with his army from the west of the valley.

65. But **Jackson** was too nimble to be caught. He slipped between his foes, and although hotly pursued, made his escape. These famous races down and up the valley occurred in the latter part of May and the early part of June. While McDowell, Banks, and Frémont were waiting to meet Jackson, should he again move northward, he quietly joined Lee before Richmond, and both fell upon McClellan.

66. Fighting began on the 25th of June, and on the following day Lee fiercely attacked the Union troops on the north side of the Chickahominy, threatened their communications with White House, and caused McClellan fully to make up his mind to change his base, and transfer his army to the James River. While McClellan was doing this, Lee continued his attacks, and terrible battles were fought. The fighting continued during seven days, known as **the seven days before Richmond**, ending July 1, in a bloody repulse of the Confederates at *Malvern Hill*. The other principal battles had been fought at *Mechanicsville*,

---

63. How did Jackson begin his valley campaign, and what did Banks do?
64. What feeling was aroused by Jackson's movements? What is said of McDowell and Frémont?
65. Result of the pursuit of Jackson? Date of these races? What more is said of Jackson?
66. What is said of Lee's operations against McClellan, and of a change of base? State what you can of the battles which took place. In what direction from Richmond are these battle-fields? (See Map, p. 172.)

Gaines's Mill, Savage's Station, and *Glendale.* McClellan's army was the stronger, numbering considerably over one hundred thousand men. The Union and Confederate losses together amounted to thirty-five thousand men.

67. While these conflicts were going on near Richmond, the armies of McDowell, Banks, and Frémont were united into one body, as the **Army of Virginia,** and placed under the command of General John Pope.

68. Lee next turned upon Pope. The forces of Jackson and Banks began the struggle, August 9, at Cedar Mountain, and it was continued by **Lee** and **Pope** in several other battles, the most sanguinary being fought near the old battle-field of Bull Run. The engagement at Chantilly,* September 1, ended the **series of conflicts** in which the Union army had been thoroughly worsted. It staggered back to the fortifications of Washington. McClellan had been ordered up with his army from the James, but he came too late to stem the tide of disaster. At Chantilly, two gallant and skilful Union generals, Stevens and Kearny (*kar'nĭ*), were slain.

69. Pope was relieved of his command, and all the troops were placed under McClellan for the defence of Washington. Lee, now resolving upon the **invasion of Maryland,** crossed the Potomac, and entered Frederick. Thence he moved westward, followed by McClellan, who marched so as to protect Washington and Baltimore. On the 14th of September the Union advance came upon part of Lee's army holding two gaps of the **South Mountain.** After severe fighting these forces of the enemy were driven from their positions.

70. On the following day, **Harper's Ferry,** with a Union garrison of near twelve thousand men, was shamefully sur-

---

* Pronounced *shan'tĭl-ĭĭ.*

---

66. What is said of the opposing forces and the losses?
67. How was the army of Virginia formed, and who commanded it?
68. What is said of battles fought by Lee and Pope? Result of these bloody conflicts? Where is Cedar Mountain? (See Map, p. 172.) What is said of McClellan? Of Stevens and Kearny?
69. Give an account of movements by Lee and McClellan in Maryland. Of conflicts at the South Mountain. Where is the South Mt.? (See Map, p. 172.)
70. What great success was gained by Jackson?

rendered to General Jackson, after a feeble resistance. Jackson immediately marched to rejoin Lee, who had placed his forces west of Antietam (*an-te'tam*) Creek, near Sharpsburg. There, September 17, was fought the great battle of **Antietam**, which raged from dawn till dark, and left both armies greatly shattered; but Lee was forced to recross the Potomac.

71. For several weeks **McClellan** did not seek his foe. At length, crossing the Potomac, in the early days of November, he moved southward, east of the Shenandoah Valley, up which Lee was now retreating. At this time the president, who had been much dissatisfied with McClellan's inactivity, sent him an order to surrender the command to **General Ambrose E. Burnside**. This general concentrated his forces on the Rappahannock, opposite Fredericksburg, intending to march upon Richmond from that point. The Union troops crossed the river, and, December 13, were defeated, with frightful loss, in an attempt to carry the works held by Lee in the rear of **Fredericksburg**. On the night of the 15th they recrossed the river.

72. The **Federal government** this year prohibited *slavery* in all the territories of the United States, abolished it in the District of Columbia, and authorized the enlistment of *colored troops*. Many thousand blacks afterwards fought on the Union side.

73. THE SIOUX WAR. — The summer of 1862, was sadly marked in **Minnesota** by terrible massacres perpetrated by bands of Sioux (*soo*) Indians, under Little Crow and other chiefs. They murdered hundreds of the inhabitants, and compelled many thousands to flee from their homes. The whites soon marched against the savages, killed or captured some hundreds of them, and drove others into Da-ko'ta. In the next year, when the Indians renewed the work of

---

70. State where Lee placed his forces, and give an account of the battle of Antietam. Where is Sharpsburg? (See Map, p. 172.)
71. After some weeks what movements of the armies were made? Who superseded McClellan, and where did the new commander place his forces? Give an account of the Union defeat at Fredericksburg.
72. What action did the government take this year in regard to slavery? What is said of colored troops?
73. What Indian massacres occurred in 1862? How were the Indians punished?

death, they were hunted down, as if they were wild beasts, and pursued far westward till they crossed the Missouri River.

74. **Events of 1863.** — On the first day of the year 1863 President Lincoln issued his **Emancipation Proclamation**, which will ever be memorable. It declared forever free all slaves in the insurgent states, except in such parts of Louisiana and Virginia as were under national authority. This New Year's Day was the beginning of a new era in the history of the colored race.

75. Late in January General Joseph Hooker took command of the **Army of the Potomac**, in place of Burnside. This army was still opposite Fredericksburg. After three months Hooker crossed the Rappahannock, and was badly defeated by Lee in a battle fought chiefly May 2 and 3, at **Chancellorsville.** Again the Union army retreated across the river, having suffered great loss. Among the Confederate loss was the famous general, "Stonewall" Jackson, who was shot by mistake by his own men, and fell mortally wounded.

76. Early in the next month, Lee put his splendid army in motion for another invasion of the loyal states. He pressed down the Shenandoah Valley, on the way capturing or dispersing a Union force, crossed the Potomac, and advanced into Pennsylvania. Hooker rapidly moved back, marching in such a manner as to cover Washington. He had reached Frederick, Maryland, when he was superseded by General George G. Meade, who met the invading host at **Gettysburg,*** Pennsylvania, and there gave battle.

77. **This decisive battle,** the greatest of the war, began July 1, and continuing through the next two days, ended in a Federal victory. On the 4th of July Lee began to

* *get'tiz-burg — g* as in *go*.

---

74. When did President Lincoln issue the Emancipation Proclamation, and what did it declare?
75. What is said of Hooker and his defeat near Chancellorsville? What was Chancellorsville? *Ans.* It was a large house about ten miles west of Fredericksburg. What famous southern general fell in this battle?
76. In the next month what movements were made by Lee and Hooker? Who superseded Hooker, and where did the armies join battle?
77. State what you can about the battle of Gettysburg, including its results. Where is Gettysburg? (See Map, p. 185.)

withdraw his broken columns towards Virginia. The mighty armies which struggled at Gettysburg lost in killed, wounded, and missing, near fifty thousand men, and of these Lee lost much more than half.

78. Crossing the Potomac, Lee retreated up the Shenandoah Valley, and at length took position on the south side of the Rapidan'. **Meade** followed, and posted the Union army north of that stream. There they confronted each other till some time in the next spring, except that both generals made some forward movements to find a chance to get the advantage. But neither allowed himself to be outmanœuvred.

79. We shall now tell of the greatest achievement in the west — the **opening of the Mississippi.** You will remember that General Sherman attacked the outworks of Vicksburg and was repulsed, at the end of last year. Efforts for its capture were soon renewed. Early in this year General Grant placed his forces on the west side of the river, a few miles above **Vicksburg**, and began to plan how best to operate against the stronghold. One scheme after another was tried and abandoned. Finally, he marched his army to a point many miles below the city, and on the last day of April crossed to the east bank of the Mississippi, by means of Admiral Porter's vessels, which had run by the rebel batteries in the night-time. While moving around to the rear of Vicksburg, Grant met the Confederates, and defeated them in **five battles** outside of their fortifications.

80. Driving the enemy, under General Pemberton, back into Vicksburg, Grant then laid **siege** to the place. General Joseph E. Johnston, with a Confederate force, hovered in the rear of the Union army, but he had too few men to attack it. Day and night the army and fleet rained shot and shell into

---

78. What movements did the rival generals make after this battle?
79. Where is Vicksburg? (See Map, p. 184.) By whom and how were efforts for the capture of Vicksburg renewed early in 1863? How did Grant get to the rear of Vicksburg, and how many battles were fought while moving to this position.
80. What did Grant then do? What is said of General Johnston? Describe the siege.

the doomed city. Assaults made by the besiegers were repulsed. For more than six weeks the siege went on; but at last, July 4, **Vicksburg was surrendered**, and its garrison, twenty-seven thousand men, became prisoners.

81. The capture of Vicksburg made **Port Hudson**, the last Confederate stronghold on the river, untenable. It was therefore surrendered, five days later, to General Banks, who for some weeks had been investing it. Banks had superseded Butler at New Orleans The fall of these fortified places opened the Mississippi through its whole length. The Confederacy was thus cut in two.

82. There were fights at various places in **Missouri** and **Arkansas**, but they had no great bearing on the war. After Vicksburg fell, Grant sent out a force under General Steele, who, in September, took possession of *Little Rock*, the capital of Arkansas. In the western part of these states bands of rebel *guerrillas* had their haunts. One of these bands dashed into **Lawrence**, Kansas, in August, burned much of the city, and murdered one hundred and forty of its inhabitants.

83. Now let us go back to **Tennessee**, where we left Rosecrans the victor at Murfreesboro'. Bragg, after his defeat, fell back southward, and took a strong position north of Duck River. It was nearly six months before **Rosecrans** was prepared to advance. He then, in the latter part of June, began a series of skilful movements, which in nine days compelled the Confederate army to abandon Middle Tennessee, and retreat over the Cumberland Mountains to Chattanooga.

84. After some weeks Rosecrans again advanced in such a manner as to compel Bragg again to retreat, and the Union general then threw part of his force into Chat-

---
80. When was Vicksburg surrendered, and how many prisoners were taken?
81. What effect did the fall of Vicksburg have on operations at Port Hudson? When and to whom was Port Hudson surrendered? What had the fall of these posts accomplished?
82. What is said of fights in Missouri and Arkansas? What of Little Rock? Of guerrillas, and the massacre at Lawrence?
83. Relate how the Confederates under Bragg were made to abandon Middle Tennessee.
84. How did Rosecrans gain Chattanooga, and what battle followed?

tanooga. Pushing on, he found the enemy only a few miles south of that place. Bragg, having received reenforcements, was now stronger than his pursuer. The bloody battle of **Chickamauga** followed, fought September 19 and 20, near a creek of that name. The Federals were beaten, and fell back to Chattanooga, where they fortified themselves. In the last day's fight General Thomas and his men saved the army from ruin. He stood like a rock when the masses of the enemy were hurled upon him.

85. The Union army was now shut up in **Chattanooga** by Bragg, who took possession of mountain ranges near the town. Soon the besieged were in danger of starving. The national government made great efforts to relieve them. Grant was appointed to the chief command of all the Union armies in the west east of the Mississippi, and Rosecrans was superseded by Thomas. Sherman came with troops from Vicksburg, and Hooker with a detachment from the army of the Potomac.

86. The siege was raised by a battle, which Grant began on the 23d of November and continued on the two following days. The Federals gained a complete victory, but it was wonderful how they gained it. They rushed up the steep sides of **Lookout Mountain and Missionary Ridge**, swept the Confederates from their strong positions, and forced them to flee southward.

87. While Rosecrans was moving against Chattanooga, late in the summer, Burnside was marching an army from Kentucky into the valley of **East Tennessee**, where he was joyfully welcomed — most of the people being Unionists. But their country had been held by armed Confederates, who had treated them with great severity. On the 1st of September Burnside occupied *Knoxville*.

---

84. Result of the battle? What is said of General Thomas? Where is Chattanooga? (See Map, p. 185.)
85. Describe the condition of the Union army at Chattanooga. What command was given to Grant, and who superseded Rosecrans? What generals brought reënforcements?
86. How did Grant raise the siege of Chattanooga? What is said of this Federal victory?
87. When and how was East Tennessee repossessed? What is said of the people of East Tennessee?

88. Bragg, after shutting up the Union army in Chattanooga, detached Longstreet and his command to regain East Tennessee. That general marched upon **Knoxville**, and laid siege to it; but Burnside stoutly held the place, and after the victory at Chattanooga, Grant sent a force under Sherman to his assistance. Learning this, Longstreet made a desperate assault, was repulsed, and then retreated towards Virginia.

89. In the summer **a daring raid** was made through Kentucky, into Indiana and Ohio, by the noted Confederate ranger, General Morgan, and his troopers. Pursuers pressed hard after him, and in less than a month his band was killed, captured, or scattered. Among the captured was Morgan himself. He, however, dug out of the prison in which he was confined, and continued his career as a raider, till one night when he was surprised by Union troopers, and shot while trying to escape.

90. Nearly forty thousand **seamen** were in the service of the government this year, most of them being employed to enforce the blockade and assist the Union armies. They captured many swift steamers, sent out by English merchants with cargoes for southern ports.

91. The government sent expeditions for the capture of **Fort Sumter** and **Charleston**. Early in April, Admiral Du Pont, with a fleet of iron-clads, assailed the defences of Charleston Harbor, but he was soon obliged to retire. Afterwards land and naval forces, under General Gillmore and Admiral Dahl'gren, attacked these defences. In July Gillmore seized part of **Morris Island**, and tried to take Fort Wagner, on the other part, by storming it, but failed with sad loss. By a siege, the Confederates were at length forced to abandon this fort. Fort Sumter was

---

88. What did Bragg do to regain East Tennessee? What is said of the siege of Knoxville?
89. What daring Confederate raid is mentioned? Result to the raiders? What further is said of Morgan?
90. How many seamen were in the service of the government? What is said of English blockade-runners?
91. Give an account of the first expedition sent against Fort Sumter. Who commanded the second expedition? Give an account of operations against Fort Wagner. What of Fort Sumter? Of Charleston?

bombarded and made a heap of ruins, but the garrison still held it, and Charleston also withstood the long siege, although Gillmore threw shells into the city from Morris Island.

92. Congress had authorized the president to obtain troops by a **draft**. Those who feared the draft or hated the war fiercely opposed this way of raising troops. In New York city it gave rise to a terrible and bloody **riot**, which broke out July 13, while the draft was going on. It lasted four days before it was put down. The fury of the mob was especially directed towards negroes, and among the buildings sacked and burned was the Asylum for Colored Orphans. So wicked and brutal were the rioters.

93. The rebellion was at the height of its power about the middle of this year; but it began to wane after the Union victories at Gettysburg and Vicksburg, on the 3d and 4th of July.

3. *From the Beginning of 1864 to the Assassination of President Lincoln.*

94. **Events of 1864.** — In February, 1864, General Sherman made a successful **raid**, on a grand scale, **from Vicksburg** eastward, nearly across the State of Mississippi. The Confederate general Forrest and his horsemen were at this time in the northern part of the state. They drove back a large cavalry force which set out from Memphis to join Sherman at Meridian.

95. Forrest, like Morgan, was a swift and daring raider. A little later he made an inroad into the western part of Tennessee and Kentucky, and among other exploits took **Fort Pillow** by storm on the 12th of April. At that time it was garrisoned by almost six hundred men, about half of them being negro troops. After the works had been carried, the assailants stained their victory by a dreadful

---

92. What is said of opposition to the draft? Of a riot in New York city?
93. When was the rebellion at the height of its power, and when did it begin to wane?
94. What great raid did Sherman make from Vicksburg, and what happened to a coöperating cavalry force?
95. A little later what did Forrest do?

massacre, and thus a large part of the garrison fell. The employment of colored troops by the national government had greatly exasperated the southern people.

96. Forrest and his troopers, some time after the affair at Fort Pillow, thoroughly routed, in **Northern Mississippi**, a large force sent against them from Memphis; but another force, in July, gave them a severe defeat.

97. Early in the year General Banks, commanding at New Orleans, led an **expedition far up the Red River**. He intended to occupy Shreveport. His army was reenforced by ten thousand men from Vicksburg, and Admiral Porter, with a fleet of iron-clad gunboats, coöperated. But the Federals did not go so far as Shreveport. After two battles, fought April 8 and 9, the first resulting in a victory for the Confederates and the second in their repulse, the expedition was given up.

98. While Porter's **gunboats** were above Alexandria the water fell so much that they could not repass the rapids at that place. They were, however, **saved** by the remarkable skill of Colonel Bailey, who built a dam below the rapids, and thus raised the water high enough to allow the vessels to pass them.

99. An expedition sent out early in the year to reclaim Florida also failed, the Union troops being disastrously defeated near **O-lus'tee**, February 20.

100. We shall now speak of much more important events—of the famous **campaigns of Grant and Sherman**. In March the rank of Lieutenant-General was conferred upon Grant, and he was given command of all the Union armies. The bulk of the **Confederate forces** formed two great armies. One, in Virginia, under Lee, was strongly

---

95. Give an account of the Fort Pillow massacre.
96. What else is related of Forrest?
97. Who led the Red River expedition, and what was the point aimed at? Where is Shreveport? (See Map, p. 184.) Where is Alexandria? What can you say of the forces? Result of the expedition?
98. Give an account of the saving of the gunboats in Red River.
99. What can you tell of a Union expedition sent to Florida? Where is Olustee? (See Map, p. 185.)
100. What rank was conferred upon Grant? What did most of the southern forces form?

posted south of the Rapidan, and shielded Richmond; the other, in Georgia, under Johnston, was intrenched at Dalton (*dawl'tun*), and shielded Atlanta, a great railroad centre of the south.

101. General Sherman was placed in command of the **Union forces west** of the Alleghany Mountains, to conquer Johnston. General Meade still held command of the **Army of the Potomac**, which had the task of conquering Lee's army. Lieutenant-General Grant had his headquarters with the Army of the Potomac, and took the general direction of military affairs.

102. This army crossed the Rapidan, May 4, and the next day Lee hurled his heavy columns upon it, in the region known as the **Wilderness**. There a terrific battle raged for two days, at the close the Confederates withdrawing behind their intrenchments. These were too strong to be assaulted. Grant, resolving to go on, therefore made a flank movement, but again found his foe before him at **Spottsylvania**, where the rival armies had a long, fierce struggle. Another flank movement was followed by a fight at the **North Anna**, and another by the bloody Federal repulse at **Cold Harbor**. Whenever Grant made a flanking advance, Lee fell back rapidly, and behind breastworks again confronted him.

103. Then, at the middle of June, the Union leader, moving to the left, threw his army **across the James**, the Confederates falling back within the defences of Richmond and Petersburg. This bloody **campaign to the James** had lasted six weeks, and cost the Union army sixty thousand men, while the Confederates, who had commonly fought behind intrenchments, lost only about one third as many.

---

100. Describe Lee's position. Johnston's.
101. What was Sherman's command and task? Meade's? What is said of Grant?
102. When did the Army of the Potomac cross the Rapidan? What did Lee then do? What is said of the battle of the Wilderness? Give an account of Grant's operations after this battle, including the battles of Spottsylvania, North Anna, and Cold Harbor. Where is the Wilderness? (See Map, p. 172.) Spottsylvania? Cold Harbor? What is said of Lee's movements?
103. Describe the movements of the two armies after the battle of Cold Harbor. How long had the campaign to the James lasted, and what were the losses?

104. In coöperation with the movement of the Army of the Potomac against Richmond, **General Butler** ascended the James River with about thirty-five thousand men, who were landed at **City Point** and **Bermuda Hundred**. These positions he fortified and held. He also marched within seven or eight miles of Richmond, but was driven back to Bermuda Hundred. When Grant had fought his way down to Cold Harbor, a large part of Butler's troops joined him, to take part in that battle.

105. Lee and his veterans were now within the long line of earthworks, which, extending from the south-west of **Petersburg** to the north-west of **Richmond**, shielded these cities. Grant, having passed the James, threw his army against these defences. Being repulsed, he sat down for a **regular siege**, and while conducting it, struck heavy blows at his vigilant antagonist. There was a great deal of **severe fighting**, sometimes north of the James, but mostly south of it, the severest battles being fought south of Petersburg, where the national troops tried to get around to the rear of the enemy's works.

106. The most remarkable attempt to get inside these works was made July 30, by exploding a **mine** under a Confederate fort before Petersburg. The fort and its garrison were thrown high in air, but the storming column, which pressed into the gap made by the explosion, was repulsed with dreadful slaughter.

107. General Sigel's army, in the **Shenandoah Valley**, was also to coöperate with the Army of the Potomac. Sigel, advancing about the time at which Grant began his march, soon came upon a Confederate force, and was defeated. General Hunter took the command in place of Sigel, and after routing a large body of the enemy, marched

---

104. Give an account of Butler's coöperating movements with an army which had been collected at Fortress Monroe. Where are City Point and Bermuda Hundred? (See Map, p. 172.) Where is Petersburg?
105. Where were Lee and his army? What did Grant do after crossing the James? What is said of the fighting during the siege of Petersburg?
106. Give an account of an attempt to break through the Confederate defences by exploding a mine.
107. What is said of Sigel's coöperation with the Army of the Potomac? Of Hunter's?

against **Lynchburg**. But he found this city too well defended to be taken, and was forced to retreat into West Virginia.

108. The way to the Potomac was thus left open, and Lee, in the hope of compelling Grant to raise the siege of Richmond and go to the defence of the national capital, sent General Early, with a strong **invading army**, northward. Early swept down the Shenandoah Valley, crossed the Potomac into Maryland early in July, and after defeating a small force under the active General Wallace (*wol'lis*), at the Mo-noc'a-cy River, near Frederick, seriously **threatened Washington** and **Baltimore**. But Grant had sent up troops to protect the capital, and Early quickly retreated into Virginia. For some time, however, he hovered near the Potomac. His cavalry made a plundering raid into Pennsylvania, and on the 30th of July burned most of **Chambersburg**.

109. On the 19th of September General Philip H. Sheridan, who had commanded Grant's cavalry, but who was now in command of the army protecting Washington, defeated Early in the battle of **Winchester**, and sent him "whirling up the valley." Pursuing his enemy southward, Sheridan, three days after, again struck him a stunning blow, and then returning, laid waste this fertile valley, so that the enemy could draw no further supplies from it.

110. Just one month from the day of the battle of Winchester, the Confederates, in the early morning, fell upon Sheridan's troops, near **Cedar Creek**, and drove them from their camp. Sheridan himself was miles away at the time, in Winchester; but soon he came riding swiftly to the front, and imparted to the men something of his own fiery spirit. They charged upon the Confederates, and put them to total rout. Early's army was ruined.

---

108. What plan did Lee adopt to raise the siege of Richmond? Relate some events of this invasion. What had Grant done? What fate befell Chambersburg?
109. When and by whom was Early defeated at Winchester? How did the Union general follow up his victory?
110. Give an account of the surprise of Sheridan's troops at Cedar Creek. Of Sheridan's arrival, and the result of the contest.

111. While such had been the progress of the war in Virginia, General Sherman, in the west, had been conducting one of the most remarkable campaigns on record. With an army of nearly one hundred thousand men, he set out from the neighborhood of Chattanooga, May 6, on his **march to Atlanta**. Confronting him was General Johnston, with an army about half as large.

112. By skilfully moving so as to threaten the enemy's flank and rear, Sherman compelled him to fall back first from one strong position, then from another, till he had pushed him across the Chat-ta-hoo'chee, and forced him, about the middle of July, to take refuge within the fortifications of Atlanta. He then laid siege to the city. During this march **heavy battles** were fought — the severest at *Resaca* (*re-sah'kah*), *Dallas*, and *Ken'e-saw Mountain*.

113. At **Atlanta**, the brave and prudent Johnston was superseded by the impetuous General Hood, who, in the latter part of July, sallied forth three times, on the 20th, 22d, and 28th, and furiously assailed the Union lines, but each time was repulsed, and suffered great loss. In the second of these battles the gallant and accomplished Union general, McPherson, was killed. At length Sherman moved his main force around south of the city, and defeating a large part of the Confederate army at **Jonesboro'**, compelled Hood to abandon Atlanta in the night of September 1. The victors occupied it, and could now take breath for a while. During the campaign both armies had been re-enforced.

114. After the fall of Atlanta, **Hood**, passing around to the north-west of the city, seriously threatened the long line of supplies of the Union army. **Sherman** followed him some distance, but in a short time marched back to

---

111. When and with how large an army did General Sherman set out from Chattanooga for Atlanta?
112. Give an account of Sherman's march to Atlanta. Name the severest battles that took place.
113. What is said of a change of Confederate commanders, and of three furious assaults upon the Union lines? What of General McPherson? Tell how and when Sherman gained Atlanta.
114. What movements of Hood and Sherman followed the fall of Atlanta?

Atlanta. He had sent troops and his best general, Thomas, to protect Tennessee, whither Hood was now tending.

115. The Confederate general invaded Tennessee, and Thomas concentrated his scattered forces at Nashville; but before this could be done the invaders overtook a strong column under General Schofield (*sko'feeld*), who made a stand at **Franklin** on the last day of November, and repulsed their assaults with great loss to the assailants. Schofield that night fell back to **Nashville**, which city the Confederates soon began to invest. On the 15th of December Thomas sallied out and drove them back, and the next day, renewing the battle, put them to total rout. He pursued them vigorously, and the fragments of Hood's army suffered terribly in their winter flight back into Alabama.

116. We will now see what Sherman had been doing meanwhile. Severing all communication with the north, and committing Atlanta to the flames, save its dwelling-houses and a few other buildings, he set out in the middle of November on his **famous march to the sea.** His way lay through the heart of Georgia. His troops, moving in separate columns, swept over a wide space, and collected their provisions from the country through which they passed. They saw no enemy who could offer serious resistance, and in less than a month reached the vicinity of Savannah. Then, by assault, Sherman quickly carried **Fort McAllister** (*mak-ăl'lis-ter*), and thus opened communication with the Federal fleet off the coast. A few days later, December 21, he took possession of **Savannah**, its garrison having fled in the night-time.

117. The last rebel invasion of **Missouri** was made in the autumn of this year. General Price entered the state from Arkansas, at the head of a large invading force, but he was soon driven back.

---

114. Whom did Sherman send to protect Tennessee?
115. Give an account of the battle of Franklin. Where is Franklin? *Ans.* Eighteen miles south-west of Nashville. Give an account of Thomas's victory at Nashville. What is said of Hood's flight?
116. State when Sherman set out on his march for the sea, and what occurred at Atlanta. What is said of the march? Of Fort McAllister and Savannah?
117. What can you tell of the last rebel invasion of Missouri?

118. In August of this year the brave Admiral Farragut won new fame. Boldly defying the fire of Forts Morgan and Gaines at the entrance to **Mobile Bay**, he steamed past them with his fleet, captured or dispersed the rebel gunboats, and, after a desperate conflict, overcame the great iron ram Tennessee. Afterwards, aided by a land force, he took the forts, and thus closed Mobile Bay to blockade-runners. But the city itself was not captured till the spring of 1865.

119. A few **English-built cruisers**, commissioned by the rebel authorities, caused immense loss to American commerce. The greatest havoc was inflicted by the *Alabama*, Captain Semmes. This steamer — built in a British ship-yard, manned chiefly by British sailors, and armed with British cannon — darted swiftly over the seas, capturing and burning American merchantmen. She long eluded pursuit, but one Sunday morning, in June, 1864, the *Ke'ar-sarge*, Captain Winslow, encountered her off the harbor of Cherbourg (*shĕr-boorg'*), France, and sunk her.

120. In the autumn of 1864 **Lincoln** was **reëlected** by the people of the loyal states, and Andrew Johnson, of Tennessee, was chosen vice-president. **Nevada*** (*ne-vah'-dah*) was admitted as a state in the same year.

121. **Events of 1865.** — The first military success of the year 1865 was the capture of **Fort Fisher**, the main defence of Wilmington, whose port had never yet been wholly closed to blockade-runners. Admiral Porter, with a powerful fleet, bombarded the fort with great effect, and then the land forces, under General Terry, carried the works by assault, January 15. The fall of Fort Fisher

---

* So named from the *Sierra Nevada*, a mountain-range partly bounding the state on the west. Sierra Nevada are Spanish words, meaning *mountain-chain snow-clad*.

---

118. Give an account of Farragut's victory in Mobile Bay. What is said of Forts Morgan and Gaines, and the city? Where is Mobile Bay? (See Map, p. 184.)
119. What is said of English-built cruisers? Give an account of the doings of the Alabama. What was her fate?
120. When was Lincoln reëlected, and who became vice-president? What territory became a state in the same year?
121. What was the first military success of the year 1865? At the mouth of what river was Fort Fisher? (See Map, p. 185.) How and when was the fort taken? Where is Wilmington? (See Map, p. 185.)

was followed in a few weeks by the fall of **Wilmington**. Union troops took the city.

122. The 1st of February saw Sherman again on the march. Moving northward, he easily brushed aside the small bodies of the enemy which offered any annoyance, and on the 17th occupied **Columbia**, the capital of South Carolina. On the same day **Charleston** was abandoned by its garrison, whose safety was now threatened by Sherman's movements. On the following day, February 18, Gillmore's troops raised the national flag over Fort Sumter, and took possession of the city.

123. From Columbia, Sherman continued his march northward for a while, and then turning, moved in a northeasterly direction to Fayetteville, North Carolina. Resuming his course, he was now first seriously opposed by the enemy. Near **Averysboro'** he beat a strong force of the enemy, and at **Bentonsville**, where a severe battle was fought, defeated his old antagonist, Johnston, who had collected troops from various quarters. On the 23d of March, Sherman entered **Goldsboro'**, to which place General Schofield had brought up a coöperating force from Newbern, and General Terry another from Wilmington.

124. The **vast injury** which Sherman had done the Confederates in his march down to the sea, and through the Carolinas, cannot be told. He had destroyed railroads, mills, workshops — everything of great use in war. There was also great destruction of private property. Through South Carolina, in particular, he had cut a wide swath of desolation. His conquering legions were now where they could coöperate with Grant's army.

125. The end was now near. Just before Grant began his final campaign (of which we are soon to tell), and while

---

121. What followed the capture of Fort Fisher?
122. Give an account of Sherman's march from Savannah to Columbia. Relate how Charleston and Fort Sumter came again under national authority.
123. Describe Sherman's march from Columbia. What battles were fought, and with what results? When did Sherman enter Goldsboro', and what junction of forces was made? In what direction is Goldsboro' from Newbern? (See Map, p. 185.) From Wilmington?
124. What can you tell about the injury Sherman had done the Confederates?
125. What is said of Confederate affairs just before and during Grant's final campaign?

he was conducting it, other Union leaders, acting under his instructions, were dealing the Confederacy hard blows. General Canby and Admiral Thatcher were assailing the strong defences of **Mobile**. These were, at length, taken, and the city fell on the 12th of April.

126. **General Wilson**, with thirteen thousand horsemen, sent out by General Thomas, was making a great raid through the heart of Alabama, capturing cities, and destroying railroads and other property useful to an enemy. **General Stoneman**, from East Tennessee, was also making a great raid with cavalry in South-western Virginia and the western part of North Carolina.

127. **General Sheridan**, with near ten thousand troopers, bursting through the Shenandoah Valley, had fallen again upon the little army of Early, and captured most of it. Then he destroyed the canal west of Richmond, and tore up the railroads north of the city. Sweeping around easterly, he joined the Union army before Petersburg.

128. Grant opened the **final campaign** on the 29th of March. On the morning of that day he set in motion strong columns of his army to pass around the end of the intrenchments south-west of Petersburg, so as to get to the enemy's rear. Fighting began on the same day, and on the 1st of April, Sheridan, in command of these flanking columns, thoroughly defeated part of Lee's army, at the cross-roads called **Five Forks**.

129. Early in the next morning Grant made **a general assault** upon the whole line of intrenchments before Petersburg, and carried it, driving the Confederates to their inner works. Jefferson Davis and his cabinet fled from Richmond. Lee's army abandoned the cities which they had so long and so bravely defended, and hurried westward, aiming to unite with Johnston's army in North Carolina.

---

125. What is said of Mobile and its defences?
126. What is said of General Wilson's raid? Of General Stoneman's?
127. Give an account of Sheridan's operations west and north of Richmond.
128. When did Grant open the final campaign? Describe the beginning of this campaign. What victory was gained April 1?
129. What did Grant do the next morning? What is said of Davis and his cabinet officers? What of Lee's army?

130. On the following morning, April 3, the Union troops occupied both **Petersburg** and **Richmond**. The Confederates were fiercely pursued. Sheridan hung upon their flank, and at length placed his columns squarely across their front, while overwhelming masses pressed upon their rear. Then, April 9, **Lee surrendered** to Grant near Appomat'tox Court-House.

131. As tidings of the capture of Richmond, and of Lee's surrender, spread through the north, the joy of the loyal people knew no bounds. But in a few days this feeling was suddenly changed to one of deep sorrow and indignation when the telegraph flashed over the land the intelligence that **President Lincoln** had been **assassinated**. This dreadful deed was done on the evening of April 14, while the president was in a theatre. A desperado, named John Wilkes Booth, stole up behind him, and shot him in the head. The president died the next morning.

132. Booth was a southern partisan, and the head of a band of conspirators. The same night another of the band forced his way into the room of William H. Seward, the Secretary of State, then lying in bed, ill, and stabbed him, but not mortally.

II. JOHNSON'S ADMINISTRATION. 1865-1869. PEACE. RECONSTRUCTION.

1. **Events of 1865, continued.** — A few hours after the death of Lincoln, the vice-president, **Andrew Johnson**, took the oath of office as **president**. The assassin, Booth, after eluding pursuit for some days, was found hidden in a barn, and refusing to give himself up, was shot. Some of the other conspirators were hanged, and some were imprisoned.

2. The decisive victory in Virginia was soon followed by the **surrender of all** the remaining Confederate forces.

---

130. When were Petersburg and Richmond occupied by Union troops ? Give an account of the pursuit and the surrender of Lee.
131. How was the joy of the loyal people changed to the utmost sorrow and indignation ? Give some particulars of the assassination and death of Lincoln.
132. What is said of Booth ? Of the attempt to assassinate Seward ?
1. Who became president after Lincoln's death ? Fate of Booth and his band of conspirators ?
2. What is said of the surrender of all the remaining Confederate forces ?

Johnston surrendered his army to Sherman. **Davis,** the ruler of the Confederacy, was stopped in his flight, in Georgia, by some of General Wilson's horsemen. He was carried to Fortress Monroe, and kept a long time as a prisoner, but finally was allowed to go at large.

3. The war, which had lasted four years and a little over, was now ended. Its **cost** had been immense. On the Union side nearly three hundred thousand men perished — killed outright in battle or dying from wounds and disease. On the Confederate side probably as many perished. We hesitate to speak of the loss of money in connection with the loss of precious human life; yet it is well for us to know that, when the war ended, the nation was in debt near three thousand million dollars, and that this was but part of the pecuniary cost of the war.

4. While the struggle was going on, the government had to issue **bonds,** that is, writings binding it to pay money at a future time; and these, to a vast amount, were bought by the people. United States **notes,** for larger or smaller sums, were also issued, and these circulated as money. Large sums were also obtained by various kinds of new taxes. Gold and silver coin ceased to be in general use, and brought a high premium.

5. The saddest story of all the war is that which tells of the cruel treatment of **Union prisoners** in the south. We would not here describe, if we could, the terrible sufferings which the captives had to endure in Libby Prison, on Belle Isle (*bel-ile'*), and above all, in that great prison-pen at Andersonville, from heat, cold, hunger, from diseases which should have been prevented, and from outrages committed by brutal guards.

6. The contest being over, the national government had to

---

2. What is said of the capture and imprisonment of Davis?
3. How long had the war lasted? How many men perished by the war? How large a debt had the United States contracted?
4. What is said of United States bonds? Of United States notes? Taxes? Gold and silver coin?
5. What statement is made concerning the treatment of Union soldiers taken prisoners? Where was Libby Prison? *Ans.* In Richmond. Where is Belle Isle? *Ans.* It is a small island in the James River, near Richmond. Andersonville? (See Map, p. 185.)
6. After the war was over, what important duty devolved upon the government?

decide upon what terms the rebel states might be restored to their former relations in the Union. In a short time it became evident that there was a disagreement between President Johnson and a large majority of Congress as to the best policy to be followed in reconstructing these states.

7. The **president** claimed that they should be allowed to have representatives in Congress, and be fully restored to their position as states of the republic as soon as they had complied with certain conditions. He required them to rescind their ordinances of secession, to declare the Confederate war-debt void, and to vote for an amendment to the Constitution abolishing slavery in the United States. Such an amendment Congress had proposed early in 1865. Three fourths of all the states ratified it, and slavery was declared abolished in December of the same year.

8. **Congress** required more than all this, and especially that the freedmen — that is, the blacks who had lately been slaves — should not only be free, but should have civil rights conceded them, so that they might enjoy the same security of person and property as the whites. Congress proved strong enough to carry out its own plan of reconstruction in spite of the president's opposition.

9. In March, 1865, Congress passed a bill for the relief of freedmen and loyal refugees. A department, known as the **Freedmen's Bureau**, with General Howard as its head, was organized under this law. Another act, passed notwithstanding the president's veto, enlarged the powers of the Bureau, which, during some years, watched over the freedmen, to give them protection and needful assistance.

10. Tennessee was the first state to comply with the requirements of Congress, and resume her political standing in the Union. On the 2d of March, 1867, Congress

---

6. What disagreement arose?
7. What did the president claim as regards the rebel states? What conditions did he require of these states? How and when was slavery constitutionally abolished?
8. What did Congress require of the rebel states? Which plan prevailed?
9. What can you tell of the Freedmen's Bureau?
10. What state was the first to comply with the requirements of Congress? What act was passed March 2, 1867?

passed a **Reconstruction Act** over the president's veto. This act and others, also passed over the veto, prescribed the conditions on which the ten states, then not represented in Congress, should be reconstructed, and made them subject to military authority till they complied with these conditions. In the following year seven of these states accepted the conditions, and were allowed to resume their political privileges. The three other states were re-admitted on the same terms, early in 1870.

11. Another bill, known as the **Tenure of Office Bill**, was passed in March, 1867, notwithstanding the president's veto. The bill declared, in effect, that those persons who had been appointed to civil offices with the advice and consent of the Senate, could not be removed by the president without the Senate's permission. The president alone could not remove even a member of his cabinet.

12. In the following summer, soon after Congress had adjourned, the president suspended from office Edwin M. Stanton, the Secretary of War, and directed General Grant to assume the duties of the department. Early in the next year, that is, in 1868, Congress reinstated Mr. Stanton, but the president soon afterwards issued an order removing him. This time, however, Mr. Stanton did not yield the place.

13. This proceeding of President Johnson brought the long and bitter controversy between the executive and Congress to a crisis. The House of Representatives **impeached the president** of high crimes and misdemeanors. Charges for violation of the Tenure of Office Act, and for other offences, were made to the Senate, which body has the sole power to try impeachments. The president sent eminent counsel to manage his cause, and the trial began on the 30th of March. After several weeks, the senators gave their decision. The president was ac-

---

10. What did this act, and others supplementary to it, effect? What more is said of the restoration of the states?
11. When was the Tenure of Office Bill passed, and what was its design?
12. In the summer of 1867 what cabinet-officer was suspended by the president? Relate what action was afterwards taken on Mr. Stanton's case.
13. What is said about the impeachment of President Johnson? His trial? Verdict of the senate? What vote is necessary to convict in impeachment? *Ans.* A two thirds vote of the members present.

quitted. Two-thirds of the members would not vote for his conviction.

14. In the summer of 1866 a **telegraphic cable**, which is a kind of wire-rope, was laid across the Atlantic from Ireland to Newfoundland (*nu'fund-land*). Since that time intelligence has been flashed through this cable along on the bed of the ocean from continent to continent. To Cyrus W. Field, of New York, it is chiefly owing that this great project was accomplished.

15. **Nebraska*** was admitted as a state in 1867; and in the same year the United States obtained a vast accession of territory, by the purchase from Russia (*rŭsh'ĭ-ah*) of the north-west part of the continent, for $7,200,000 in gold. This region, then known as Russian America, was named **Alaska** after it came into our possession.

16. The presidential canvass of 1868 resulted in the election of the Republican candidates, **General Grant**, of Illinois, as **president**, and Schuyler Colfax (*skī'ler kōl'fax*), of Indiana, as vice-president.

III. GRANT'S ADMINISTRATION. 1869-1877.

1. The **inauguration** of Grant took place on the 4th of March, 1869. In May of that year a gigantic enterprise was successfully completed in our country. This was the construction of the **Pacific Railroad** from Omaha (*o'ma-haw*), on the Missouri River, to the Pacific coast. We can hardly estimate the great results which will come from opening this highway across the continent.

2. In the summer of the same year **another cable** was laid beneath the waters of the Atlantic. This one stretches from France to America, and successfully carries telegraphic messages from one country to the other.

---

* An Indian name, said to signify *water-valley*.

---

14. When and how was telegraphic communication between Ireland and America effected? To whom is the successful accomplishment of this project chiefly due?
15. When was Nebraska admitted as a state? What is said of the purchase of Alaska?
16. Who were elected president and vice-president in 1868?
1. When was Grant inaugurated? What can you state about the Pacific Railroad?
2. What is said of the Atlantic cable which connects France and America?

3. A few days before the end of Johnson's administration Congress proposed the famous **Fifteenth Amendment**, which declares that the right of any citizen of our country to vote shall not be denied or abridged on account of race, color, or previous condition of servitude. Three fourths of the states having agreed to this, the amendment was declared, on the 30th of March, 1870, to be part of the Constitution.

4. The month of October, 1871, is memorable to the citizens of **Chicago** for the great fire which destroyed half the city and burned out of house and home nearly one hundred thousand people. No other American city has ever been visited by so destructive a fire. A year and a month later the great **fire in Boston** burned down between seven and eight hundred buildings, many of them spacious warehouses, with a vast quantity of merchandise.

The burnt districts of both cities were **rebuilt** with wonderful quickness, and the new buildings are much stronger and better than the old.

5. During the civil war the Alabama and other English-built cruisers had done great injury to our commerce. As these vessels had been fitted out in British ports, our government claimed compensation from the English government for the losses they had inflicted. After much discussion, a treaty was made at Washington by which the **Alabama claims** were referred to five arbitrators.* This board of arbitration met at Geneva, Switzerland, and finally decided, in September, 1872, that Great Britain should pay fifteen and a half millions of dollars to the United States in

---

* One named by the President, one by the Queen, one by the King of Italy, one by the President of the Swiss Confederation, and one by the Emperor of Brazil.

---

3. When did Congress propose the Fifteenth Amendment? What does this Amendment declare? When was it declared part of the Constitution?
4. What can you tell about the Chicago fire? About the great fire in Boston? About the rebuilding of the burnt districts?
5. Tell what the Alabama and other English-built cruisers had done. What did our government do? How were the Alabama claims finally settled?

settlement of the claims. The money was paid in accordance with this decision.

6. When the time came to select the presidential candidates for 1872, General Grant was nominated by the republicans for re-election. Henry Wilson, of Massachusetts, was nominated for the vice-presidency. The republicans were successful. **General Grant** became **president** for a second term, and **Henry Wilson** became vice-president.

7. The year 1876 is known in the history of our country as the **centennial year.** The Republic was then a hundred years old. As a fitting celebration of this memorable year, an exposition, on a grand scale, of the products of the industry of all nations was held in Philadelphia, where a hundred years before the Declaration of Independence had been signed. The **Centennial Exhibition,** as it was called, was opened in Fairmount Park on the 10th of May, and for six months was thronged by visitors. The main building covered twenty acres, and besides this immense structure about two hundred other buildings were erected for the purposes of the Exhibition.

8. The **results** of the Exhibition were in the highest degree successful. It brought together from all parts of the country a far greater number of American people than were ever gathered on any other occasion; and these millions of visitors could not fail to learn much of interest and importance from so vast a display of the products of the industry and skill of all nations.

9. **Colorado** was admitted as a state in 1876. This made the number of states in the Union thirty-eight.

10. When the time for the election of president came around again in 1876, **Governor Rutherford B. Hayes,** of Ohio, was nominated by the republicans. Governor

---

6. Who became president and who vice-president in 1873?
7. When was the Centennial Year? What great celebration was held, and where? What can you tell about the Centennial Exhibition?
8. What can you tell of the results of the Exhibition?
9. When did Colorado become a state?
10. What nominations for the presidency were made in 1876?

Samuel J. Tilden, of New York, was nominated by the democrats.

11. The canvass was closely contested, and the **result of the election** remained, for a long time, uncertain. Some of the electoral votes in three of the southern states (South Carolina, Louisiana, and Florida), and in Oregon, were claimed by both parties.

12. Both sides declared themselves the victors, and each charged the other with unfairness, or worse — the **republicans** that the democrats had intimidated colored voters in the three southern states whose electoral votes were in dispute, the **democrats** that republican officials had fraudulently changed the election returns in those states.

13. The successful candidate must have one hundred and eighty-five electoral votes. Tilden had one hundred and eighty-four which were undisputed. In the states whose votes were in dispute, certificates of electors for both Hayes and Tilden were sent to the Senate.

14. The question was complicated, and as nothing of the kind had ever occurred before, there was no precedent to follow. Finally a way was found out of the difficulty. Leading men of both political parties agreed upon a bill which was passed by Congress. It provided for a tribunal, known as the **Electoral Commission**,* which should decide who were the true electors from the states about which there was any dispute.

15. The Commission met, and after a session continued for many days, all the questions were settled. The candidates of the republicans were declared elected, Ruther-

---

* This Commission was composed of five members of the Senate, five members of the House of Representatives, and five of the Associate Justices of the Supreme Court.

---

11. What can you tell about the canvass and the result of the election?
12. What did both the republicans and the democrats claim, and what charges were made?
13. What is said about the electoral votes? What about the states whose electoral votes were claimed by both parties?
14. What is said about the matter in dispute? Finally what plan was decided on?
15. What did the Electoral Commission do?

ford B. Hayes, of Ohio, president, and William A. Wheeler, of New York, vice-president. They were inaugurated March 5, 1877, the 4th being Sunday.

IV. HAYES'S ADMINISTRATION. 1877 ——.

1. The summer of 1878 was sadly marked in several of the southern states by the prevalence of the **yellow fever**. It broke out in New Orleans, and thence spread over a large part of the south-west. The people suffered terribly. Benevolent people of the north and west sent much money, and in other ways gave substantial aid to the sufferers. The hearts of the southern people were filled with gratitude for this kindness and sympathy. When cold weather came, the scourge ceased, but it had carried off twenty thousand persons.

2. While the war was going on, and for several years after its close, labor readily found employment. Land and merchandise — whatever men had to sell — were sold at a high price, and most business enterprises were prosperous.

But this season of prosperity came to an end in the autumn of 1873. Then began a general **prostration of business**, which continued for several years. A considerable shrinkage of values took place, followed by numerous failures in all kinds of business. Many who supposed themselves rich, suddenly found themselves poor. Laboring men were thrown out of employment, and the hard times caused much distress among the poorer classes. It was not till the year 1879 that a change for the better could be clearly seen.

3. During all these years, from the early part of the war till 1879, the **circulating money** had been government

---

15. Who were declared elected? When were Hayes and Wheeler inaugurated?
1. What can you tell about the yellow fever in 1878?
2. What can you tell about labor and business during the war and after? About a prostration of business and the result? When did a change for the better take place?
3. What kind of money had circulated from the early part of the war till 1879?

notes, called greenbacks, and bank-notes. Gold and silver were held at a premium, and did not circulate as money.

Some thought an increased issue of this paper money would give renewed prosperity to business; others thought the paper money should be made redeemable in coin. The latter opinion prevailed in Congress, which passed a bill known as the **Resumption Act.** This provided for the resumption of specie payments on the 1st of January, 1879. The provisions of the bill were carried out; coin came into circulation once more, and the paper money became as valuable as gold.

4. One result of the prostration of business was the great **railroad riots** which occurred in July, 1877. These began by a strike on the Baltimore and Ohio Railroad, at Martinsburg, in West Virginia. The immediate cause of the outbreak was a reduction of wages. The strikers would not work themselves or let others work.

5. The strike spread rapidly from road to road, and a horde of the idle and vicious joined the working-men. In Pittsburgh, Baltimore, Chicago, and in other cities ferocious mobs gathered in the streets. In Pittsburgh, especially, there were wild scenes of riot, and a vast deal of railroad property was destroyed and pillaged.

6. The governors of several states called upon the president of the United States to aid in putting down the insurrections, as it was found that the local troops or state militia could not always be relied on.

United States troops were dispatched to the places where serious outbreaks occurred, and the riots quickly came to an end. They lasted barely two weeks, but a vast amount of property was destroyed and many lives were lost.

---

3. What is said of gold and silver? What opinions were held about money, and which prevailed in Congress? Tell what you can about the Resumption Act and the result.
4. When did the railroad riots occur? Where did the strike first break out?
5. What further can you tell of the strike? What is said about mobs?
6. What aid was asked? What is said about the United States troops?

7. The prompt and vigorous action of the president proved that our republican government is not weak or halting when it has to deal with popular violence and insurrection.

8. Within a few years there have been many improvements in machinery, and other inventions which have added to the comfort of mankind. One of the most curious and wonderful of these has very lately come into use in our country. This is the telephone, an apparatus for reproducing sound. By the aid of electricity, articulate speech is transmitted, for long distances, with great distinctness.

Our History here comes to an end. Looking back, we see from what feeble beginnings we have arisen, and how we have grown to giant strength. To-day we stand in the front rank of nations; and when we consider the intelligence and energy of the people, the vast extent of our country, and the form of our government, we cannot but believe that the Great Republic, giving freedom and just laws to all, is destined to have a grander career than the world has ever witnessed. But we should not feel proud because of our strength and prosperity, which are derived in no inconsiderable degree from great natural advantages. Rather let us remember that the real glory of a nation comes not from riches or power, or lands of vast extent, but from the love of Right and Truth.

---

7. What is said about the action of the president?
8. What can you tell about the telephone?

THE GROWTH OF THE UNITED STATES IN EXTENT OF TERRITORY.

1. **The boundaries of the United States**, at the close of the Revolutionary War, were established by the treaty of 1783, on the north and the east, essentially as at present; on the west, the Mississippi River was made the boundary, and on the south, Florida,* which then extended west to the Mississippi, having parallel 31° as its northern limit.

2. In the year 1803, **Louisiana** was purchased of France for fifteen millions of dollars. The Louisiana Purchase was a vast region extending west from the Mississippi River to the Spanish province of Mexico, and north to British America. The western and northern boundaries were indefinite.† Several large states and territories have been formed from this purchase.

3. **Oregon**, a region of much greater extent than the present state, lying north from Mexico and west from the Rocky Mountains to the Pacific, was for a long time claimed both by the United States and by Great Britain.‡ The present boundary line, the forty-ninth parallel, was agreed upon in 1847.

4. In the year 1819 Spain sold **Florida** to the United

---

* By this treaty Florida was conveyed by England to Spain.

† The boundaries between Louisiana and the Spanish province of Mexico were not settled till 1821 Then it was agreed that the dividing line should follow the Sabine River from its mouth to the thirty-second parallel, thence a meridian to the Red River, that river to the one hundredth meridian west from Greenwich, that meridian to the Arkansas, that river to its source, thence north to the forty-second parallel, and that parallel to the Pacific.

On the north, it was agreed in 1819, between Great Britain and the United States, that parallel forty-nine should be the boundary between the United States and British America from the Lake of the Woods to the Rocky Mountains.

On the east, after a few years, the United States claimed Florida as far as the Perdido River, that being the eastern limit of the old French province of Louisiana. Just before the war of 1812 they took possession of their claim — being the part of Florida between the Pearl and Perdido rivers.

‡ The United States claimed Oregon, from the exploration of its principal river, the Columbia, in 1792, by Captain Robert Gray, also from the expedition of Lewis and Clark, sent out by the president in 1804, also from the purchase of Louisiana. The English claimed the country from the operations of British fur-traders within the territory.

States for five millions of dollars. The country was not given up by Spain till 1821, when the treaty was finally ratified.

5. **Texas**, which had separated from Mexico, was annexed to the United States in 1847.

6. A vast country, including **California**, and extending south to the river Gila and west to the Pacific, was acquired from Mexico by conquest and by treaty.* By the treaty in 1848 our government agreed to pay fifteen millions of dollars to Mexico, and to assume debts to the amount of more than three millions, due by that country to citizens of the United States.

7. In 1853 the United States purchased of Mexico a region including the Mesilla Valley, south of the river Gila. This is sometimes called the **Gadsden Purchase**, from General James Gadsden, who negotiated the purchase for the United States.

8. Russian America, afterwards called **Alaska**, was purchased from Russia for seven million two hundred thousand dollars, in the year 1867.

9. Thus by purchase, annexation, and conquest, the **area of our national domain** has become four and one half times as much as at the close of the Revolutionary War — or an increase from 800,000 square miles in 1783 to 3,600,000 in 1879. This vast expanse is nearly thirty times that of Great Britain and Ireland together, or very nearly eighteen times that of all France.

* The boundary between the United States and Mexico was to be the Rio Grande from its mouth to New Mexico; thence to the river Gila; that river to its junction with the Colorado; thence in a straight line to the Pacific, at a point ten miles south of San Diego.

See **Map** following this page.

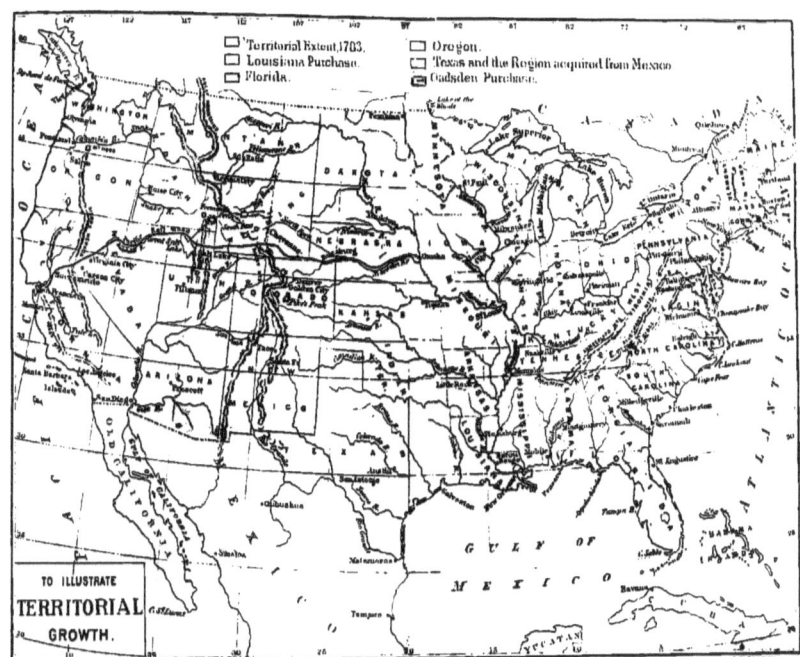

CHRONOLOGICAL REVIEW.

NOTE. — The figures in the paragraphs, and at the end of them, refer to the pages upon which the events are mentioned.

1861—1879.

Lincoln became president in 1861, 169. He entered upon a second term in 1865, but, April 14, was assassinated, and Vice-President **Johnson** succeeded to the presidency, 208. During these administrations the most formidable rebellion known to history was subdued, and slavery in the United States was abolished by an amendment of the Constitution.

1861. The rebels attacked *Fort Sumter*, and compelled Major Anderson to evacuate it, April 14. The president called for troops, 170. Jefferson Davis offered to commission privateers, and a blockade of the southern ports was established, 177. Four more slave states joined the Confederacy, 170.

The Federals, in Virginia, were disastrously defeated at *Bull Run* (July 21), 173, and in the autumn at *Ball's Bluff*, 174. In West Virginia, General McClellan, in July, gained victories over the Confederates at *Rich Mountain* and *Carrick's Ford*, and before the end of the year that region was nearly cleared of armed Confederates, 174, 175.

In Kentucky, the Confederates, in September, seized and fortified Columbus, and the Union troops, under General Grant, then occupied Paducah, 176.

In Missouri, Lyon captured a camp of disloyalists near St. Louis, in May, but lost the hard-fought battle of *Wilson's Creek* (August 10), 175.

On the Atlantic coast the Federals captured the Confederate works at *Hatteras Inlet* (August 29), and those at *Port Royal Entrance*, November 7, 177.

Mason and Slidell were taken from the British steamer Trent, 178.

1862. The Federal government prohibited slavery in the territories, abolished it in the District of Columbia, and authorized the enlistment of colored troops, 192.

1862. In the west, east of the Mississippi, the Federals gained a victory at *Mill Spring* (January 19); captured *Fort Henry* and *Fort Donelson*, and occupied *Nashville*, 179; were victorious, under General Grant, at *Shiloh* (April 6 and 7), and, under General Halleck, compelled the enemy to evacuate *Corinth* (May 29), 180. In the autumn, the Federals, under General Rosecrans, defeated the enemy at *Iuka*, 181, and at *Corinth*. The Confederates fell back after the battle of *Perryville* (October 8), 181; and at *Murfreesboro'* they were beaten by General Rosecrans in a three days' battle, which began December 31, 182.

West of the Mississippi, a Union victory was won at *Pea Ridge* (March 7 and 8), and nine months afterwards, another at *Prairie Grove*, 182.

The Confederate posts on the Mississippi, as far as Vicksburg, successively yielded to the Federals, 183, and Admiral Farragut opened the river from its mouth to *New Orleans* (April 25), of which city General Butler took military possession, 186.

On the Atlantic coast General Burnside and Commodore Goldsborough captured *Roanoke Island*, 186, and before the end of April nearly the whole coast of North Carolina was at the mercy of the Federals, who also had reduced *Fort Pulaski*. The Confederate ram *Merrimack*, after a day's havoc among the Union vessels in Hampton Roads (March 8), was driven back to Norfolk by the *Monitor*, 187.

In Virginia, the army of the Potomac, under McClellan, compelled the Confederates to evacuate *Yorktown*, beat them at *Williamsburg*, repulsed them near *Fair Oaks* and *Seven Pines* (May 31). 189. Meanwhile Stonewall Jackson drove the Federals from the Shenandoah Valley, and then joined General Lee before Richmond, 190. Lee then, in a *seven days' campaign* of almost constant fighting, raised the siege of the Confederate capital, pursuing McClellan to the James, where the latter repulsed the Confederates, with great loss, at *Malvern Hill* (July 1), 190. The Confederates next moved against the Army of Virginia, commanded by General Pope, and, after a series of conflicts, beginning at *Cedar Mountain* and ending at *Chantilly* (September 1), compelled Pope to fall back within the defences of Washington, 191. Lee next invaded Maryland. McClellan gained a victory

1862. over him at *South Mountain*, and by the great battle of *Antietam* (September 17) forced the Confederates, who had meanwhile captured *Harper's Ferry*, back to Virginia, 191, 192. Burnside superseded McClellan, and was badly defeated at *Fredericksburg* (December 13), 192.

During the summer the Sioux War broke out. It was suppressed the next year, 192.

1863. President Lincoln signalized the opening of the new year by issuing the Emancipation Proclamation, 193.

In Virginia, General Hooker superseded Burnside, and was severely beaten at *Chancellorsville* (May 2, 3) by Lee, who soon after set out for a second invasion of the loyal states. General Meade superseded Hooker, beat Lee in the great and decisive battle of *Gettysburg* (July 1, 2, 3), and pursued him into Virginia, 193.

Vicksburg was surrendered to General Grant (July 4), and a few days later *Port Hudson* to General Banks, 195.

The Federals, under Rosecrans, were defeated at the *Chickamauga* (September 19 and 20), and besieged in *Chattanooga*. The siege was raised, and the enemy thoroughly defeated by Grant, in a three days' battle, beginning November 23, 196. Soon after the Confederates were repulsed before *Knoxville*, by Burnside, 197.

1864. Among the earlier events were the expedition to *Meridian*, 198, the *Fort Pillow Massacre*, the *Red River* expedition, 199, and a Federal defeat at *Olustee*, Florida.

Grant was appointed to the chief command of the Union armies, 199, and, crossing the Rapidan with the Army of the Potomac (May 4), met the enemy in bloody conflicts in the *Wilderness*, at *Spottsylvania*, the *North Anna*, and *Cold Harbor*, 200. Then crossing the James (June 14), joined by Butler from Fortress Monroe, he laid siege to *Petersburg* and *Richmond*, 201. The Confederates made a third invasion of Maryland. They were soon obliged to retreat, but hovered near the Potomac till General Sheridan, in a brilliant campaign, ending in the victory of *Cedar Creek* (October 19), closed the war in the Shenandoah Valley, 202.

In the west, General Sherman made his famous *march to the sea*. Setting out (May 6) from Chattanooga, he fought heavy battles, the severest being at *Resaca, Dallas*, and

1864. *Kenesaw Mountain*, and captured *Atlanta* (September 2), 203; then sweeping through Georgia to the sea, he carried *Fort McAllister* by assault, and took *Savannah* (December 21), 204. Meanwhile the Confederates had been successfully resisted at *Franklin*, and disastrously routed at *Nashville* (December 15 and 16) by General Thomas, 204.

In June the notorious privateer *Alabama* was sunk, 205.

In August Admiral Farragut won a victory in *Mobile Bay*, 205.

1865 *Fort Fisher*, North Carolina, was captured (January 15), 205. Sherman swept northward through South Carolina; drove the Confederates from *Columbia*; compelled them to evacuate *Charleston*; then pressing forward into North Carolina, beat them at *Averysboro'* and at *Bentonsville*, and entered *Goldsboro'* (March 23), 206.

Grant's army began the final campaign (March 29), gave the Confederates a crushing defeat at *Five Forks*, 207; captured *Richmond* and *Petersburg*, and compelled Lee to surrender (April 9), near *Appomattox Court-House*, 208. *Mobile* was taken, 207. Before the end of May all the Confederate armies had surrendered.

1866. The Atlantic cable, from Ireland to Newfoundland, was laid, 212.

1867. The Reconstruction Act became a law, 211.

Alaska was purchased from Russia, 212.

1868. The House of Representatives having impeached President Johnson, his trial began (March 30), 211.

1869. **Grant** became president, 212.

The Pacific Railroad was completed, 212.

1870. The Fifteenth Amendment was declared adopted, 213.

1871. Half of Chicago was burned down (Oct. 8, 9, 10), 213.

1876. The International Centennial Exhibition was held in Philadelphia (opened May 10, closed Nov. 10), 214.

Colorado became a state, 214.

1877. **Hayes** became president (March 5), 216.

1879. Specie payments were resumed (Jan. 1), 217.

PRESIDENTS AND VICE-PRESIDENTS OF THE UNITED STATES.

	PRESIDENTS.	RESIDENCE.	INAUGURATED.	VICE-PRESIDENTS.	RESIDENCE.
1st,	George Washington,	Virginia,	April 30, 1789,	John Adams,	Massachusetts.
2d,	John Adams,	Massachusetts,	March 4, 1797,	Thomas Jefferson,	Virginia.
3d,	Thomas Jefferson,	Virginia,	March 4, 1801,	{ Aaron Burr,	New York.
				{ George Clinton,	New York.
4th,	James Madison,	Virginia,	March 4, 1809,	{ George Clinton,	New York.
				{ Elbridge Gerry,	Massachusetts.
5th,	James Monroe,	Virginia,	March 4, 1817,	Daniel D. Tompkins,	New York.
6th,	John Quincy Adams,	Massachusetts,	March 4, 1825,	John C. Calhoun,	South Carolina.
7th,	Andrew Jackson,	Tennessee,	March 4, 1829,	{ John C. Calhoun,	South Carolina.
				{ Martin Van Buren,	New York.
8th,	Martin Van Buren,	New York,	March 4, 1837,	Richard M. Johnson,	Kentucky.
9th,	William H. Harrison,	Ohio,	March 4, 1841,	John Tyler,	Virginia.
10th,	John Tyler,	Virginia,	April 6, 1841.		
11th,	James K. Polk,	Tennessee,	March 4, 1845,	George M. Dallas,	Pennsylvania.
12th,	Zachary Taylor,	Louisiana,	March 5, 1849,	Millard Fillmore,	New York.
13th,	Millard Fillmore,	New York,	July 10, 1850.		
14th,	Franklin Pierce,	New Hampshire,	March 4, 1853,	William R. King,	Alabama.
15th,	James Buchanan,	Pennsylvania,	March 4, 1857,	Jno. C. Breckinridge,	Kentucky.
16th,	Abraham Lincoln,	Illinois,	March 4, 1861,	{ Hannibal Hamlin,	Maine.
				{ Andrew Johnson,	Tennessee.
17th,	Andrew Johnson,	Tennessee,	April 15, 1865.		
18th,	Ulysses S. Grant,	Illinois,	March 4, 1869,	Schuyler Colfax,	Indiana.
				Henry Wilson,	Massachusetts.
19th,	Rutherford B. Hayes,	Ohio,	March 5, 1877,	William A. Wheeler,	New York.

AREAS, SETTLEMENT, AND ADMISSION OF THE STATES.

STATES.	AREAS. SQ. MILES.	WHEN, WHERE, AND BY WHOM SETTLED.			ADMITTED.
Virginia,*	38,352	1607	Jamestown,	English,	
New York,	47,000	1614	New York,	Dutch,	
Massachusetts,	7,800	1620	Plymouth,	English,	
New Hampshire,	9,280	1623	Portsmouth,	English,	
Connecticut,	4,750	1633	Windsor,	English,	The Thirteen Original States.
Maryland,*	11,124	1634	St. Mary's,	English,	
Rhode Island,	1,306	1636	Providence,	English,	
Delaware,*	2,120	1638	Wilmington,	Swedes,	
North Carolina,*	50,704		Albemarle Sd.,	English,	
New Jersey,	8,320	1664	Elizabeth,	English,	
South Carolina,*	34,000	1670	Ashley River,	English,	
Pennsylvania,	46,000	1682	Philadelphia,	English,	
Georgia,*	58,000	1733	Savannah,	English,	
Vermont,	10,212	1724	Brattleboro',	English,	1791
Kentucky,*	37,680	1774	Harrodsburg,	English,	1792
Tennessee,*	45,600	1768	Watauga River,	English,	1796
Ohio,	39,964	1788	Marietta,	Americans,	1802
Louisiana,*	41,346	1700		French,	1812
Indiana,	33,809		Vincennes,	French,	1816
Mississippi,*	47,156	1699	Biloxi,	French,	1817
Illinois,	55,410	1693	Kaskaskia,	French,	1818
Alabama,*	50,722	1702	Mobile Bay,	French,	1819
Maine,	35,000			English,	1820
Missouri,*	65,350	1755	St. Genevieve,	French,	1821
Arkansas,*	52,189	1685	Arkansas Post,	French,	1836
Michigan,	56,451	1701	Detroit,	French,	1837
Florida,*	59,268	1565	St. Augustine,	Spaniards,	1845
Texas,*	274,356	1715		Spaniards,	1845
Iowa,	55,045	1833	Dubuque,	French,	1846
Wisconsin,	53,924	1745	Green Bay,	French,	1848
California,	188,981	1769	San Diego,	Spaniards,	1850
Minnesota,	83,531	1838	St. Paul,	Americans,	1858
Oregon,	95,274	1811	Astoria,	Americans,	1859
Kansas,	81,318				1861
West Virginia,	23,000				1863
Nevada,	112,090				1864
Nebraska,	75,995				1867
Colorado,	104,500				1876
Dist. of Columbia,	60				

The TERRITORIES have an area of about 938,000 square miles. ALASKA has an area of 577,390 square miles.

* Slaveholding in 1861.

DECLARATION OF INDEPENDENCE.

IN CONGRESS, July 4, 1776.

A Declaration by the Representatives of the United States of America, in Congress assembled.

WHEN, in the course of human events, it becomes necessary for one people to dissolve the political bands which have connected them with another, and to assume, among the powers of the earth, the separate and equal station to which the laws of nature and of nature's God entitle them, a decent respect to the opinions of mankind requires that they should declare the causes which impel them to the separation.

We hold these truths to be self-evident : — That all men are created equal ; that they are endowed by their Creator with certain unalienable rights ; that among these are life, liberty, and the pursuit of happiness. That, to secure these rights, governments are instituted among men, deriving their just powers from the consent of the governed ; that, whenever any form of government becomes destructive of these ends, it is the right of the people to alter or to abolish it, and to institute a new government, laying its foundation on such principles, and organizing its powers in such form, as to them shall seem most likely to effect their safety and happiness. Prudence, indeed, will dictate, that governments long established should not be changed for light and transient causes ; and accordingly all experience hath shown that mankind are more disposed to suffer while evils are sufferable, than to right themselves by abolishing the forms to which they are accustomed. But when a long train of abuses and usurpations, pursuing invariably the same object, evinces a design to reduce them under absolute despotism, it is their right, it is their duty, to throw off such government, and to provide new guards for their future security. Such has been the patient sufferance of these colonies ; and such is now the necessity which constrains them to alter their former systems of government. The history of the present King of Great Britain is a history of repeated injuries and usurpations, all having in direct object the establishment of an absolute tyranny over these States. To prove this, let facts be submitted to a candid world.

He has refused his assent to laws the most wholesome and necessary for the public good.

He has forbidden his governors to pass laws of immediate and pressing importance, unless suspended in their operation till his assent should be obtained ; and when so suspended, he has utterly neglected to attend to them.

He has refused to pass other laws for the accommodation of large districts of people, unless those people would relinquish the right of representation in the Legislature — a right inestimable to them, and formidable to tyrants only.

He has called together legislative bodies at places unusual, uncomfortable, and distant from the depository of their public records, for the sole purpose of fatiguing them into compliance with his measures.

He has dissolved representative houses repeatedly, for opposing, with manly firmness, his invasions on the rights of the people.

He has refused, for a long time after such dissolutions, to cause others to be elected ; whereby the legislative powers, incapable of annihilation, have returned to the people at large for their exercise, the State remaining, in the mean time, exposed to all the dangers of invasion from without and convulsions within.

He has endeavored to prevent the population of these States ; for that purpose, obstructing the laws for naturalization of foreigners, refusing to pass others to encourage their migration hither, and raising the conditions of new appropriations of lands.

He has obstructed the administration of justice, by refusing his assent to laws for establishing judiciary powers.

He has made judges dependent on his will alone for the tenure of their offices, and the amount and payment of their salaries.

He has erected a multitude of new offices, and sent hither swarms of officers to harass our people and eat out their substance.

He has kept among us, in times of peace, standing armies, without the consent of our Legislatures.

He has affected to render the military independent of, and superior to, the civil power.

He has combined with others to subject us to a jurisdiction foreign to our Constitution, and unacknowledged by our laws; giving his assent to their acts of pretended legislation, —

For quartering large bodies of armed troops among us:

For protecting them, by a mock trial, from punishment for any murders which they should commit on the inhabitants of these States:

For cutting off our trade with all parts of the world:

For imposing taxes on us without our consent:

For depriving us, in many cases, of the benefits of trial by jury:

For transporting us beyond seas to be tried for pretended offences:

For abolishing the free system of English laws in a neighboring province, establishing therein an arbitrary government, and enlarging its boundaries, so as to render it at once an example and fit instrument for introducing the same absolute rule into these colonies:

For taking away our charters, abolishing our most valuable laws, and altering, fundamentally, the forms of our governments:

For suspending our own Legislatures, and declaring themselves invested with power to legislate for us in all cases whatsoever.

He has abdicated government here, by declaring us out of his protection, and waging war against us.

He has plundered our seas, ravaged our coasts, burned our towns, and destroyed the lives of our people.

He is, at this time, transporting large armies of foreign mercenaries, to complete the works of death, desolation, and tyranny, already begun with circumstances of cruelty and perfidy scarcely paralleled in the most barbarous ages, and totally unworthy the head of a civilized nation.

He has constrained our fellow-citizens, taken captive on the high seas, to bear arms against their country, to become the executioners of their friends and brethren, or to fall themselves by their hands.

He has excited domestic insurrections amongst us, and has endeavored to bring on the inhabitants of our frontiers the merciless Indian savages, whose known rule of warfare is an undistinguished destruction of all ages, sexes, and conditions.

In every stage of these oppressions we have petitioned for redress in the most humble terms; our repeated petitions have been answered only by repeated injury. A prince whose character is thus marked by every act which may define a tyrant, is unfit to be the ruler of a free people.

Nor have we been wanting in attention to our British brethren. We have warned them, from time to time, of attempts by their Legislature to extend an unwarrantable jurisdiction over us. We have reminded them of the circumstances of our emigration and settlement here. We have appealed to their native justice and magnanimity, and we have conjured them, by the ties of our common kindred, to disavow these usurpations, which would inevitably interrupt our connections and correspondence. They, too, have been deaf to the voice of justice and consanguinity. We must, therefore, acquiesce in the necessity which denounces our separation, and hold them, as we hold the rest of mankind, enemies in war, in peace friends.

We, therefore, the Representatives of the United States of America, in General Congress assembled, appealing to the Supreme Judge of the world for the rectitude of our intentions, do, in the name and by the authority of the good people of these colonies, solemnly publish and declare, That these united colonies are, and of right ought to be, FREE and INDEPENDENT STATES; that they are absolved from all allegiance to the British crown, and that all political connection between them and the State of Great Britain is, and ought to be, totally dissolved; and that, as free and independent States, they have full power to levy war, conclude peace, contract alliances, establish commerce, and to do all other acts and things which independent States may of right do. And, for the support of this declaration, with a firm reliance on the protection of Divine Providence, we mutually pledge to each other our lives, our fortunes, and our sacred honor.

The foregoing Declaration was, by order of Congress, engrossed, and signed by the following members:—

JOHN HANCOCK.

NEW HAMPSHIRE.
Josiah Bartlett,
William Whipple,
Matthew Thornton.

MASSACHUSETTS BAY.
Samuel Adams,
John Adams,
Robert Treat Paine,
Elbridge Gerry.

RHODE ISLAND, &C.
Stephen Hopkins,
William Ellery.

CONNECTICUT.
Roger Sherman,
Samuel Huntington,
William Williams,
Oliver Wolcott.

NEW YORK.
William Floyd,
Philip Livingston,
Francis Lewis,
Lewis Morris.

NEW JERSEY.
Richard Stockton,
John Witherspoon,
Francis Hopkinson,
John Hart,
Abraham Clark.

PENNSYLVANIA.
Robert Morris,
Benjamin Rush,
Benjamin Franklin,
John Morton,
George Clymer,
James Smith,
George Taylor,
James Wilson,
George Ross.

DELAWARE.
Cæsar Rodney,
George Read,
Thomas M'Kean.

MARYLAND.
Samuel Chase,
William Paca,

Thomas Stone,
Charles Carroll,
of Carrollton.

VIRGINIA.
George Wythe,
Richard Henry Lee,
Thomas Jefferson,
Benjamin Harrison,
Thomas Nelson, Jr.,
Francis Lightfoot Lee,
Carter Braxton.

NORTH CAROLINA.
William Hooper,
Joseph Hewes,
John Penn.

SOUTH CAROLINA.
Edward Rutledge,
Thomas Heyward, Jr.,
Thomas Lynch, Jr.,
Arthur Middleton.

GEORGIA.
Button Gwinnett,
Lyman Hall,
George Walton.

CONSTITUTION OF THE UNITED STATES.

PREAMBLE.

WE, the people of the United States, in order to form a more perfect Union, establish justice, insure domestic tranquillity, provide for the common defence, promote the general welfare, and secure the blessings of liberty to ourselves and our posterity, do ordain and establish this CONSTITUTION for the United States of America.

ARTICLE I.

SECTION I.

All Legislative powers herein granted shall be vested in a Congress of the United States, which shall consist of a Senate and House of Representatives.

SECTION II.

1st clause. The House of Representatives shall be composed of members chosen every second year, by the people of the several States; and the electors in each State shall have the qualifications requisite for electors of the most numerous branch of the State Legislature.

2d clause. No person shall be a Representative who shall not have attained to the age of twenty-five years, and been seven years a citizen of the United States, and who shall not, when elected, be an inhabitant of that State in which he shall be chosen.

Preamble. — Who ordained and established our Constitution, and for what purposes? What is a Constitution? ANS. *A body of laws which constitute the basis or foundation for a form of government.* What are the three great departments of government? (See p. 114.)

Article I. — SEC. I. Of what does the first article of the Constitution treat? ANS. *Of the legislative department.* In what body are the legislative powers vested? Of what does Congress consist?

SEC. II. — *1st clause.* By whom and how often are representatives chosen? Qualifications of electors of representatives?

2d clause. How old at least must a representative be? How long must he have been citizen of the United States, and of what state must he be an inhabitant?

3d clause. Representatives and direct taxes shall be apportioned among the several States which may be included within this Union, according to their respective numbers, which shall be determined by adding to the whole number of free persons, including those bound to service for a term of years, and excluding Indians not taxed, three fifths of all other persons. The actual enumeration shall be made within three years after the first meeting of the Congress of the United States, and within every subsequent term of ten years, in such manner as they shall by law direct. The number of Representatives shall not exceed one for every thirty thousand, but each State shall have at least one Representative; and until such enumeration shall be made, the State of New Hampshire shall be entitled to choose three; Massachusetts, eight; Rhode Island and Providence Plantations, one; Connecticut, five; New York, six; New Jersey, four; Pennsylvania, eight; Delaware, one; Maryland, six; Virginia, ten; North Carolina, five; South Carolina, five; and Georgia, three.

4th clause. When vacancies happen in the representation from any State, the executive authority thereof shall issue writs of election to fill such vacancies.

5th clause. The House of Representatives shall choose their Speaker and other officers, and shall have the sole power of impeachment.

SECTION III.

1st clause. The Senate of the United States shall be composed of two Senators from each State, chosen by the

---

3d clause. How are representatives and direct taxes to be apportioned among the states? What are taxes? ANS. *Sums of money exacted by government.* How may all taxes be divided? ANS. *Into direct and indirect.* What is a direct tax? ANS. *A tax laid directly on the person or on property, as a poll-tax or a tax on land.* What is an indirect tax? ANS. *A tax laid on articles of consumption or expenditure. Duties, imposts, &c., are indirect taxes.* How is the representative population of a state to be determined? Who are referred to in the phrase, "three fifths of all other persons"? ANS. *Slaves.* When was the first enumeration or census to be made, and how often thereafter? In what year was the first census taken? ANS. *In 1790.* What limit was put to the apportionment of representatives? What representation at least shall each state have?

4th clause. How are vacancies in the representation of a state to be filled?

5th clause. By whom are the speaker and other officers of the house chosen? What do you understand by the speaker of the house? ANS. *The presiding officer.* What body has the sole power of impeachment? What is impeachment? ANS. *An accusation charging a civil officer with official misconduct.*

SEC. III.— *1st clause.* How many national senators does each state have? How

Legislature thereof, for six years; and each Senator shall have one vote.

2d clause. Immediately after they shall be assembled in consequence of the first election, they shall be divided, as equally as may be, into three classes. The seats of the Senators of the first class shall be vacated at the expiration of the second year; of the second class, at the expiration of the fourth year; and of the third class, at the expiration of the sixth year, so that one third may be chosen every second year; and if vacancies happen, by resignation or otherwise, during the recess of the Legislature of any State, the Executive thereof may make temporary appointments until the next meeting of the Legislature, which shall then fill such vacancies.

3d clause. No person shall be a Senator who shall not have attained to the age of thirty years, and been nine years a citizen of the United States, and who shall not, when elected, be an inhabitant of that State for which he shall be chosen.

4th clause. The Vice-President of the United States shall be President of the Senate, but shall have no vote, unless they be equally divided.

5th clause. The Senate shall choose their other officers, and also a President pro tempore, in the absence of the Vice-President, or when he shall exercise the office of President of the United States.

6th clause. The Senate shall have the sole power to try all impeachments. When sitting for that purpose, they shall be on oath or affirmation. When the President of the

---

are the senators chosen, and for how many years? Each senator has how many votes? Have the large states more senators than the small states?

2d clause. Into how many classes were the senators at first divided? How long did the senators of the first class hold their offices? Of the second class? Of the third class? By this plan, what part of the senate is chosen every second year? Can you tell any advantage of this plan over the plan of electing all the senators at one time? When may the governor of a state fill a vacancy in the senate? How long do such appointments continue?

3d clause. How old at least must a senator be? How long must he have been a citizen of the United States, and of what state an inhabitant?

4th clause. Who is president of the senate? What vote has he?

5th *clause.* How are other officers of the senate chosen? What is a president pro tem'po-re? ANS. *A president for the time being.*

6th clause. What sole power has the senate? What conditions are required of the senate when sitting as a court of impeachment? What is an affirmation?

United States is tried, the Chief Justice shall preside; and no person shall be convicted without the concurrence of two thirds of the members present.

7th clause. Judgment, in cases of impeachment, shall not extend further than to removal from office, and disqualification to hold and enjoy any office of honor, trust, or profit, under the United States; but the party convicted shall, nevertheless, be liable and subject to indictment, trial, judgment, and punishment, according to law.

SECTION IV.

1st clause. The times, places, and manner of holding elections for Senators and Representatives, shall be prescribed in each State by the Legislature thereof; but the Congress may, at any time, by law, make or alter such regulations, except as to the places of choosing Senators.

2d clause. The Congress shall assemble at least once in every year; and such meeting shall be on the first Monday in December, unless they shall by law appoint a different day.

SECTION V.

1st clause. Each House shall be the judge of the elections, returns, and qualifications of its own members; and a majority of each shall constitute a quorum to do business; but a smaller number may adjourn from day to day, and may be authorized to compel the attendance of absent members, in such manner and under such penalties as each House may provide.

2d clause. Each House may determine the rules of its proceedings, punish its members for disorderly behavior, and, with the concurrence of two thirds, expel a member.

ANS. *A solemn declaration made by those who conscientiously decline taking an oath?* Who presides when the president of the United States is impeached? How large a part of the senate is necessary for conviction?

7th clause. In case of impeachment, how far may judgment extend? To what is the convicted party further liable?

SEC. IV. — *1st clause.* What does the legislature of each state prescribe as regards elections for senators and representatives? But what power is reserved to Congress?

2d clause. How often shall Congress assemble? When?

SEC. V. — *1st clause.* Of what is each house the judge? What constitutes a quorum? Meaning of quorum? ANS. *Such a number as is sufficient to do business.* What may a smaller number do?

2d clause. What power has each house as to rules of its proceedings, and the punishment for disorderly conduct?

3d clause. Each House shall keep a journal of its proceedings, and from time to time publish the same, excepting such parts as may, in their judgment, require secrecy; and the yeas and nays of the members of either House, on any question, shall, at the desire of one fifth of those present, be entered on the journal.

4th clause. Neither House, during the session of Congress, shall, without the consent of the other, adjourn for more than three days, nor to any other place than that in which the two Houses shall be sitting.

SECTION VI.

1st clause. The Senators and Representatives shall receive a compensation for their services, to be ascertained by law, and paid out of the treasury of the United States. They shall, in all cases except treason, felony, and breach of the peace, be privileged from arrest during their attendance at the session of their respective Houses, and in going to and returning from the same; and for any speech or debate in either House they shall not be questioned in any other place.

2d clause. No Senator or Representative shall, during the time for which he was elected, be appointed to any civil office, under the authority of the United States, which shall have been created, or the emoluments whereof shall have been increased, during such time; and no person holding any office under the United States shall be a member of either House during his continuance in office.

SECTION VII.

1st clause. All bills for raising revenue shall originate

3d clause. What is required of each house in respect to keeping and publishing a journal? When are the yeas and nays to be entered on the journal?

4th clause. What regulation is there as to adjournment?

SEC. VI. — *1st clause.* What is said of the payment of members of Congress for their services? What is the present compensation of a member? ANS. *Five thousand dollars a year, with twenty cents for every mile of travel by the most usually travelled post route to and from the national capital.* In what cases and when are members privileged from arrest? For what are they not to be questioned?

2d clause. What restriction is placed upon members as regards civil offices? Can a person holding any office under the United States be at the same time a member of either house?

SEC. VII. — *1st clause.* In which house must bills for raising revenue originate? What is the senate allowed to do?

in the House of Representatives; but the Senate may propose or concur with amendments, as on other bills.

2d clause. Every bill which shall have passed the House of Representatives and the Senate shall, before it become a law, be presented to the President of the United States. If he approve, he shall sign it; but if not, he shall return it, with his objections, to that House in which it shall have originated, who shall enter the objections at large on their journal, and proceed to reconsider it. If, after such reconsideration, two thirds of that House shall agree to pass the bill, it shall be sent, together with the objections, to the other House, by which it shall likewise be reconsidered; and if approved by two thirds of that House, it shall become a law. But, in all such cases, the votes of both Houses shall be determined by yeas and nays, and the names of the persons voting for and against the bill shall be entered on the journal of each House respectively. If any bill shall not be returned by the President within ten days (Sundays excepted) after it shall have been presented to him, the same shall be a law, in like manner as if he had signed it, unless the Congress by their adjournment prevent its return, in which case it shall not be a law.

3d clause. Every order, resolution, or vote, to which the concurrence of the Senate and House of Representatives may be necessary (except on a question of adjournment), shall be presented to the President of the United States; and, before the same shall take effect, shall be approved by him, or, being disapproved by him, shall be repassed by two thirds of the Senate and House of Representatives, according to the rules and limitations prescribed in the case of a bill.

2d clause. After a bill has passed both houses, what shall be done with it? What shall the president do with it? What is the returning of a bill with the president's objections called? ANS. *A veto.* Meaning of the word veto? ANS. *I forbid.* Object of the veto? *To enable the president to check the passage of improper laws.* After the president has vetoed a bill, how may it become a law? How may a bill which has been neither signed by the president nor vetoed become a law?

3d clause. What must be done before any order, resolution, or vote requiring the concurrence of both houses can take effect? How may an order, resolution, or vote be passed over the veto? On a question of adjournment has the president the veto power?

SECTION VIII.

The Congress shall have power —

1st clause. To lay and collect taxes, duties, imposts, and excises, to pay the debts and provide for the common defence and general welfare of the United States; but all duties, imposts, and excises shall be uniform throughout the United States:

2d clause. To borrow money on the credit of the United States:

3d clause. To regulate commerce with foreign nations, and among the several States, and with the Indian tribes:

4th clause. To establish a uniform rule of naturalization, and uniform laws on the subject of bankruptcies throughout the United States:

5th clause. To coin money, regulate the value thereof, and of foreign coin, and fix the standard of weights and measures:

6th clause. To provide for the punishment of counterfeiting the securities and current coin of the United States:

7th clause. To establish post-offices and post-roads:

8th clause. To promote the progress of science and useful arts, by securing, for limited times, to authors and inventors, the exclusive right to their respective writings and discoveries:

SEC. VIII. — *1st clause.* What power has Congress in regard to taxes, duties, imposts, and excises? What are duties? ANS. *Taxes on articles imported or exported.* What are imposts? ANS. *Taxes laid on imported goods.* What are excises? ANS. *Taxes on commodities made or produced within the country.* What are to be uniform?

2d clause. What power has Congress as to borrowing money?

3d clause. As to regulating commerce?

4th clause. As to naturalization and bankruptcies? Meaning of naturalization? ANS. *The act by which an alien becomes a citizen of the United States.* How long does the law require an alien to live in our country before he can become a citizen of the United States? ANS. *At least five years.*

5th clause. What power has Congress in regard to coining money, &c.? Where is the mint of the United States situated? ANS. *At Philadelphia.*

6th clause. What power has Congress in regard to counterfeiting?

7th clause. In regard to post-offices and post-roads?

8th clause. What power has Congress to promote the progress of science and useful arts? How long is the author of a book entitled to the exclusive right of publishing it? ANS. *Twenty-eight years, with the privilege of a renewal of the copyright for fourteen years longer.* What is a patent? ANS. *A document, issued by government, granting to the applicant the exclusive right to an invention or discovery.* How long does a patent hold good? ANS. *Fourteen years; and at the end of that period the commissioner of patents may extend the patent for seven years longer.*

9th clause. To constitute tribunals inferior to the Supreme Court:

10th clause. To define and punish piracies and felonies committed on the high seas, and offences against the law of nations:

11th clause. To declare war, grant letters of marque and reprisal, and make rules concerning captures on land and water:

12th clause. To raise and support armies; but no appropriation of money to that use shall be for a longer term than two years:

13th clause. To provide and maintain a navy:

14th clause. To make rules for the government and regulation of the land and naval forces:

15th clause. To provide for calling forth the militia to execute the laws of the Union, suppress insurrections, and repel invasions:

16th clause. To provide for organizing, arming, and disciplining the militia, and for governing such part of them as may be employed in the service of the United States, reserving to the States respectively the appointment of the officers, and the authority of training the militia according to the discipline prescribed by Congress:

17th clause. To exercise exclusive legislation, in all cases whatsoever, over such district (not exceeding ten miles square) as may, by cession of particular States, and the acceptance of Congress, become the seat of the government of the United States; and to exercise like authority over all

---

9th clause. What power has Congress in regard to tribunals?
10th clause. In regard to piracies, &c.?
11th clause. In regard to declaring war, &c.? What are "letters of marque and reprisal"? ANS. *Commissions granted by the government to particular citizens, authorising them to seize the ships, goods, &c., of a hostile nation, on the high seas.*
12th clause. What power has Congress in regard to armies?
13th clause. In regard to a navy?
14th clause. In regard to the land and naval forces?
15th clause. In regard to calling forth the militia?
16th clause. In regard to the militia, &c.? What powers, however, are reserved to the states?
17th clause. What power has Congress as regards legislation over the seat of the national government, and all places purchased for the erection of forts, &c.? What district became the seat of the national government? ANS. *The District of Columbia — a tract of land originally ten miles square, lying on both sides of the Potomac, and ceded to the government by Maryland and Virginia. In* 1846

places purchased by the consent of the Legislature of the State in which the same shall be, for the erection of forts, magazines, arsenals, dockyards, and other needful buildings : and

18th clause. To make all laws which shall be necessary and proper for carrying into execution the foregoing powers, and all other powers vested by this Constitution in the government of the United States, or in any department or officer thereof.

SECTION IX.

1st clause. The migration or importation of such persons as any of the States now existing shall think proper to admit, shall not be prohibited by the Congress prior to the year one thousand eight hundred and eight; but a tax or duty may be imposed on such importation, not exceeding ten dollars for each person.

2d clause. The privilege of the writ of habeas corpus shall not be suspended, unless when, in cases of rebellion or invasion, the public safety may require it.

3d clause. No bill of attainder, or ex post facto law, shall be passed.

4th clause. No capitation, or other direct, tax shall be laid, unless in proportion to the census or enumeration hereinbefore directed to be taken.

---

the part of this District on the Virginia side of the Potomac was ceded back to that state. Before the national government can purchase property within a state, whose consent must be obtained?

18th clause. What general powers are, by the 18th clause, conferred upon Congress?

SEC. IX.—*1st clause.* What restriction as regards the migration or importation of certain persons was placed on Congress? Who were the persons spoken of in this clause? ANS. *Slaves.* What duty might be imposed on such importation? Did Congress afterwards forbid the importation of slaves into the United States? ANS. *In* 1807 *a law was enacted forbidding the importation of slaves after the* 1st *of January,* 1808.

2d clause. What is said of the writ of habeas corpus? Meaning of habeas corpus? ANS. *You may have the body.* What is a writ of habeas corpus? ANS. *A writ commanding the body of the person, in whose favor it is issued, to be brought before a court or judge. The object of the writ is to set at liberty any person who is illegally confined.*

3d clause. What is said of a bill of attainder, or ex post facto law? What is a bill of attainder? ANS. *In the sense of the Constitution, it is a special act of the legislature inflicting punishment upon a person without trial or conviction in the ordinary course.* What is an ex post facto law? ANS. *A law which makes an act punishable in a manner in which it was not punishable when committed.*

4th clause. How are capitation taxes or other direct taxes to be laid? What is a capitation tax? ANS. *A direct tax laid upon each individual; a poll-tax.*

5th clause. No tax or duty shall be laid on articles exported from any State.

6th clause. No preference shall be given, by any regulation of commerce or revenue, to the ports of one State over those of another; nor shall vessels bound to or from one State be obliged to enter, clear, or pay duties in another.

7th clause. No money shall be drawn from the treasury but in consequence of appropriations made by law; and a regular statement and account of the receipts and expenditures of all public money shall be published from time to time.

8th clause. No title of nobility shall be granted by the United States; and no person holding any office of profit or trust under them shall, without the consent of the Congress, accept of any present, emolument, office, or title of any kind whatever, from any king, prince, or foreign State.

SECTION X.

1st clause. No State shall enter into any treaty, alliance, or confederation; grant letters of marque and reprisal; coin money; emit bills of credit; make anything but gold and silver coin a tender in payment of debts; pass any bill of attainder, ex post facto law, or law impairing the obligation of contracts; or grant any title of nobility.

2d clause. No State shall, without the consent of the Congress, lay any imposts or duties on imports or exports, except what may be absolutely necessary for executing its inspection laws; and the net produce of all duties and imposts, laid by any State on imports or exports, shall be for

---

5th clause. What is said of duties on articles exported from any state?

6th clause. What commercial preference shall not be given? What is said of vessels bound to one state from another?

7th clause. What restriction is placed upon the drawing of money from the treasury? What statement and account shall be published from time to time?

8th clause. Can the United States grant any title of nobility? What are officeholders forbidden to accept?

SEC. X.— *1st clause.* What can you say of the power of any state as to making a treaty, &c.? As to letters of marque and reprisal? As to coining money? As to bills of credit? What are bills of credit? ANS. *In the sense of the Constitution they are bills issued by a state, on the mere faith and credit of the state, and designed to circulate as money.* What can you say of the power of a state as to a legal tender? As to a bill of attainder, &c.? As to a title of nobility?

2d clause. What prohibition is there as to imposts and duties? What are inspection laws? ANS. *Laws under which certain articles of trade are inspected*

the use of the treasury of the United States; and all such laws shall be subject to the revision and control of the Congress.

3d clause. No State shall, without the consent of Congress, lay any duty of tonnage, keep troops or ships of war in time of peace, enter into any agreement or compact with another State, or with a foreign power, or engage in war, unless actually invaded, or in such imminent danger as will not admit of delay.

ARTICLE II.
SECTION I.

1st clause. The Executive power shall be vested in a President of the United States of America. He shall hold his office during the term of four years, and, together with the Vice-President, chosen for the same term, be elected as follows :

2d clause. Each State shall appoint, in such manner as the Legislature thereof may direct, a number of Electors equal to the whole number of Senators and Representatives to which the State may be entitled in the Congress; but no Senator or Representative, or person holding any office of trust or profit under the United States, shall be appointed an Elector.

THE TWELFTH AMENDMENT.*

The Electors shall meet in their respective States, and vote by ballot for President and Vice-President, one of whom, at least, shall not be an inhabitant of the same State with themselves; they shall name in their ballots

* The *3d clause* has been superseded by the *Twelfth Amendment*, which was proposed in 1803, and declared adopted in 1804.

---

by officers appointed for that purpose. What is said of the net produce of all duties and imposts laid by a state? What power has Congress over inspection laws?

3d clause. What is said of the power of a state relative to a duty of tonnage? What is a tonnage duty? ANS. *A tax on vessels at a certain rate each ton.* What is said of the power of a state as to keeping troops or war-vessels? As regards an agreement with another state, or a foreign power? As regards making war?

Article II.—SEC. I. *1st clause.* Of what does the second article of the Constitution treat? ANS. *Of the executive department.* In whom is the executive power vested? What is the length of a presidential term?

2d clause. State how presidential electors are appointed, and what number each state is entitled to. Who are excluded from being electors?

TWELFTH AMENDMENT.—Where do the electors meet? How is the vote taken? What provision prevents the president and vice-president from being inhabitants of the same state? How do the electors proceed to vote? What

the person voted for as President, and in distinct ballots the person voted for as Vice-President; and they shall make distinct lists of all persons voted for as President, and of all persons voted for as Vice-President, and of the number of votes for each, which lists they shall sign and certify, and transmit, sealed, to the seat of the government of the United States, directed to the President of the Senate; the President of the Senate shall, in presence of the Senate and House of Representatives, open all the certificates, and the votes shall then be counted; the person having the greatest number of votes for President shall be the President, if such number be a majority of the whole number of Electors appointed; and if no person have such majority, then from the persons having the highest numbers, not exceeding three, on the list of those voted for as President, the House of Representatives shall choose immediately, by ballot, the President. But, in choosing the President, the votes shall be taken by States, the representation from each State having one vote; a quorum for this purpose shall consist of a member or members from two thirds of the States, and a majority of all the States shall be necessary to a choice. And if the House of Representatives shall not choose a President, whenever the right of choice shall devolve upon them, before the fourth day of March next following, then the Vice-President shall act as President, as in the case of the death or other constitutional disability of the President. The person having the greatest number of votes as Vice-President shall be the Vice-President, if such number be a majority of the whole number of Electors appointed; and if no person have a majority, then from the two highest numbers on the list the Senate shall choose the Vice-President; a quorum for the purpose shall consist of two thirds of the whole num-

else are they required to do? Before whom are the votes counted? What portion of the electoral votes is required for an election? What course is pursued, provided there is no choice by the electors? When the duty of choosing the president devolves on the house of representatives, how is an equal voice given to each state? For the purpose of choosing a president, what constitutes a quorum? What is necessary to a choice? In case no choice is made before the 4th of March following, who is to act as president? How is the vice-president chosen? How is he chosen in case of not receiving a majority of the electoral

ber of Senators, and a majority of the whole number shall be necessary to a choice. But no person constitutionally ineligible to the office of President shall be eligible to that of Vice-President of the United States.

4th clause. The Congress may determine the time of choosing the Electors, and the day on which they shall give their votes; which day shall be the same throughout the United States.

5th clause. No person, except a natural-born citizen, or a citizen of the United States at the time of the adoption of this Constitution, shall be eligible to the office of President; neither shall any person be eligible to that office who shall not have attained to the age of thirty-five years, and been fourteen years a resident within the United States.

6th clause. In case of the removal of the President from office, or of his death, resignation, or inability to discharge the powers and duties of the said office, the same shall devolve on the Vice-President; and the Congress may, by law, provide for the case of removal, death, resignation, or inability, both of the President and Vice-President, declaring what officer shall then act as President; and such officer shall act accordingly, until the disability be removed, or a President shall be elected.

7th clause. The President shall, at stated times, receive for his services a compensation, which shall neither be increased nor diminished during the period for which he

---

votes? Can a person who is ineligible to the office of president become vice-president?

4th clause. What power has Congress as to the time of choosing the electors and the day on which they shall vote? Do the electors cast their votes on the same day throughout the United States? When are the electors chosen? ANS. *On the Tuesday next after the first Monday in the last November of a presidential term.* On what day do the electors cast their votes? ANS. *On the first Wednesday in December following their election.*

5th clause. What qualifications are required of a president? Can an alien become president of the United States?

6th clause. In what cases does the vice-president act as president? What provision has been made in case of vacancies in the offices of both president and vice-president? ANS. *The president of the senate pro tempore, and in case there is no president of the senate, then the speaker of the house of representatives, shall act as president.* How long shall such officer act?

7th clause. What is said about the president's compensation? What is the salary of the president? ANS. $50,000 *a year, together with the use of the presidential mansion and its furniture.* Of the vice-president? ANS. $8,000 *a year.*

shall have been elected; and he shall not receive within that period any other emolument from the United States, or any of them.

8th clause. Before he enter on the execution of his office, he shall take the following oath or affirmation: —

"I do solemnly swear (or affirm) that I will faithfully execute the office of President of the United States, and will, to the best of my ability, preserve, protect, and defend the Constitution of the United States."

SECTION II.

1st clause. The President shall be Commander-in-Chief of the army and navy of the United States, and of the militia of the several States when called into the actual service of the United States; he may require the opinion, in writing, of the principal officer in each of the executive departments, upon any subject relating to the duties of their respective offices; and he shall have power to grant reprieves and pardons for offences against the United States, except in cases of impeachment.

2d clause. He shall have power, by and with the advice and consent of the Senate, to make treaties, provided two thirds of the Senators present concur; and he shall nominate, and by and with the advice and consent of the Senate shall appoint, ambassadors, other public ministers, and consuls, judges of the Supreme Court, and all other officers of the United States, whose appointments are not herein otherwise provided for, and which shall be established by law; but the Congress may, by law, vest the appointment

---

8th clause. What is the president's oath?

Sec. II. — *1st clause.* What power has the president in relation to the army, navy, and militia? Whose opinion may the president require in writing, and upon what subjects? What executive departments have been created by Congress to aid the president? Ans. *Seven — Department of State, of the Treasury, of War, of the Navy, of the Interior (the heads of these being called Secretaries), the Post-office Department, at the head of which is the postmaster general, and the Department of Justice, at the head of which is the attorney general.* How is the chief officer in each of these departments appointed? Ans. *By the president, with the approval of the senate.* What do these officers constitute? Ans. *The president's cabinet.* What is the salary of a cabinet officer? Ans. *$8000 a year.* In what cases can the president grant reprieves and pardons?

2d clause. What power has the president in respect to treaties? In whom is the appointing power vested? What officers shall the president nominate and appoint? What may Congress do in reference to inferior officers?

of such inferior officers, as they think proper, in the President alone, in the courts of law, or in the heads of departments.

3d clause. The President shall have power to fill up all vacancies that may happen during the recess of the Senate, by granting commissions which shall expire at the end of their next session.

SECTION III.

He shall, from time to time, give to the Congress information of the state of the Union, and recommend to their consideration such measures as he shall judge necessary and expedient; he may, on extraordinary occasions, convene both Houses, or either of them, and, in case of disagreement between them with respect to the time of adjournment, he may adjourn them to such time as he shall think proper; he shall receive ambassadors and other public ministers; he shall take care that the laws be faithfully executed, and shall commission all the officers of the United States.

SECTION IV.

The President, Vice-President, and all civil officers of the United States, shall be removed from office on impeachment for, and conviction of, treason, bribery, or other high crimes and misdemeanors.

ARTICLE III.

SECTION I.

The Judicial power of the United States shall be vested in one Supreme Court, and in such inferior courts as the Congress may, from time to time, ordain and establish.

3d clause. What vacancies can the president fill? When do such appointments expire?

SEC. III.— Duties of the president in respect to Congress? In what manner is it customary for the president to recommend measures? ANS. *By written messages.* When may the president convene Congress? When adjourn it? His duty in respect to public ministers? the execution of the laws? the granting of commissions?

SEC. IV.— Under what circumstances shall civil officers of the United States be removed?

Article III.— SEC. I. Of what does the third article of the Constitution treat? ANS. *Of the judicial department.* In what is the judicial power of the United States vested? How long shall the judges hold their offices?

The judges, both of the supreme and inferior courts, shall hold their offices during good behavior, and shall, at stated times, receive for their services a compensation which shall not be diminished during their continuance in office.

SECTION II.

1st *clause.* The Judicial power shall extend to all cases in law and equity arising under this Constitution, the laws of the United States, and treaties made, or which shall be made, under their authority; to all cases affecting ambassadors, other public ministers, and consuls; to all cases of admiralty and maritime jurisdiction; to controversies to which the United States shall be a party; to controversies between two or more States; between a State and citizens of another State; between citizens of different States; between citizens of the same State claiming lands under grants of different States; and between a State, or the citizens thereof, and foreign States, citizens, or subjects.

2d *clause.* In all cases affecting ambassadors, other public ministers, and consuls, and those in which a State shall be party, the Supreme Court shall have original jurisdiction. In all the other cases before mentioned, the Supreme Court shall have appellate jurisdiction, both as to law and fact, with such exceptions, and under such regulations, as the Congress shall make.

3d *clause.* The trial of all crimes, except in cases of impeachment, shall be by jury; and such trial shall be held in the State where the said crimes shall have been commit-

---

What is said of their compensation? Of what is the supreme court composed? ANS. *Of one chief justice and eight associate justices, any six of whom constitute a quorum.* Salaries of the justices? ANS. *The chief justice receives* $10,500 *a year; each associate justice* $10,000 *a year.*

SEC. II. — 1st *clause.* State the first of the nine subjects to which the judicial power of the United States extends; the second; the third; the fourth; the fifth; the sixth; the seventh; the eighth; the ninth. What is the meaning of admiralty and maritime jurisdiction? ANS. *Jurisdiction of affairs which have to do with the sea.* Can a suit be brought against a state by citizens of another state? ANS. *It cannot.* See *Amendment, Art.* XI.

2d *clause.* In what cases has the supreme court original jurisdiction? In all other cases, what jurisdiction? What is meant by appellate jurisdiction? ANS. *Jurisdiction in cases first brought in an inferior court and then carried up.*

3d *clause.* How are impeachments tried? (See p. 8, *6th clause.*) How all other crimes? Where shall the trial be held?

ted; but when not committed within any State, the trial shall be at such place or places as the Congress may by law have directed.

SECTION III.

1st clause. Treason against the United States shall consist only in levying war against them, or in adhering to their enemies, giving them aid and comfort. No person shall be convicted of treason, unless on the testimony of two witnesses to the same overt act, or on confession in open court.

2d clause. The Congress shall have power to declare the punishment of treason; but no attainder of treason shall work corruption of blood, or forfeiture except during the life of the person attainted.

ARTICLE IV.
SECTION I.

Full faith and credit shall be given in each State to the public acts, records, and judicial proceedings of every other State. And the Congress may, by general laws, prescribe the manner in which such acts, records, and proceedings shall be proved, and the effect thereof.

SECTION II.

1st clause. The citizens of each State shall be entitled to all privileges and immunities of citizens in the several States.

2d clause. A person charged in any State with treason, felony, or other crime, who shall flee from justice, and be

---

SEC. III.—*1st clause.* In what does treason against the United States consist? What testimony is requisite to a conviction of treason?

2d clause. What restriction is there upon the power of Congress to punish treason? Meaning of attainder? ANS. *Stain, taint.* What is meant by "corruption of blood"? ANS. *Taint of blood, which disables a person from inheriting any estate or transmitting it to others.*

Article IV.—SEC. I. How are the public acts, records, and judicial proceedings of each state to be treated? What is said about the manner of proving them, and their effect?

SEC. II.—*1st clause.* What is said of the privileges of the citizens of one state in other states?

2d clause. What is said of a person who is charged with crime in one state and flees into another?

found in another State, shall, on demand of the Executive authority of the State from which he fled, be delivered up, to be removed to the State having jurisdiction of the crime.

3d clause. No person held to service or labor in one State, under the laws thereof, escaping into another, shall, in consequence of any law or regulation therein, be discharged from such service or labor; but shall be delivered up on claim of the party to whom such service or labor may be due.

SECTION III.

1st clause. New States may be admitted by the Congress into this Union; but no new State shall be formed or erected within the jurisdiction of any other State; nor any State be formed by the junction of two or more States, or parts of States, without the consent of the Legislatures of the States concerned, as well as of the Congress.

2d clause. The Congress shall have power to dispose of, and make all needful rules and regulations respecting the territory or other property belonging to the United States; and nothing in this Constitution shall be so construed as to prejudice any claims of the United States, or of any particular State.

SECTION IV.

The United States shall guarantee to every State in this Union a republican form of government, and shall protect each of them against invasion; and on application of the Legislature, or of the Executive (when the Legislature cannot be convened), against domestic violence.

3d clause. What is said of persons held to service or labor who flee from one state into another? What persons are here referred to? ANS. *Fugitive slaves and apprentices.*

SEC. III. — *1st clause.* What body has the power to admit new states? How is the power restricted? How many states have been admitted since the adoption of the Constitution? (See Table, p. 226.)

2d clause. What power has Congress over the national territory or other property? How is this power restricted?

SEC. IV. — What shall the United States guarantee to each state? What power and duties result from this provision?

ARTICLE V.

The Congress, whenever two thirds of both Houses shall deem it necessary, shall propose amendments to this Constitution; or, on the application of the Legislatures of two thirds of the several States, shall call a convention for proposing amendments, which, in either case, shall be valid to all intents and purposes, as part of this Constitution, when ratified by the Legislatures of three fourths of the several States, or by conventions in three fourths thereof, as the one or the other mode of ratification may be proposed by the Congress; provided that no amendment which may be made prior to the year one thousand eight hundred and eight shall in any manner affect the first and fourth clauses in the ninth section of the first article; and that no State, without its consent, shall be deprived of its equal suffrage in the Senate.

ARTICLE VI.

1st clause. All debts contracted and engagements entered into before the adoption of this Constitution shall be as valid against the United States under this Constitution, as under the Confederation.

2d clause. This Constitution, and the laws of the United States which shall be made in pursuance thereof, and all treaties made, or which shall be made, under the authority of the United States, shall be the supreme law of the land; and the judges in every State shall be bound thereby, anything in the Constitution or laws of any State to the contrary notwithstanding.

3d clause. The Senators and Representatives before mentioned, and the members of the several State Legislatures,

---

Article V. — How may amendments to the Constitution be proposed? What is required before amendments become part of the Constitution? Can any state be deprived of its equal suffrage in the senate?
Article VI. — 1*st clause.* What is said of certain debts and engagements?
2*d clause.* What constitutes the supreme law of the land? Who are specially mentioned as being bound thereby?
3*d clause.* Who are required to be bound by oath or affirmation to support the Constitution? What is said of religious tests?

and all Executive and Judicial officers, both of the United States and of the several States, shall be bound by oath or affirmation to support this Constitution ; but no religious test shall ever be required as a qualification to any office or public trust under the United States.

ARTICLE VII.

The ratification of the Conventions of nine States shall be sufficient for the establishment of this Constitution between the States so ratifying the same.

AMENDMENTS.

THE FIRST TEN AMENDMENTS.—1791.

Article I. — Congress shall make no law respecting an establishment of religion, or prohibiting the free exercise thereof; or abridging the freedom of speech, or of the press; or the right of the people peaceably to assemble, and to petition the government for a redress of grievances.

Article II. — A well-regulated militia being necessary to the security of a free State, the right of the people to keep and bear arms shall not be infringed.

Article III. — No soldier shall, in time of peace, be quartered in any house, without the consent of the owner ; nor in time of war, but in a manner to be prescribed by law.

Article VII. — What number of states was required for carrying the Constitution into operation? How many ratified it before it went into effect? (See p. 113.) What two states ratified it afterwards? When?

What is the character of the first ten amendments? ANS. *They are general restrictions upon the powers of Congress, their objects being to secure the rights of the people and to preserve the Federal system.* When were they proposed, and when declared adopted? ANS. *They were proposed in 1789, in the first session of the first Congress, and were declared adopted in 1791.*

Article I. — What restrictions are laid upon Congress in respect to religion? What is said of the freedom of speech or of the press? Of the right to petition the government?

Article II. — Have the people the right to keep and bear arms?

Article III. — What is said of quartering soldiers?

Article IV. — The right of the people to be secure in their persons, houses, papers, and effects, against unreasonable searches and seizures, shall not be violated; and no warrants shall issue but upon probable cause, supported by oath or affirmation, and particularly describing the place to be searched, and the persons or things to be seized.

Article V. — No person shall be held to answer for a capital or otherwise infamous crime, unless on a presentment or indictment of a grand jury, except in cases arising in the land or naval forces, or in the militia, when in actual service in time of war or public danger; nor shall any person be subject for the same offence to be twice put in jeopardy of life or limb; nor shall be compelled, in any criminal case, to be a witness against himself; nor be deprived of life, liberty, or property, without due process of law; nor shall private property be taken for public use, without just compensation.

Article VI. — In all criminal prosecutions the accused shall enjoy the right to a speedy and public trial, by an impartial jury of the State and district wherein the crime shall have been committed, which district shall have been previously ascertained by law, and to be informed of the nature and cause of the accusation; to be confronted with the witnesses against him; to have compulsory process for obtaining witnesses in his favor; and to have the assistance of counsel for his defence.

Article VII. — In suits at common law, where the value in controversy shall exceed twenty dollars, the right of

---

Article IV.— What is said of searches and seizures? What of the issuing of warrants?

Article V.— What is said about holding a person to answer for crimes? What is meant by a grand jury? ANS. *A jury of not less than twelve men, nor generally more than twenty-three, whose duty it is to examine into accusations and decide whether there is sufficient evidence of guilt to require the accused to be put on trial.* What is meant by capital crimes? ANS. *Crimes the punishment of which is death.* What is said of a second trial for the same offence? What is meant by this provision? ANS. *That a person cannot be tried a second time for the same offence in case he has been once legally acquitted or convicted.* Can a criminal be compelled to be a witness against himself? What important provision is there as to life, liberty, and property? Can private property be taken for public use?

Article VI.— What right shall a person accused of crime enjoy as to time and kind of trial? By whom shall he be tried? Of what shall he be informed? What is said of witnesses against him? Of witnesses for him, and of counsel?

Article VII.— In what suits shall the right of trial by jury be preserved? What is said of the reëxamination of a fact tried by a jury?

trial by jury shall be preserved ; and no fact tried by a jury shall be otherwise reëxamined, in any court of the United States, than according to the rules of the common law.

Article VIII. — Excessive bail shall not be required, nor excessive fines imposed, nor cruel and unusual punishments inflicted.

Article IX. — The enumeration in the Constitution of certain rights shall not be construed to deny or disparage others retained by the people.

Article X. — The powers not delegated to the United States by the Constitution, nor prohibited by it to the States, are reserved to the States respectively, or to the people.

THE ELEVENTH AMENDMENT. — 1798.

Article XI. — The judicial power of the United States shall not be construed to extend to any suit in law or equity, commenced or prosecuted against one of the United States, by citizens of another State, or by citizens or subjects of any foreign State.

THE TWELFTH AMENDMENT. — 1804. (See p. 16.)

THE THIRTEENTH AMENDMENT. — 1865.

Article XIII. — SECTION 1. Neither slavery nor involuntary servitude, except as a punishment for crime, whereof the party shall have been duly convicted, shall exist within the United States, or any place subject to their jurisdiction.

SECTION 2. Congress shall have power to enforce this article by appropriate legislation.

THE FOURTEENTH AMENDMENT. — 1868.

Article XIV. — SECTION I. All persons born or naturalized in the United States, and subject to the jurisdiction there-

---

Article VIII. — What is said of bail, fines, and punishments?
Article IX. — What is said of rights retained by the people?
Article X. — What is said of powers not delegated to the United States?
Article XI. — Can a suit be brought against a state by citizens of another state or by subjects of a foreign power?
Article XIII. — Sec. I. What is said of slavery or involuntary servitude?
Article XIV. — Sec. I. Who are citizens of the United States? What is said about a state's abridging the privileges of citizens? What other restrictions are laid upon states for the sake of protecting persons and property?

of, are citizens of the United States and of the State wherein they reside. No State shall make or enforce any law which shall abridge the privileges or immunities of citizens of the United States ; nor shall any State deprive any person of life, liberty, or property, without due process of law, nor deny to any person within its jurisdiction the equal protection of the laws.

SECTION II. Representatives shall be apportioned among the several States according to their respective numbers, counting the whole number of persons in each State, excluding Indians not taxed. But when the right to vote at any election for the choice of Electors for President and Vice-President of the United States, Representatives in Congress, the executive and judicial officers of a State, or the members of the Legislature thereof, is denied to any of the male inhabitants of such State, being twenty-one years of age, and citizens of the United States, or in any way abridged, except for participation in rebellion or other crime, the basis of representation therein shall be reduced in the proportion which the number of such male citizens shall bear to the whole number of male citizens twenty-one years of age in such State.

SECTION III. No person shall be a Senator or Representative in Congress, or Elector of President and Vice-President, or hold any office, civil or military, under the United States, or under any State, who, having previously taken an oath as a member of Congress, or as an officer of the United States, or as a member of any State Legislature, or as an executive or judicial officer of any State, to support the Constitution of the United States, shall have engaged in insurrection or rebellion against the same, or given aid or comfort to the enemies thereof. But Congress may, by a vote of two thirds of each House, remove such disability.

SEC. II.— How shall representatives be apportioned among the several states? Before this amendment took effect what was the law? (See p. 7, 3d *clause*.) For what cause shall the basis of representation of a state be reduced, and in what way?

SEC. III.— What persons are prohibited from holding any national or state office? But how may this disability be removed?

SECTION IV. The validity of the public debt of the United States, authorized by law, including debts incurred for payment of pensions and bounties for services in suppressing insurrection or rebellion, shall not be questioned. But neither the United States nor any State shall assume or pay any debt or obligation incurred in aid of insurrection or rebellion against the United States, or any claim for the loss or emancipation of any slave, but all such debts, obligations, and claims shall be held illegal and void.

SECTION V. Congress shall have power to enforce, by appropriate legislation, the provisions of this article.

THE FIFTEENTH AMENDMENT.—1870.

Article XV.—SECTION I. The right of citizens of the United States to vote shall not be denied or abridged by the United States, or by any State, on account of race, color, or previous condition of servitude.

SECTION II. Congress shall have power to enforce this article by appropriate legislation.

SEC. IV.—What declaration is made regarding the validity of the national debt? What debts, obligations, and claims shall be held illegal and void? Is the national government or any state allowed to pay any such debts or claims?

Article XV.—SEC. I. Recite the fifteenth amendment.

REVIEW QUESTIONS.

                                                                                                       PAGE

1. Give some account of the discovery and colonization of Iceland and Greenland by the Northmen. 6
2. What is said of voyages made to the southern coast of New England by the Northmen? 6

PERIOD I. DISCOVERIES.

1. Give some account of Columbus, and his voyages. . 9, 10
2. Of the discovery and naming of the Pacific Ocean. . 10, 11
3. Give some account of the discovery of Florida, and the attempt of the discoverer to colonize it. . . . 11, 12
4. Of the expedition of De Soto. 12
5. Of the founding of the first European town in the United States. 13
6. Give an account of the earliest exploring voyages made to America by the French. 13, 14
7. Give some particulars of two attempts made by the Huguenots to plant colonies in our country. . . . 14
8. Relate what you can concerning the first permanent French settlement in America. 15
9. Concerning the voyages of the Cabots. . . . 15
10. Concerning the voyage of Francis Drake. . . . 15
11. Give an account of Raleigh's attempts to plant colonies in America. 16
12. Give an account of territorial grants made by King James I., and state what was done by the companies receiving the grants. . 17
13. State what was the foundation of the English claim to territory in America. 15, 18
14. Of the Spanish claim. . . . 9, 11, 12, 13, 18
15. Of the French claim. 14, 18, 54
16. Of the Dutch claim. 41
17. Give a brief description of the aborigines, and name some of the principal groups or families. . . . 18, 20, 21

PERIOD II. SETTLEMENTS AND INTERCOLONIAL WARS.

1. Give some account of the settlement of Virginia. . . 23
2. Of the first legislative assembly in America. . . 25
3. How and when was negro slavery introduced into the English colonies? 26
4. What attempt was made to enslave the Indians a hundred years before? 12

(31)

5. Relate some particulars of Bacon's Rebellion. . 27
6. State what you can of Captain John Smith. 24, 25, 28, 29
7. Give the history of the Plymouth Colony. . . 29, 30
8. State what you can of the founding of the oldest towns by the colonists of Massachusetts Bay. 31
9. What is said of the persecution of the Quakers? . . 33
10. Of the early history of education in the Colony of Massachusetts Bay? 33
11. State what you can of the Confederacy of the New England Colonies. 33
12. Give an account of King Philip's War. . . 34
13. What war occurred in Virginia about the same time? . 27
14. When were the Plymouth and Massachusetts Bay Colonies united, and who was the first governor under the new charter? . 35
15. Give some particulars of a strange delusion which prevailed in Massachusetts at this time. 35
16. Give an account of the settlement of New Hampshire. . 36
17. State some other events in the history of New Hampshire. 37
18. Relate what you can of the Connecticut Colony. . 37, 38
19. Of the Saybrook Colony. 38
20. Give an account of the Pequot War. . . . 38
21. Of the founding of the New Haven Colony. . . 39
22. What is said of a charter granted by Charles II.? . . 39
23. Give an account of the founding of the Providence and Rhode Island Colonies. 40
24. What is said of two charters granted to the settlers? . 41
25. Give an account of the settlement of New York. . 41, 42
26. What can you tell of Stuyvesant's administration, and of the conquest of the country by the English? . . 42, 43
27. Give some account of the first settlements in New Jersey, and of the beginning of colonization. 45
28. What is said of East and West Jersey? . . . 45
29. Give an account of the settlement of Delaware. . . 46
30. Relate its subsequent history till the Revolution. . 46, 47
31. Give some particulars relating to the settlement of Maryland. 47
32. What is said of the contests between the Protestants and Roman Catholics in Maryland? 48
33. What is said concerning the grant of Pennsylvania to Penn? 49
34. What is said of the treaty made with the Indians, and of the founding of Philadelphia? 50
35. Give some further account of Penn and his province. 50, 51
36. Give an account of the settlement of North Carolina. . 51
37. Of the settlement of South Carolina. . . 51, 52
38. What more can you tell of the early history of North and South Carolina? 52, 53
39. Give the early history of Georgia. . . . 53, 54
40. State when, where, and by whom each of the thirteen colonies was settled, naming them in the order of their settlement. 23–54
41. Give an account of French explorations in America. . 54

REVIEW QUESTIONS. 33

42. What is said of the domain of the French in America; of their settlements, and chain of posts? . . . 55
43. Name five events which occurred in 1682. . 45, 47, 49, 50, 54
44. State the cause of King William's War, and give the principal events of the war in America. 58
45. When did King William's War begin, and how long did it last? 58
46. Give the principal events, in America, of Queen Anne's War. 59
47. When did Queen Anne's War begin, and how long did it last? 59
48. What was this war called in Europe? ANS. It was called the *War of the Spanish Succession*, — the French monarch, in violation of a treaty with England, having placed his grandson on the throne of Spain.
49. Give an account of King George's War in America. 60, 61
50. What was King George's War called in Europe? ANS. The *War of the Austrian Succession*, from its having chiefly originated in disputes regarding the succession to the throne of Austria.
51. State the cause of the French and Indian War. . . 61
52. What was this war called in Europe? . . . 61
53. Relate what was done by Washington in 1753 and 1754. 62, 63
54. Give an account of Braddock's defeat in 1755. . . 63
55. What can you tell of other events in this year? . 63, 64
56. What successes were gained by the Marquis de Montcalm in 1756 and 1757? 64, 65
57. Give some account of three expeditions sent out by the English in 1758. . . . . 65, 66
58. Of the capture of Niagara, Ticonderoga, and Crown Point. 67
59. Of Wolfe's expedition, and the battle on the Plains of Abraham. 67, 68
60. When was peace made, and what were the provisions of the treaty? 68
61. Name, with the dates of their beginning, the wars in which the English and French colonists were engaged. . 58, 59, 60, 61
62. Give an account of the Navigation Acts. . . . 71

PERIOD III. THE REVOLUTION.

1. What was the cause of the Revolutionary War? . . 76
2. Give an account of the Stamp Act, with date of its passage. 76, 77
3. What principle as regards taxation did the colonists maintain? 76
4. Give an account of the Colonial Congress. . . . 76
5. By what measures did Parliament again excite indignation in the colonies? 77
6. What is said of the duty on tea? 78
7. Of tea sent to America, and the result? . . 78, 79
8. In what way did Parliament punish the Bostonians for throwing the tea into the harbor? 79
9. What is said of the first Continental Congress? . . 79
10. Give an account of what took place April 19, 1775. 82, 83
11. When and where did the second Continental Congress meet, and what did it do? 84

12. Give an account of the battle of Bunker Hill. . . 84
13. Describe the invasion of Canada. 85
14. How and when were the British compelled to evacuate Boston ? 86
15. Give an account of the British expedition sent against Charleston, South Carolina. 87
16. Give an account of the adoption of the Declaration of Independence. 87
17. Give an account of the battle of Long Island. . . 88
18. Of events to December 25 of this year. . . . 89
19. Give an account of Washington's successes at Trenton and Princeton. 90
20. Mention some of the foreigners who served as officers in the American army. 91
21. Give an account of operations, including a battle, which resulted in the capture of Philadelphia by the British. . . 92
22. Give an account of the battle which followed. . . 92
23. Where did Washington's army go into winter quarters, and what was its condition ? 93
24. Give an account of Burgoyne's advance from Canada to the Hudson. 93
25. Of the battle of Bennington. 94
26. Of operations in the Mohawk Valley. 94
27. Of two battles fought near Saratoga, and of the surrender of Burgoyne. 95
28. What event, which produced great joy in America, resulted from Burgoyne's surrender ? 96
29. Give an account of the battle of Monmouth, . 96, 97
30. What is said of Indian massacres ? 97
31. How were the Indians afterwards chastised ? . . 100
32. Give an account of the capture of Savannah by the British. 98
33. Of an attempt to retake the place. 99
34. What naval victory was gained this year ? . . . 100
35. What successes were gained in South Carolina by Clinton ? 100, 101
36. Give an account of the battle of Sanders's Creek. . . 101
37. Give an account of the battle of King's Mountain. . . 102
38. What is said of American finances ? 102
39. Give an account of the arrival of a French fleet and army. 102
40. Give an account of the treason of Arnold. . . 102, 103
41. Give an account of the operations of the southern army under General Greene. 102, 104, 105
42. Give an account of the siege of Yorktown and the surrender of Cornwallis. 106, 107
43. When was the final treaty signed ? 107
44. What were the boundaries of the United States ? . 107, 108
45. Give the dates of the following events — the passage of the Stamp Act; the battle of Lexington; the adoption of the Declaration of Independence; the surrender of Burgoyne; the surrender of Cornwallis. 76, 82, 87, 95, 107

46. State some of the reasons which led to the adoption of the Federal Constitution. 108, 109
47. Give some account of the Constitutional Convention. . 109
48. Write a brief account of Benj. Franklin. 70, 77, 96, 107, 109
49. When did the new government go into operation? . 109
50. Give an account of the North-west Territory. . . 110

PERIOD IV. NATIONAL GROWTH.

1. Give an account of an Indian war in Washington's administration. 115
2. Of an insurrection. 116
3. Of two treaties. 117
4. Of a difficulty with France in Adams's administration. . 118
5. Name four memorable events of Jefferson's first term, and give particulars of the Louisiana purchase. . . 119, 120
6. State what you can of English "Orders in Council" and French "Decrees," and of the "right of search." . . . 121
7. Relate what you can of the affair of the Chesapeake and the Leopard. 121, 122
8. Name the principal causes which led to The Second War with Great Britain. 121, 123
9. When was war declared, and who was president? . . 123
10. Give an account of Hull's campaign. . . 123, 126
11. Relate what occurred at Queenstown. . . . 126
12. What is said of the naval contests of 1812?. . 126, 127
13. Give an account of Perry's victory. 128
14. Of Harrison's invasion of Canada. . . . 128, 129
15. Relate what occurred at York and on the Niagara frontier in 1813. . . . . 129, 130
16. Tell what you can of the expedition against Montreal. . 130
17. Of the action between the Chesapeake and the Shannon. . 131
18. Of two battles on the Niagara frontier in 1814. . . 132
19. Of the land and naval battles at Plattsburg. . . 133
20 What is said of the expeditions against Washington and Baltimore? 133, 134
21. Give an account of the expedition against New Orleans, and of Jackson's great victory. 135, 136
22. When and where was the treaty of peace signed? . . 136
23. What is said of the war with Algiers? . . . 137
24. State what you can about the Missouri Compromise. 138, 158
25. Give some account of the purchase of Florida. . . 139
26. State what you know about the "Monroe doctrine." . 139
27. Give some of the leading features of John Quincy Adams's administration. 139, 140
28. Give particulars of the South Carolina ordinance of nullification. 141
29 State what you can about the U. S. Bank. . 137, 141, 142
30. Give an account of the Florida War. . . 142, 143
31. Give an account of three important events in Van Buren's administration. 143, 144

32. What caused the war with Mexico, and what is said of a dispute as to boundaries? 146
33. Give some account of two battles fought by General Taylor east of the Rio Grande. 148
34. Of Taylor's other military operations during 1846. . . 150
35. Of the battle of Buena Vista. . . . 150, 151
36. What is said of the conquest of New Mexico? . . 151
37. Of the conquest of California? 152
38. Give some particulars of the capture of Vera Cruz and the battle of Cerro Gordo. 152, 153
39. What can you tell of Scott's march towards the city of Mexico. 153
40. Give an account of battles fought near the city. . 153, 154
41. What is said of the capture of the city of Mexico? . . 154
42. Give some particulars of the treaty with Mexico. . . 154
43. Give a brief account of questions which came up in reference to slavery. 155, 156
44. Of the Compromise Measures of 1850. . . . 157
45. What two leading statesmen died in 1852? . . 157
46. What can you relate concerning the Kansas-Nebraska Bill? 158
47. Give some account of the struggle in Kansas. . 158, 159
48. Give some account of the slavery question.
   26, 71, 110, 117, 138, 145, 155, 156, 157, 158, 159, 160, 164
49. Give an account of the presidential contest of 1860. . 161
50. Of secession and the organization of the Southern Confederacy. 161
51. What is said of Forts Sumter and Pickens? . 161, 162
52. Of the government at Washington during this crisis? . 162

PERIOD V. THE GREAT REBELLION.

1. Give an account of the attack upon Fort Sumter. . 169, 170
2. Name three events which occurred April 19. . 82, 108, 170
3. How many and what states formed the Southern Confederacy? 161, 170
4. What slave states did not join the Confederacy? . . 170
5. Give what particulars you can of the battle of Bull Run. . 173
6. Give an account of events in West Virginia. . . 174
7. Of events in Missouri till Lyon's death. . . . 175
8. Of affairs in Kentucky in 1861. . . . 176, 177
9. Relate what you can of two expeditions which gained footholds on the southern coast in 1861. 177
10. What is said of the national navy and of Confederate privateers? 177, 178
11. What can you say of the action of the British and the French governments, and of the Trent affair? . . . 178
12. Describe the position of the opposing forces in Kentucky and Tennessee at the beginning of 1862. . . . 179
13. Give an account of the capture of Forts Henry and Donelson. 179

14. What were some of the consequences of the capture of Fort Donelson? 179
15. Relate what you can of the battle of Shiloh. . . 180
16. Of the taking of Corinth. 180
17. Of Bragg's invasion of Tennessee and Kentucky. . 181
18. Give some account of two victories won by Rosecrans while Bragg was engaged in his expedition. . . . 181, 182
19. Give the date, occasion, and result of the battle of Murfreesboro'. 182
20. Give an account of two battles fought in Arkansas in 1862. 182
21. Of the opening of the Mississippi from Columbus to Vicksburg. 183
22. Give the date of the surrender of Island No. 10, and state what great battle was won on the same day. . . 180, 183
23. Give the particulars in relation to the capture of New Orleans. 186
24. In relation to the capture of Roanoke Island. . . 186
25. Relate what you can about the Merrimack and the Monitor. 187, 188
26. State two important events which occurred March 8, 1862. . . . . 182, 187
27. Give an account of McClellan's Peninsular campaign till May 31. . . . . 188, 189
28. Relate what occurred on the last day of May and the first day of June, 1862. 189
29. Give an account of "Stonewall" Jackson's campaign in the Shenandoah Valley. 190
30. Of the "seven days before Richmond." . . 190, 191
31. State what command was given to General Pope. . 191
32. Give an account of the series of contests between Lee and Pope. 191
33. Of operations of Lee and McClellan in Maryland, including the capture of Harper's Ferry and the battle of Antietam. 191, 192
34. Of subsequent movements of the Army of the Potomac under McClellan and Burnside. 192
35. What is said of the Emancipation Proclamation? . 193
36. Give an account of the battle of Chancellorsville. . 193
37. Of the movements of the hostile armies afterwards till Hooker was superseded by Meade. 193
38. Give an account of the battle of Gettysburg. . 193, 194
39. Relate particulars of the capture of Vicksburg. . 194, 195
40. What other attempts had been made to take Vicksburg? 183, 186
41. Consequences of the fall of Vicksburg ? . . 195
42. Give some account of Rosecrans's campaign, including the battle of Chickamauga. 195, 196
43. Of the siege and battle of Chattanooga. . . 196
44. What can you tell of Burnside in East Tennessee? . 196
45. Give some account of Federal operations against Fort Sumter and Charleston. 197, 198
46. When did the power of the Rebellion begin to wane ? . 198

47. What events occurred in Mississippi and Florida in February, 1864? 198, 199
48. What is said of Forrest and Fort Pillow? . . 198, 199
49. Give an account of the Red River expedition. . . 199
50. Give an account of Grant's campaign to the James. . 200
51. Of the siege of Petersburg and Richmond. . . . 201
52. Of Early's invasion of Maryland. 202
53. Of Early's defeats by Sheridan. 202
54. Give an account of Sherman's march to Atlanta. . . 203
55. Of the siege and capture of Atlanta. . . . 203
56. Of Hood's invasion of Tennessee and his defeat by Thomas. 204
57. Give some particulars of Sherman's march from Atlanta to the sea. 204
58. Of Farragut's exploits in Mobile Bay. . . . 205
59. Of the career and fate of the Alabama. . . . 205
60. What can you tell of the capture of Fort Fisher and Wilmington? 205
61. Relate particulars of Sherman's march from Savannah to Goldsboro'. 206
62. Give an account of some military operations just before and during Grant's final campaign. 207
63. Give some particulars of the final campaign, including the battle of Five Forks, the capture of Petersburg and Richmond, and Lee's surrender. 207, 208
64. When was President Lincoln assassinated, and who succeeded him as President? 208
65. What is said of the surrender of the Confederate forces? 208, 209
66. What can you say of the cost of the war ? . . . 209
67. Give some account of the disagreement between President Johnson and Congress. 210
68. Of the Tenure of Office Bill, and the impeachment and trial of President Johnson. 211, 212
69. What can you tell of the purchase of Alaska? . . 212
70. Name the Presidents of the United States in their order. (See Table, 225.)
71. What Presidents died in office? . . 144, 157, 208
72. Name the Thirteen Original States. (See Table, 226.)
73. How many states were in the Union at the beginning of Washington's administration? 113
74. What states of the Original Thirteen joined the Union after the government went into operation? 113
75. How many states were in the Union at the beginning of Grant's administration? (See Table, 226.)

INDEX OF PERSONS.

an(g) ŏn(g), and awn(g), indicating, in this list, French nasals, are uttered as spelled, except that the sounds stop before the sound of *ng* is formed.

Abercrombie, James (ab'er-krum-bī), born 1706, died 1781. 66.
Adams, John, born 1735, died 1826. 77, 107, 109, 117, 119, 139.
Adams, John Quincy, born 1767, died 1848. 139, 140.
Adams, Samuel, born 1722, died 1803. 77.
Allen, Ethan. 83.
Amherst, Sir Jeffrey (am'erst). 65, 67, 68.
Amidas, Philip (am'I-das). 16.
Ampudia, Pedro de (ahm-poo'de-ah, pā'dro dā). 150.
Anderson, Robert. 161, 170.
Andre, John (an'drā), born 1751, died 1780. 103.
Andros, Sir Edmund. 35, 39, 41, 44.
Arista, Mariano (ah-rees'tah, mah-re-ah'no). 148.
Arnold, Benedict, born 1740, died 1801. 83, 85, 94, 95, 102, 103, 105, 106.
Ashe, John (ash). 98.
Ayllon, Vasquez de (ile-yōne', vahs'-keth dā). 12.

Bacon. Nathaniel. 27.
Bailey, Joseph. 199.
Bainbridge, William, born 1774, died 1833. 120, 127.
Baker, Edward D. 174.
Balboa, Vasco Nunes de (bahl-bo'ah, vahs'ko noon'yeth dā). 10.
Baltimore. See CALVERT.
Banks, Nathaniel P. 190, 191, 195, 199.
Barclay, R. H. 128.
Barlow, Arthur. 16.
Baum, Friedrich (bowm, free'drik). [94.

Beauregard, Peter G. T. (bo're-gard). 169, 173, 180.
Behring, Vitus (beer'ing vī'tus). 69.
Bellamont, Richard, Earl of. 44.
Benton, Thomas H., born 1782, died 1858. 142.
Berkeley, John, Lord (berk'lĭ). 45.
Berkeley, Sir William. 27.
Bienville, Lemoyne (be-an(g)-veel', le-moin'). 55.
Black Hawk. 140.
Bonaparte, Napoleon, born 1769, died 1821. 119, 121, 133.
Booth, John Wilkes. 208.
Braddock, Edward, born about 1715, died 1755. 63.
Bradford, William. 30.
Bradstreet, John. 66.
Bragg, Braxton. 180, 181, 195, 196, 197.
Brewster, William (broo'ster), born 1560, died 1644. 30.
Brock, Sir Isaac. 126.
Brooke, Robert, Lord (brŏŏk). 37, 38.
Brown, Jacob, born 1775, died 1828. 130, 132.
Brown, John, born 1800, died 1859. 160.
Buchanan, James (buk-an'an), born 1791, died 1868. 159, 162.
Buell, Don Carlos. 179, 180, 181.
Burgoyne, John (bur-goin'). 84, 93, 94, 95.
Burke, Sir Edmund, born 1729, died 1797. 77.
Burnside, Ambrose E. 186, 192, 193, 196, 197.
Burr, Aaron, born 1756, died 1836. 120
Butler, Benj. F. 171, 177, 186, 195, 201.
Butler, John. 97.

hāte, pōle, hăt, těn, tĭn, gŏŏd, noon, ow-l, thin, ch-op, matter.

39

INDEX OF PERSONS.

Cabot, John (kab'ut). 15, 18, 42.
Cabot, Sebastian. 15, 18, 42.
Calhoun, John C. (kal-hoon'), born 1782, died 1850. 141, 156.
Calvert, Sir George, 1st Lord Baltimore, born about 1582, died 1632. 47.
Calvert, Sir Cecil (se'sil), 2d Lord Baltimore. 47, 48, 50.
Calvert, Sir Charles, 3d Lord Baltimore. 49.
Calvert, Leonard (len'ard). 47.
Campbell, Archibald (kam'bel). 98.
Canby, Edward R. S. 207.
Canonicus (ka-non'e-kus). 30, 40.
Carteret, Philip (kar'ter-et). 45.
Carteret, Sir George. 45.
Cartier, James (kar-te-ā'). 14.
Carver, John. 30.
Champlain, Samuel de (sham-plane', sam'u-el dę), born 1567, died 1635. 15, 54.
Charles I., King, died 1649. 31, 47.
Charles II., King, died 1685. 34, 39, 41, 42, 45, 51.
Chauncey, Isaac (chahn'sī). 129.
Clarendon, Edward, Earl of. 51.
Clay, Henry, born 1777, died 1852. 141, 156, 157.
Clayborne, William (klā'burn). 48.
Clinton, Sir Henry. 84, 87, 88, 95, 96, 97, 99, 100, 101, 106.
Cockburn, Sir George (ko'burn). 130, 131.
Colfax, Schuyler (kōl'fax, skī'ler). 212.
Coligny, Gaspard de (ko-leen'ye, gahs-par' dę), born 1517, died 1572. 14.
Columbus, Christopher, born, some suppose, about 1435, others, about 1447, died 1506. 9, 10.
Cornwallis, Charles, Lord (korn-wol'lis). 89, 90, 101, 102, 104, 105, 106, 107.
Coronado, Vasquez de (ko-ro-nah'do, vahs'keth dä). 13.
Cortes, Hernando (kor'tĕz). 11.
Croghan, George (kro'gan). 128.
Curtis, Samuel R. 182.

Dade, Francis L. 142.
Dahlgren, John A. (dal'gren), born 1809, died 1870. 197.
Dare, Virginia. 16.

Davenport, John. 39.
Davis, Charles H. 183.
Davis, Jefferson. 161, 177, 207. 209.
Dearborn, Henry (deer'burn), born 1751, died 1829. 123, 127, 129, 130.
Decatur, Stephen (de-ka'tur), born 1779, died 1820. 120, 127, 137.
De Grasse, Count (dę gras'). 106, 107
De Kalb, Baron (dä kalb). 91, 101.
Delaware, Lord, died 1618. 25.
De Monts (dę mawn(g)'). 15.
De Soto, Fernando (dā so'to), born 1500, died 1542. 12, 13.
De Rochambeau (dę ro-shŏn(g)-bo'). 102, 106.
D'Estaing, Count (des-tan(g)'). 97, 99.
De Ternay (dę tĕr-nā'). 102.
Dieskau, Baron (dees'kow). 64.
Dinwiddie, Robert (din-wid'dī). 61, 62.
Doniphan, Alexander W. (don'ī-fan). 151.
Dorr, Thomas W. 144, 145.
Douglas, Stephen A. (dug'las), born 1813, died 1861. 158.
Downie, George. 133.
Drake, Sir Francis, born 1545, died 1596. 15, 16.
Drummond, Sir Gordon. 132, 133.
Dunmore, Lord. 86.
DuPont, Samuel F., born 1803, died 1865. 177, 197.

Early, Jubal A. 202, 207.
Eaton, Theophilus (the-of'ī-lus). 39.
Eaton, William. 120.
Elizabeth, Queen, died 1603. 15, 16.
Endicott, John. 31.

Farragut, David G., born 1801, died 1870. 186, 205.
Ferdinand V., King, died 1516. 9.
Ferguson, Patrick. 101.
Field, Cyrus W. 212.
Fillmore, Millard. 155, 157.
Fitch, John, born 1743, died 1798. 121.
Foote, Andrew H. (fŏŏt), born 1806, died 1863. 179, 183.
Forbes, John (forbz). 66.
Forrest, Napoleon B. 198, 199.
Franklin, Benjamin, born 1706, died 1790. 70, 77, 96, 107, 109.

---

hāte, pōle, hĭt, tĕn, tĭn, gŏŏd, noon, ow-l, thĭn, ch-op. matter.

INDEX OF PERSONS.

Fremont, John C. 152, 176, 190, 191.
Fulton, Robert (fŏŏl'tʼn), born 1765, died 1815. 121.

Gage, Thomas. 79, 82, 86.
Gates, Horatio. 95, 101, 102.
George II., King, died 1760. 53, 60.
George III., King, died 1820. 77, 82.
Gilbert, Sir Humphrey, born 1539, died 1584. 16.
Gillmore, Quincy A. 187, 197, 206.
Goldsborough, Louis M. (gōldz'-bur-o). 186.
Gorges, Sir Ferdinando (gor'jĕz). 36.
Gosnold, Bartholomew (goz'nuld). 16, 23.
Gourgues, Dominique de (goorg, do-me-ncek' dẹ). 14.
Grant, Ulysses S. 176, 179, 180, 181, 194, 195, 196, 197, 199, 200, 201, 202, 207, 211, 212.
Greene, Nathanael, born 1742, died 1786. 102, 104, 105.
Gustavus Adolphus, King, died 1632. 46.

Halleck, Henry W. 176, 180, 181.
Hamilton, Alexander, born 1757, died 1804. 115, 119, 120.
Hampton, Wade. 127, 130, 132.
Hancock, John, born 1737, died 1793. 82.
Harmar, Josiah. 115.
Harrison, William H., born 1775, died 1841. 122, 127, 128, 129, 144.
Harvard, John, died 1638. 33.
Henry, Patrick, born 1736, died 1799. 76, 77, 86.
Herkimer, Nicholas (her'kĭ-mer). 94.
Holmes, William (hōmz). 37.
Hood, John B. (hŏŏd). 203, 204.
Hooker, Joseph (bŏŏk'er). 193, 196.
Hooker, Thomas. 38.
Howard, Oliver O. 210.
Howe, George Augustus, (brother of Admiral Howe and Sir William). 66.
Howe, Admiral Lord. 88, 97.
Howe, Sir Wm. 84, 86, 88, 91, 92, 96.
Howe, Robert. 98.
Hudson, Henry. 41.
Hull, Isaac. 126.
Hull, William. 123, 126.

Hunter, David. 176, 201.
Hutchinson, Mrs. Ann. 32, 40.

Isabella, Queen, died 1504. 9.

Jackson, Andrew, born 1767, died 1845. 131, 135, 136, 138, 140, 141, 143.
Jackson, Claiborne F. (klā'burn). 175.
Jackson, Thomas J., born 1826, died 1863. 189, 190, 191, 192, 193.
James I., King, died 1625. 17, 29.
James II., King, died 1701. 35, 42, 44, 58.
Jay, John, born 1745, died 1829. 107, 117.
Jefferson, Thomas, born 1743, died 1826. 87, 118, 119, 122, 130.
Jesup, Thomas S. (jes'up). 142.
Johnson, Andrew. 205, 208, 210, 211.
Johnson, Sir William, born 1715, died 1774. 63, 64, 67.
Johnston, Albert S., born 1803, died 1862. 180.
Johnston, Joseph E. 173, 189, 194, 200, 203, 206, 209.
Joliet, Louis (jo'lĭ-ct *or* zho-le-ā'). 54.
Jones, Jacob. 127.
Jones, John Paul, born 1747, died 1792. 100.

Kalb. See DE KALB.
Kearny, Philip (kär'nĭ), born 1815, died 1862. 101.
Kearny, Stephen W. (uncle of Philip), born 1794, died 1848. 151, 152.
Kidd, William. 44.
Kieft, Sir William (keeft). 42.
King Philip. 34.
Kosciusko, Thaddeus (kos-sĭ-us'ko, thad'ĭ-us). 91.

Lafayette, Marquis de (mar'kwis dẹ lah-fā-et'), born 1757, died 1834. 91, 102, 105, 106, 139.
Lane, Ralph. 16.
La Salle (lah sahl'), born about 1635, died 1687. 54.
Laurens, Henry. 107.
Lawrence, James. 131.
Ledyard, William (lej'urd). 106.
Lee, Charles. 96.

hāte, pōle, hăt, tĕn, tĭn, gŏŏd, noon, ow-l, thin, ch-op, matter.

INDEX OF PERSONS.

Lee, Henry. 99, 105.
Lee, Richard Henry. 87.
Lee, Robert E. (son of General Henry Lee), born 1806, died 1870. 189, 190, 191, 192, 193, 194, 199, 200, 201, 202, 207, 208.
Lincoln, Abraham (link'un), born 1809, died 1865. 161, 169, 170, 193, 205, 208.
Lincoln, Benjamin. 98, 99, 100.
Little Crow. 192.
Longstreet, James. 197.
Loudoun, Lord (low'dun). 65.
Louis XIV., King, died 1715. 54, 58.
Louis XVI., King, died 1793. 102.
Lyon, Nathaniel, born 1819, died 1861. 175.

Macdonough, Thomas (mak-don'uh), born 1784, died 1825. 133.
Macomb, Alexander (ma-koom'). 133.
Madison, James, born 1751, died 1836. 122, 127.
Magellan, Fernando (ma-jel'lan). 10.
Marion, Francis (măr'ĭ-un), born 1732, died 1795. 101, 105.
Marquette, James (mahr-ket'). 54.
Mason, John (proprietor of New Hampshire). 36, 37.
Mason, John (of Connecticut). 38.
Mason, James M. 178.
Massasoit (mas-sa-soit'). 30.
McClellan, George B. 173, 174, 188, 189, 190, 191, 192.
McCulloch, Benj. (mak-kul'luh). 175.
McDowell, Irvin, 173, 189, 190, 191.
McPherson, James B., born 1828, died 1864. 203.
Meade, George G. (meed). 193, 194, 200.
Menendez, Pedro (mā-nen'deth, pā'dro). 13, 14.
Miantonomoh (mi-an-ton'o-mo). 40.
Miller, James. 132.
Minuit, Peter (min'u-it). 42, 46.
Monro, George (mun-ro'). 65.
Monroe, James (mun-ro'), born 1758, died 1831. 137, 138, 139.
Montcalm, Marquis de (mont-kahm'), born 1712, died 1759. 64, 66, 67, 68.
ontgomery, Richard (mont-gum'-ĭ), born 1736, died 1775. 85.

Morgan, Daniel. 95, 104.
Morgan, John H. 197.
Morris, Lewis. 46.
Morris, Robert. 103.
Morse, Samuel F. B. 164
Moultrie, William (mole'trĭ). 87.
Mulligan, James A. 175.
Narvaez, Pamphilo de (nar-vah'eth pahm-fe'lo dā). 12.
Nicolls, Richard (nik'ulz). 42, 44.

Oglethorpe, James Edward (o'gl thorp). 53, 60.
Opechancanough (op-e-kan'ka-no). 26.
Osceola (os-se-ō'lah). 142.
Otis, James, born 1725, died 1783. 77.

Pakenham, Sir Edward (pak'n-am). 136.
Parker, Sir Peter. 87.
Pemberton, John C. 194.
Penn, William, born 1644, died 1718. 46, 47, 49, 50, 51.
Pepperrell, Sir William (pep'er-el), born 1697, died 1759. 61.
Perry, Oliver Hazard, born 1785, died 1820. 128.
Phillips, William. 105.
Phipps, Sir William. 35, 58.
Pickens, Andrew. 98.
Pierce, Franklin (peerce), born 1804, died 1869. 157, 158, 159.
Pike, Zebulon Montgomery. 129.
Pinckney, Charles C., born 1746, died 1825. 118.
Pitcairn, John (pit'kārn). 82.
Pitt, William, 1st Earl of Chatham, born 1708, died 1778. 65, 77.
Pizarro, Francisco (pe-zär'ro). 11.
Pocahontas (po-ka-hon'tas). 24.
Polk, James K. (pōke), born 1795 died 1849. 145, 146, 154.
Polk, Leonidas (le-on'ĭ-das). 176.
Ponce de Leon (pōne'thā dā lā-ōne') born about 1460, died 1521. 11, 12.
Pontiac (pon'te-ak). 69.
Pope, John, 183, 191.
Popham, George (pop'am). 28.
Porter, David (pōr'ter). 134.
Porter, David D. (son of Com. David Porter). 186, 194, 199, 205.

bāte, pōle, hăt, těn, tĭn, gŏŏd, noon, ow-l, thin, ch-op, matter.

INDEX OF PERSONS. 43

Porter, Fitz-John. 189.
Powhatan (pow-hă-tan'). 24.
Preble, Edward (preb'l). 120
Prescott, William. 84.
Prevost, Augustine (pre'vost, aw-gus'tin). 98.
Prevost, Sir George (son of Gen. Augustine Prevost). 130, 133.
Price, Sterling. 175, 181, 182, 204.
Prideaux, John (prid'o), 67.
Proctor, Henry A. 128, 129.
Pulaski, Count (pu-las'kĭ). 91, 99.
Putnam, Israel, born 1718, died 1790. 88.

Raleigh, Sir Walter (raw'lĭ), born 1552, died 1618. 16.
Rawdon, Lord Francis. 105.
Riall, Phineas (ri'al). 132.
Ribault, John (re-bo'). 14.
Rochambeau. See DE ROCHAMBEAU.
Rodgers, John. 120.
Rolfe, John (rolf). 24.
Rosecrans, William S. (rōz'krantz). 174, 175, 181, 182, 195, 196.
Ross, Robert. 134.

Santa Anna (san'tah an'nah). 150, 153, 154.
Say and Seal, Lord. 37, 38.
Schofield, John M. (skō'feeld). 204, 206.
Schuyler, Philip (skī'ler), born 1733, died 1804. 85, 93, 95.
Scott, Dred. 160.
Scott, Winfield, born 1786, died 1866. 126, 132, 150, 152, 153, 171, 174.
Semmes, Raphael (semz, raf'a-el). 178, 205.
Seward, William H. 208.
Shays, Daniel, 109.
Sheridan, Philip H. 202, 207, 208.
Sherman, Thomas W.. 177.
Sherman, William T. 183, 196, 197, 198, 199, 200, 203, 204, 206, 209.
Shirley, William. 64.
Sigel, Franz (seeg'el). 201.
Slemmer, Adam J. 161, 162.
Slidell, John (sli-del'). 178.
Sloat, John D. 152.
Smith, E. Kirby. 191.

Smith, Capt. John, born 1579 died 1631. 24, 25, 28.
Standish, Miles. 30.
Stanton, Edwin M., born 1814, died 1869. 211.
Stark John. 94.
St. Clair, Arthur. 93, 115.
Steele, Frederick (steel). 195.
Steuben, Baron (stu'ben or stol'ben, born 1730, died 1794. 91.
Stevens, Isaac I. (ste'vnz). 191.
Stewart, Alexander. 105.
Stewart, Charles, born 1778, died 1869. 137.
St. Leger, Barry (sānt lej'er). 94.
Stockton, Robert F. 152.
Stone, Charles P. 174.
Stoneman, George. 207.
St. Pierre (sānt pe-are'). 62.
Stringham, Silas H. (string'am). 177.
Stuyvesant, Peter (sti'ves-ant), born 1602, died 1682. 42, 43, 47.
Sullivan, John, born 1740, died 1795. 97, 100.
Sumter, Thomas. 101, 105.

Taney, Roger B. (taw'nĭ), born 1777, died 1864. 160.
Tarleton, Banastre (tarl'tun, ban'as-tr). 101, 104, 106.
Taylor, Zachary, born 1784, died 1850. 143, 146, 148, 150, 151, 155, 156, 157.
Tecumseh (te-kum'sĕ). 122, 129, 131.
Ternay. See DE TERNAY.
Terry, Alfred H. (těr'rĭ). 205, 206.
Thatcher, Henry K. 207.
Thomas, George H. (tom'us), born 1816, died 1870. 179, 196, 204, 207.
Thornton, Seth B. 148.
Tryon, William (tri'un). 90, 99.
Twiggs, David E. 162.
Tyler, John, born 1790, died 1862. 144, 145.

Van Buren, Martin, born 1782, died 1862. 143, 144.
Van Dorn, Earl. 181, 182.
Van Rensselaer, Stephen (rens'el-er). 126.
Van Twiller, Wouter (wow'ter). 42.

---

hāte, pōle, hĭt, tēa, tin, good, noon ow-l, thin, ch-op, matter.

INDEX OF PERSONS.

Vespucci, Amerigo (ves-poot'che, ah-mä-re'go). 10.
Verrazzano, John (vĕr-rat-sah'ne). 13.
Wadsworth, Joseph. 40.
Wallace, Lewis (wol'lis). 202.
Warren, Joseph, born 1741, died 1775. 85.
Warwick, Earl of. 37.
Washington, George, born 1732, died 1799. 62, 63, 66, 83, 85, 86, 88, 89, 90, 91, 92, 93, 96, 97, 99, 102, 103, 106, 107, 108, 109, 114, 116, 117, 118, 119.
Wayne, Anthony (wāne, an'to-nĭ), born 1745, died 1796. 99, 115.
Webb, Daniel. 65.
Webster, Daniel, born 1782, died 1852. 141, 157.
White, John. 16.
Wilkes, Charles (wĭlks). 178.
Wilkinson, James. 130, 132.

William III., King (husband of Mary), died 1702. 35, 48, 58.
Williams, Roger, born 1606, died 1683. 32, 40.
Wilson, James H. 207, 209.
Wingfield, Edward Maria. 24.
Winchester, James. 127.
Winslow, Edward (winz'lo). 30.
Winslow, John A. 205.
Winthrop, John (win'thrup), born 1588, died 1649. 31.
Winthrop, John (son of Gov. John Winthrop of Mass.). 38.
Wolfe, James (wŏŏlf), born 1726, died 1759. 67, 68.
Wool, John E. (wŏŏl), born 1789, died 1869. 126, 150, 189.
Worth, William J. 154.

Yeardley, Sir George (yard'lĭ). 25.
Young, Brigham (brig'am). 159.

hāte, pōle, hăt, tĕn, tĭn, gŏŏd, noon, ow-l, thin, ch-op matter

www.ingramcontent.com/pod-product-compliance
Lightning Source LLC
Chambersburg PA
CBHW032113230426
43672CB00009B/1722